My Love Affair with a Theatre
Derek Salberg

To Hazel,
with best wishes
Derek Salberg

My Love Affair
with a Theatre

Derek Salberg

Foreword by Lord Olivier

CORTNEY PUBLICATIONS LUTON

Published in 1978
by
Cortney Publications Luton

ISBN 0 9043 78 04 7

Printed in Great Britain by
INPRINT OF LUTON (Designers & Printers) LIMITED
95-115 Windmill Road, Luton, LU1 3XS

CONTENTS

Foreword   by Lord Olivier

Author's Note

Chapter   *Page*

1   In The Beginning — The Lyceum   1
2   Enter Lester Collingwood — A Showman   4
3   Leon Salberg — The New Regime   8
4   Repertory Begins — Then Briefly Cabarevue   13
     And Tours
5   About Me — Before I Joined The Alex   17
6   Momentous Years For The Alex And For Me   27
7   Joan   31
8   Curtain Down For The Old Alex — Up For The New   37
9   Our Association With The Grand Theatre,   40
     Wolverhampton
10   Basil   44
11   Passing Of An Era — My Father Dies   47
12   The Theatre And Sport — Mostly Cricket   50
13   I Become The New 'Guvnor' — Then War Comes   56
14   My Years In Uniform   62
15   1943-1946 — Basil At The Helm   69
16   Back In Harness   73
17   The Alex Golden Jubilee Year   79
18   Audiences   82
19   Committees — Theatre And Others   91
20   1952-1963 — Halcyon Years For Repertory   98
     And Tours
21   Repertory Declines And Ends In 1975   112
22   The Bridge Extension   120
23   1964-1973 — Touring Seasons   124

CONTENTS (continued)

Chapter		Page
24	Crisis Years — We Survive	131
25	The Alex Becomes Entirely A Touring Theatre	145
26	Pantomime	152
27	Future Of The Alex And Other Touring Theatres	178
28	My Curtain Call	189
Appendix 'A'	The Council Of Management	196
Appendix 'B'	Repertory Players From 1927	199
Appendix 'C'	Pantomime Casts	220
Appendix 'D'	Gala Programme	228
Index		

ACKNOWLEDGEMENTS

The author wishes to express his appreciation for permission to reproduce the following photographs:

The Birmingham Post and Mail for the photographs of Bishop Laurence Brown; Ted Rogers, Jack Tripp and Beryl Reid in "Mother Goose"; George Robey and the author; Peggy Mount and Rosamund Burne in "What about Stanley?"; Michael Bullock.

The Birmingham Despatch and Mercury for the Pantomime Dress Rehearsal.

Houston Rogers and Triumph Productions for "The Ideal Husband".

Sophie Baker and Triumph Productions for "Laburnum Grove".

Mel Figures for the "Gala" photographs.

The photograph of "Uncle Vanya" is reproduced by permission of the Harvard Theatre Collection, Massachusetts, U.S.A., and of the photographer Angus McBean.

'Basil's' photograph by Armstrong Jones.

Acknowledgement of Mr. Derek Salberg's photograph '4 Gov'nors' Alan Hill.

The author apologises for unwittingly omitting to acknowledge the source of other photographs contained herein.

FOREWORD

I am very grateful to Lord Olivier for giving me permission to use, as a foreword to this book, the message he wrote for the programme which was printed on the occasion of my retirement Gala Performance. It read as follows:

Derek Salberg should find himself nesting snugly in a beautiful soft cloud of gratefully affectionate thoughts these days, having spent a good life in good work in valuable service. I think many people find something attractive about a family business, and the same sense of security adheres to a dynastic theatre.

I remember his father, Leon, when I was still in my teens, at the Alex. A few of us would visit the last half of the second house there every week, when I was at the Rep in Station Street.

Derek was a splendid choice as one of the first Board Members of The National and I, perhaps particularly, was most sad to see him go.

Let me join with hundreds of others in grateful greetings to him at this time.

Laurence Olivier

AUTHOR'S NOTE

This book tells, for the most part, the story of a theatre and its associated activities. My original intention had been to extend M.F.K. Fraser's *Alexandra Theatre*, published in 1947, in which some of the earlier details in this book are to be found.

But whilst writing it I found I was including a great deal of my own life, with occasional excursions beyond strictly theatrical boundaries. It is, therefore, partly autobiographical and I hope that in the process it has not fallen between two stools. I also hope that it will give the reader at least some of the pleasure I have derived from recalling so many happy (and inevitably, just a few less happy) times at the Alex and elsewhere.

I am particularly indebted to Jackie, for so long my secretary, and now the theatre's assistant manager, who typed most of the original manuscript from my long-hand. She possesses the ability denied to most people, including myself, of being able to read my writing and without her this book would probably never have been completed.

I would also like to place on record my appreciation of the co-operation I received from Mrs. Allen of the Midland Secretarial Bureau in Birmingham, and from Norman Gurney and the staff of Cortney Publications, Luton, who are publishing this book. Norman's advice and help have been invaluable.

My only regret is that it has been impossible to mention so many of those people who have enriched both my theatre and my private life.

Birmingham   DEREK SALBERG
February, 1978

CHAPTER 1

IN THE BEGINNING — THE LYCEUM

When my retirement was announced, Anthony Everitt, the features editor, dramatic critic and man of many parts with the *Birmingham Post*, wrote — "the Alexandra has long been counted as one of England's most popular and highly rated theatres" and J.C. Trewin commented, a few days later, in the same newspaper — "it was always a genuine pleasure to go to the Alexandra. Some theatres are immediately welcoming, some, emphatically, are not . . . . My predecessor, Tom Kemp, used to say that the Alex under Derek Salberg — following family tradition — was a theatre that, with Barrie's Island, liked to be visited. He was right. You did feel in the atmosphere of the Alex that playgoing was an event . . . . Such a house as the Alexandra is respected far beyond any regional limit".

These remarks clearly indicate that the Alex (or Alec) as it is affectionately known, has become to public and artistes alike, a much loved and respected theatre. Probably now, however, few members of the public or actors are aware of its very humble beginnings. But one can glean some idea of its early status from a book written by E. Lawrence Levy around 1919, entitled *Birmingham Theatrical Reminiscences*. In that book of 272 pages, the Alex rated only 28 lines. I quote the opening ones —

> "I have not had very much to do with the popular Alex. When Lester Collingwood ran it, I hardly ever went there, not from any lack of courtesy at the hands of that very warm-hearted gentleman, whom I often met in circles extra-theatrical, but simply because the stage ways of the Alexandra were not my ways. When Mr. Leon Salberg took over the theatre, the personality of this singularly charitable, broad-minded, open-hearted manager captured me."

This reaction was demonstrated when I was at my somewhat

1

select Birmingham preparatory school, Chigwell House (now, alas, no more), for the parents of my fellow pupils would only visit the Alex, if at all, at Pantomime time, for which it already had a high reputation. In earlier days, however, I imagine their grandparents might not have been too anxious even to be seen standing outside the theatre!

The theatre's early history is briefly as follows: it was built in 1901 by William Coutts and was known as The Lyceum. Coutts, who had been Richard Cadbury's secretary, was intensely interested in the temperance movement, and in 1895 ran the People's Hall in Hurst street, then in 1896 moved on to the Palace of Delight, known for some reason as the 'Mucker' and in 1897 to the Old Museum in Birmingham's famous and now, to my way of thinking, much spoilt Bull Ring. Here he prospered until the local magistrates demanded structural alterations which he could not meet.

So he decided to build his own theatre, and with a loan of £5,000 from a Mr. Mitchell, a brewer (no doubt he felt this was a good way of using money gained from the sale of alcohol!) and with a further £5,000 from other friends he built and opened The Lyceum on May 27th, 1901 — proudly boasting that "electric light was used throughout Birmingham's beautiful new theatre". The opening play was "The Workman" which, said the advertisement in the Birmingham Daily Gazette, "will be presented by a capable company". Prices 2/- to 4d (old money).

To deviate a moment from the main story: (and I mention this because it is typical of the remarkable loyalty and devotion which this theatre has always been able to command from its staff) he brought with him from the 'Mucker' a lady who will still be remembered with affection by our older patrons. Her name was Lizzie Hand; she came as an usherette and when she died in the nineteen fifties, had been for many years in charge of the Ladies Cloakroom. Not a quick promotion one might say, but she was as much a part of Birmingham's Theatre scene as was Geordie at the Birmingham Rep. During the last years of her life, although crippled with rheumatism, she was so devoted to her job, that she arrived at the theatre each night in a taxi. The fare probably cost her more than she received in wages. On the occasion of one Theatre outing (once annual events, but

2

discontinued just before World War II) she won the wheelbarrow race with me as her partner. She possessed a photograph taken at the winning post, of which she was very proud and would show to people on the slightest, or even no provocation!

When she came to the Lyceum the cost of running a theatre was infinitesimal for in those days coal was 1/- a cwt., whisky 3/6d a bottle, tobacco 3½d an oz. and a meal could be obtained at Miles near the Market Hall for 3d. Nor did it have to fight the competition of Radio, TV, Cinemas, Nightclubs, or holidays abroad. But it must be borne in mind that around the City centre there were no less than nine other theatres and many suburbs had at least one, some, such as Smethwick and Aston, possessed two, and adjacent towns such as Dudley, Walsall and many others all possessed their own theatres. Furthermore, there was opposition in the shape of such entertainements as "combined circus, fair and menagerie" at Bingley Hall, "Savage South Africa" presented at Aston Lower Grounds with "over 100 horses, zebras, five elephants and other wild beasts" and "100 natives composed of Zulus, Basutos, Kaffirs, Matabeles, etc." But of course it was very minor opposition compared with that of the present day, to which must now be added the fear of mugging and car parking problems.

Mr. Coutts tried to give his public, who in fact demanded lurid melodramas, something rather better; a typical example is contained in his programme dated Monday, July 8th, 1901, in which he announced that—

> "in response to many requests, Mr. Coutts has pleasure in announcing that he has arranged for an attractive revival of the weirdly fascinating hypnotic play "Trilby" which is now engaged on a new lease of prosperity."

(whatever that last bit meant!)

As was the custom in those days, it was preceded by a curtain raiser "Ben Bolt" described as a famous nautical drama. Prices were —

> 2/-, 1/6d, 1/-, 9d, 6d and 4d, with early doors 3d, extra to all parts, but only 2d to the gallery.

But public support proved insufficient and the gallant venture failed and in November 1902, after a little over a year, the theatre was offered for sale.

So ended the first era.

CHAPTER 2

ENTER LESTER COLLINGWOOD — A SHOWMAN

The sale attracted no great interest and for the sum of £4,450 (the cost nowadays of about two hundred theatre chairs) the theatre was sold to Lester Collingwood.

He was a man with a large theatre experience and a flamboyant personality, who was best known as the owner of a melodrama called 'When London Sleeps' which for some time he toured and played the part of the moustachioed villain. He was a character: he sported a magnificent moustache, usually wore a large homburg hat, always smoked a huge cigar and was impeccably dressed. He loved the good things of life, which certainly included the ladies of his companies, especially those of the chorus, who were not necessarily engaged for their terpsichorean abilities. Very different from dear Madam Lehmiski's ladies of later years to whom she always referred as 'her babes' . . . . irrespective of age or type! His motto was reported as being "f . . k 'em and run". Not one to give a theatre a reputation such as that established by Philip Rodway, who for so long successfully controlled the destinies of the Theatre Royal and Prince of Wales, Sir Barry Jackson at the Rep., or my father when his turn came to put his stamp on the Alex.

Lester Collingwood's first deed on buying the Lyceum was to re-name it the 'Alexandra', after Queen Alexandra, for in those days theatres were usually named after royalty or had a royal connotation. It is interesting that to this day, probably because the Alexandra's name is nearly always abbreviated, roughly half the letters received are addressed to the Alexander Theatre.

He launched his regime in December 1902 with a melodrama called 'The Fatal Wedding'. Prices were still two shillings to fourpence and "early doors" were extra. The theatre was

4

aimed at a public who clearly wanted this type of attraction and the standard fare included plays with similar titles.

It was very much the people's theatre and so in a sense it has always remained. Whereas, at the Theatre Royal and Prince of Wales in the old days, evening dress was often worn in the Dress Circle and Stalls, this would have been totally out of character, and indeed unthinkable, at the Alex. where we have always tried to maintain a family and informal atmosphere and to bear in mind how intimidating even the act of buying a ticket at the box office can be to some people. As far as dress is concerned, and here not everyone would agree with me, I feel that the day it was accepted that one could go to the theatre dressed in jeans if one so wished was a great step forward. Although I prefer to see people more formally dressed, and especially if their girl friend or wife has taken the trouble to look smart, I am always mindful of the fact that to many young (and not so young) people, the theatre has an image of being middle-class, middle-aged and rather stuffy, an image which is gradually being broken down.*

The orchestra, however, did wear evening dress (at least down to the waist!) in Lester Collingwood's Alex where, as we have seen, the fare offered was hardly of the highest class, and the audiences, who bore no relation to the present ones, were from all accounts composed largely of noisy, often raucous people, and regularly included the now extinct type 'the lads of the town'. Oranges were in great demand and the peel scattered far and wide, some of it onto the stage itself.

Lester Collingwood started the Alex tradition for pantomime and his first, 'Aladdin', ran for eight weeks, but before his reign ended the pantomimes occupied as many as twelve weeks of the year. Future stars who appeared in them included Hetty King, the famous Dorothy Ward (still very much alive) whose song

*Just after I wrote these words, I read in an article about Lord Harewood's work for the English National Opera at the Coliseum, that he felt during his period as chairman one special achievement was that no longer did young people feel that opera was stuffy and that they must dress up for it; they now knew they were welcome just because they were opera lovers, irrrespective of dress. I might be a little biased on the subject though, for I am not noted for my sartorial elegance. Whilst in Moscow I almost created a record by being the first Englishman to be approached by a Russian to sell me *his* clothes!

5

"How'd you like to spoon with me" was the rage of the day; Fred Barnes, a local lad, whose 'Black Sheep of the Family' is still remembered by just a few older patrons. It is reputed that Charlie Chaplin appeared in one of Collingwood's early panto-mimes, as one of the Eight Lancashire Lads, but I have been unable to find verification of this. Great Alex favourites of his later pantomimes were a double act called Barrett and Knowles. They split later and one of my early theatrical recollections concerned Harry Barrett when he was appearing in 'Aladdin' for my father. I, then very young, and a staunch Villa fan, was watching the pantomime from my father's box on the day they were playing a Cup Tie. Harry Barrett had arranged to let me know from the stage how they had fared. Alas, he brought bad news. Whereupon I burst into floods of tears and had to be ignominiously removed from the box.

But I go ahead of the story of Lester Collingwood. He was giving his public what they wanted with melodramas titled "The Sin of Her Childhood", "From Convent to Throne", "The Old Folks at Home", "A Woman's Redemption", and "The Modes of Marriage". Audiences were flocking in and he had, in his own way, certainly established the Alex and his own personality on Birmingham until the day when, in keeping with the way he lived, he met his death. For, at the age of 56 — when on his way to see an actress in Sheffield, his car collided with a milk float and he died instantly. He thus became one of the first people to be killed in the then new fangled invention, the motor car.

Incidentally, Allen Rowland, the G.O.M. of the Rocket Club* recalls hearing the news during a performance at the nearby Bordesley Palace**, and the tremendous stir it caused. I have a picture taken when his cortege stopped outside the

---

* A famous Birmingham club of which I am proud to say both my father and I have been Presidents. Its objects are charity and good fellow-ship in about equal proportions. Its status is clearly indicated by the fact that two of its most recent presidents have been the late Chief Constable, Sir Derrick Capper and the recently retired Bishop of Birmingham, the Rt. Rev. Laurence Brown, and that the Lord Mayor annually takes the chair at one concert.

**The play was "From Millgirl to Millionairess".

Theatre, the streets were thronged with people who wished to pay their resepcts and was almost identical with the scene many years later when my father's cortege stopped at the same spot. When he died, Lester Collingwood, by concentrating on melodramas and his own style of pantomime, had amassed what was in those days a fortune — £12,000.

His methods were not necessarily ideal ones, but he loved life and the theatre. Quite possibly with the passing of his style of manager, the Theatre has lost something of its glamour and personality.

CHAPTER 3

LEON SALBERG — THE NEW REGIME

So on March 20th, 1911 (the year Warwickshire first won the County Cricket Championship) the Alexandra was put up for sale. The brochure which was issued was drawn up by Herbert Pepper and Rudland, still our Auditors now known as Pepper, Rudland, Cotterill & Co.

The details stated that the property included a phrenologist's shop let at £31. 4s. 0d per annum, an oyster shop at £39. 5s. 0d and a rustic woodyard (I do not know where that was situated) at £40, and three bars (non-alcoholic), let at £60 per annum. The annual Ground Rent was £316. In fact the seating capacity in that considerably smaller theatre (we were rebuilt in 1935) was stated as 2,300 whereas today it is 1,562. This was accounted for by the fact that very few of the seats were tip-ups and the pit and gallery, with the aid of expert 'packers in' employed in those days, could accommodate, in great discomfort, several hundred people, as both these parts of the theatre were unbookable. People would queue for several hours before the doors opened in order to obtain a good seat.

The theatre takings for the last year of Lester Collingwood's regime were given as £12,770. 18s. 11d. (It is a sobering thought that on a recent visit of the D'Oyly Carte Opera Company over £16,000 was taken at the box office in the course of a week, and such is the present economic climate that only a marginal profit was achieved, even after taking into account profit from bars, coffee, ice-cream, programmes and the subsidy from the City and the Arts Council. But more of that in a later chapter.)

The property was bought by my father, who till then had no experience of the theatre, in association with his two brothers-in-law Joshua and Julius Thomas (his widow I am delighted to say is still alive and well). My father was, in due

8

course, to alter the theatre's reputation for he was a gentleman in every sense of the word; a quiet, not always easy person with whom to communicate, but as honourable a man as one could meet. As Sandy Powell said recently, neither he, nor many other artistes ever had a contract with him (what would Equity say about that?), for his word was as good as his bond.

I think the following description by M.F.K. Fraser in his book *Alexandra Theatre* gave a very good brief picture of him. I quote—

> "Leon Salberg was about thirty six years old. The son of a Warsaw Jew, and nephew of the first Jewish mayor of that city, he had an unhappy childhood, after his father's early death. Eventually he was shipped, like Hamlet, to England, and came to Birmingham where he had a brother in business. Soon he saved enough money to go to South Africa, where his industry and resource enabled him to make good headway. He was a volunteer soldier against the Boers in that little unhappy war and was wounded and returned to England where he married the daughter of Myer Thomas, a leading furniture dealer in Birmingham. After another spell, accompanied by his wife, in South Africa, he settled in Birmingham for good.
>
> Mrs. Salberg, who he adored, died in 1918 soon after the birth of her third son. Leon Salberg remained a widower — there was no other woman for him. He was, indeed, not at his happiest (though always at his most kindly and considerate) in women's company. He got on better with men, and best with children.
>
> His partners were wise to leave the control of the new enterprise entirely in his hands. He went into the theatre business, as he used to say, knowing nothing about it, except that there was money in it, and he applied the qualities which had already marked his career to the job of finding out what must be done — and what should be avoided — in order to make money out of it.
>
> In the process, which continued for a quarter of a century, he transformed the Alexandra out of all recognition. He found it an obscure, stuffy Blood Tub. He left it a handsome, modern home of reputable drama and outstanding pantomime. He wrote its name in capital letters on the theatrical maps of Birmingham and England. Concurrently, he made his own name honoured, as that of a shrewd businessman whose word was his bond, and who, while frankly out for financial success, strove all the time to raise the quality of the entertainment he sold."

I would add that he had great theatrical flair, especially for discovering artistes, could usually sense if a production would succeed, but hardly ever read a play himself. His speeches I always thought were rather indifferent but made with such sincerity that it did not really matter. He retained a slight* foreign accent, called the Villa the 'Willa' — to our great amusement — and was famous for a fabulous expression — "The what'm you call it up down dere"! This was used for a whole range of reasons and how his secretary for so many years, Gladys Lutman, a sweet person, interpreted this correctly, was a never ending source of mystery to us all.

I never heard him tell an even slightly risque joke, he didn't smoke, drank only in moderation, and loved his fellow man. Bridge was his great relaxation and he played almost daily at the Birmingham Press Club, alternating with the occasional game of snooker at which he excelled. He was reasonably fond of cricket and often visited the County Ground until he fell out with Mr. Ryder, the autocratic but brilliant Warwickshire secretary of those days, a man very unlike his successor, that doyen of Secretaries, Leslie Deakins, or Alan Smith, his recent successor, who is doing such a splendid job. He was a devoted Mason and derived much joy from it, was, as stated, a past president of the Rocket Club to which he was very attached. He also did much work for Jewish and other charitable organisations, and privately for many individuals.

As Micky Fraser wrote, he had no previous experience of the theatre and so at first he sat back and watched. Again, to quote M.F.K. Fraser —

> "He observed that the theatre was often a lot fuller than it should have been, according to the box office returns. One day he called his attendants together, and said, 'Now, you all know me and you all know my wife. Well, nobody, whoever it is, is to come in this evening without paying, bar my wife and myself.' 'When the curtain went up' said Leon, 'the house was nearly empty, but there was an indignant meeting, hundreds strong outside the doors in John Bright Street, and my good lieutenants were running about tearing their hair and telling me I had offended so many people for life that they'd never come near the Alexandra again. When I asked whether any of these people ever paid for admission, they looked blank, as though wondering what that had to do with it!'"

*It sounded slight to me but I am assured it was in fact a 'thick' one.

10

During his early years, the Alex remained the purveyor of melodrama and when the 1914-18 war came a number of the plays had titles which reflected the era: "Tommy Atkins", "Home from the Trenches", "It's a long way to Tipperary", "On Leave for his Wedding" to name but a few.

Pantomime, however, remained the mainstay of the theatre, usually running thirteen to fourteen weeks and, of course, with an audience swelled by numbers of soldiers on leave, with their sweethearts and (as in World War II) with factory workers and others anxious to escape from the grim realities of life, even if only for a brief moment and, especially in that war, from the increasing horror of the mounting casualty lists. Special free performances were given for wounded soldiers.

The theatre continued to thrive even when, in 1916, entertainment tax was introduced as a war-time measure. In spite of strenuous efforts (I was part of two delegations which in later years put our plea to the House of Commons) it remained in force with variation until 1945. Not many years later it was replaced by the only slightly less crippling Value Added Tax!

The tours were weekly but around 1918 the "Raynor Repertoire Company" played a season at the theatre and was destined to do so for many years to come, presenting melodramas such as "A Bunch of Violets" and the "Silver King", with the occasional inclusion of Oscar Wilde's "Lady Windermere's Fan", then considered very daring.

The leading lady, who was idolised by Alex audiences, was Ennis Lawson. She and the rest of the company certainly worked very hard for a different play was presented almost every night of the week and obviously standards varied, but they gave great pleasure to the unsophisticated audiences of those days. These seasons, I believe, sowed a seed in my father's mind which resulted in the policy of repertory in time to come.

After the war, play titles reflected the fact that 'peace had broken out'; such as "The Tommy Came Home", "Safe Home Again", and "Discharged with Honour". But around 1921 melodrama was gradually replaced by touring revues which all had very much the same formula, with titles such as "Flirts and Skirts"; "High Heels and Stockings"; "Spare Parts" with Randolph Sutton, a great artiste born in Smethwick; "Nelly Dean" featuring Gertie Gitana whose song "By the Old Millstream" became so famous; "Hello Wembley" during the year of the great Wembley Exhibition; "Here's to You" with Florrie Ford and a then unknown young comedian called Bud Flanagan, and by no means least, "Mr. Tower of London" in which Gracie Fields made her name.

Some were good, some were quite awful as the Alex, being what was then known as a No. 2 theatre, found it very hard to compete with the several No. 1 theatres who took the cream of these shows. In the straight field it would have been in direct competition with the Royal and Prince of Wales theatres, with no hope whatsoever of obtaining the top class attractions.

But my father was very much aware of the great change in people's tastes and of the inadequacy of much of the entertainment offered, although his pantomimes were achieving a higher standard year by year. He had for a long time felt that a change was due; but in what form he hardly knew.

After much hard thinking, on 28th March, 1927, at the end of the run of "Babes in the Wood" he took a bold and progressive step which was to alter the future course of the Alex's history . . . . . . REPERTORY was about to replace the revues and melodramas.

CHAPTER 4

REPERTORY BEGINS -- THEN BRIEFLY CABAREVUE AND TOURS

The play which inaugurated repertory at the Alex was "Under Cover" followed successively by Frederick Lonsdale's "The Fake" and "The Manxman" by Hall Caine. These plays set the pattern for the immediate future, and were presented twice nightly at 6.40 p.m. and 8.50 p.m. thus necessitating cuts, a task which I was occasionally allowed to undertake after I joined the theatre, when the producer was under excessive pressure. Each play ran for a week and the two main parts were always played by the leading man and leading lady respectively, whether or not they were suited to them.

In the first season Henry Hallatt was the leading man. He was an actor of tremendous personality who was paid by my father £25 a week, a prodigious sum for a repertory actor at a time when £10 was considered a good salary. Henry was a splendid serious actor but totally unsuited to very many of the parts he played, for he was never very strong on comedy. Furthermore, he frequently only knew his lines imperfectly but, as he said on one occasion when reproached by the producer, he could not be expected to open bazaars and learn his lines at the same time, anyway.....he 'liked opening bazaars!' Prudence Vanbrugh, the leading lady, left half way through the season to tour abroad with her famous aunt, Irene, and was replaced by Karen Stanley-Alder, who became a great favourite and remained for two seasons.

The system was obviously imperfect and gave no time for creating a part or for a producer to do more than sketch the play out, especially as he and the stage manager quite often played parts, whereas nowadays the stage manager is not allowed, by Equity, to speak even one line on the stage and, quite rightly, rarely, if ever, does a producer play and direct. The sets, later such a feature of Alex repertory seasons, were mainly permanent ones and when they were not, were built against time by that magnificent carpenter Sidney Jones, who would also be working on the pantomime, which was his true love. Some years later two entirely separate staffs were employed which, although much more costly, was absolutely essential.

Although such a system could not be accepted today, it represented a distinct advance for the Alex of those days and was really the first step towards its emergence as a serious theatre.

But in spite of the great help given by the local newspapers, who admired the efforts which were being made, albeit they had defects, the company often played to audiences of less than a hundred; so few that I am reminded of the football director of a Division IV club who said sadly that their gates were so small that his was the only club where the players were informed of the crowd changes!

Then, for no apparent reason, the tide turned in July and audiences increased considerably, so repertory survived that first season and the future pattern of the Alex for years to come was established.

Henry Hallatt stayed for a second season and by the time he left the system was firmly entrenched and the theatre was being accepted by a much wider range of public. To Henry must go a great deal of the credit for this.

When the next season opened, and at prices which still ranged from two shillings to sixpence, Henry's successor was Bruce Belfrage, an excellent actor who later achieved much fame when, during the war, he continued to read the BBC News after the building had been hit by a bomb and the explosion heard by all his listeners. He was very popular and one of the few actors who could have replaced Henry, and business got better and better. The range of plays was widening and gradually the names of authors such as Barrie, Shaw and Galsworthy appeared on the play bills. Bruce Belfrage left at the end of the season and Rupert Harvey replaced him in a company which included that superb actor Frank Pettingell, but although business still remained good, it did show a slight falling off. This was accentuated the following season, with Raymond

Huntley (now one of England's outstanding character actors), who had already made such a big success both in England and America as the vampire in "Dracula", as leading man. The company, for all round standard, was probably the best to date and yet repertory lost its initial grip.

What went wrong? There were many reasons. For one thing the audiences of those days were very much geared to the leading man, leading lady system, and Raymond Huntley, a top class actor, was basically a character actor rather than a conven tional leading man in which capacity he did not capture the rather 'obvious' taste of those days. Furthermore, England was then going through a bad financial crisis (where have we heard that before!) and to make matters worse, silent films had just been replaced by the 'talkies' which made an even bigger impact on the theatre than TV in years to come. It also saw the boom in Greyhound racing which drew huge crowds including many potential theatre goers.

My father was, naturally, very worried and thought long and hard before taking a decision which, on the face of it, appeared to have a great chance of success. He decided to bring back Henry Hallatt and Ennis Lawson, the idol of earlier days. But it rarely pays to look back and it quite definitely did not on this occasion. So appalling was business that in July it was decided to discard repertory, a policy which since 1927 had over two hundred weeks to its credit, given work to hosts of actors and pleasure to thousands of people. When he made a speech on the last night of the shortened season, he was greeted, for the only time in his life, with some booing, which seemed a little hard. This was a desperate time for the Alex — so what next?

This question, of course, had been exercising the mind of my father for some considerable time for, with the knowledge that repertory was failing, he had already considered how to occupy the remainder of the year. Finally, reluctantly and under pressure from his partners who were backed up by his manager, Freddie Finch, on whom he had rightly come to rely to a great degree, he decided to adopt a form of entertainment known as 'non-stop' variety. Then the rage, it had originated at the Windmill Theatre where nudity was permitted so long as the girls did not move. This law created a curious anomaly, for at

15

the time it was not permitted for 'costumes' to be worn on Sundays. Apparently this meant that it was in order for a girl to work in the nude if she did not move, but if she wore a top hat prosecution would follow! Not perhaps as ludicrous as the insistence many years later by the Watch Committee that the famous ballerina, Pavlova, must wear tights. George Robey, who appeared the following week at the same theatre, insisted on covering the legs of the piano!

None of this, of course, has any connection with Cabarevue as it was named, which was launched in July with a basic permanent company, including a resident comedian, Dan Leno Jnr., who was clearly not in the same class as his father, with the addition each week of guest artistes.

Prices ranged from 6d to 2/- and performances continued from noon, and a patron could stay all day if he wished to do so. For a week or two things looked hopeful, but the novelty soon wore off as material became progressively more scarce and Birmingham, unlike London, had little influx of visitors to fall back upon. So, after a few weeks, and severe losses, the venture closed and there were still several months to fill before the annual pantomime.

As a stop-gap, the best touring companies available were booked but they were few and far between after the Royal and Prince of Wales had taken first choice. They included a touring version of a London Musical and a good revival of "The Chocolate Soldier" which coincided with my arrival on the staff of the theatre, and was the first production since pantomime to make a profit. Perhaps it was a good omen? This was followed by a week of Shakespeare by the Alexander Marsh Company and as a contrast, to wind up the season, a Circus!

But this solved nothing, and my father had, once again, to consider very seriously the question — what next?

CHAPTER 5

ABOUT ME — BEFORE I JOINED THE ALEX

I was born in 1912, the year after my family acquired the theatre and received for the most part a conventional middle-class upbringing and, although I never thought about it at the time, I realise now that we were more than comfortably off. We had a large house, servants, possessed a car, which was not so common in those days, and with it, as my father did not drive himself, a chauffeur, Jock, who was with us for years and having played football for Glasgow Celtic, was idolised by us. We had three chauffeurs in all, the last, George Manley, became a close friend of the family and, after my father died, worked at the theatre until he became a cinema manager. His daughter used to join my brother Reggie, my cousin Basil (of whom more later in this book) and myself in games of cricket on the lawn and was rather better than we were! (My father frowned on these games, which did nothing to improve the lawn.)

Although it would be wrong to say that my childhood was unhappy, it was nonetheless in some respects unfulfilled for the atmosphere at home was often inclined to be heavy as my father, who did not go in for small talk, was in no way an extrovert and belonged, as I do, to that half of the world which cannot don a funny hat even at Christmas. Sundays, however, were very jolly for on that day my father, who loved to be surrounded by his family and friends, held open house and was joined by dozens of them; some to play bridge, others snooker, but most just to talk and devour the prodigious teas provided.

Unhappily, my mother, whom I hardly remember, died when I was nearly six and my father never recovered from her loss, so we were deprived of a mother at a time when we most needed one. Also, as a result of not having a sister and of spending a long time at boarding school, although I had three splendid girl cousins, Audrey, Betty and Myra, it was many years before I felt at ease in female company, in fact I'm not absolutely sure that I do now!

At first a maiden aunt we knew as 'Mim' came to run the house, accompanied by a bachelor uncle, Tim. Mim and Tim and my father did not really get on together which caused a heavy atmosphere and she was superseded by housekeepers, none of whom would have won prizes either for beauty or 'joie de vivre'. But eventually there arrived a relation, separated from her husband (and somewhat disapproved of by a section of the family), who brought gaiety into the home and to my father who, unfortunately, was persuaded by some female members of the family that she was extravagant, which was certainly true; and feathering her own nest, which was possibly true. So she departed and with her a lot of sunshine and we reverted to housekeepers, the first of whom, a worthy lady, sported a splendid cavalry moustache.

But fortunately, my brothers, Stanley, Reggie and I were devoted to each other. Especially Reggie and I, for Stanley was many years older and we were both very impressed and slightly overawed by his seniority.

Stanley was, and remained until he died much too young, an amazing person, as different as possible from my father, Reggie and myself. I had to admit, if only to myself, that he did not quite match up to my, then, boyhood heroes of the *Magnet* and *The Gem*, Harry Wharton and Bob Cherry, for he not only smoked in his very early teens but drank and actually went out with girls, not always of the highest moral integrity! He was eventually barred from the stage door of the Alex by my father, who was especially displeased when, whilst at finishing school in Switzerland, he sent him a photograph taken in his bedroom in which, prominently featured by his bedside, was a picture of the previous year's pantomime principal girl who was not only somewhat notorious, but married into the bargain! He knew every policeman and bus conductor in Birmingham and, had the King and Queen visited Birmingham, it is most likely that he would very quickly have been on speaking terms with them! I slightly disapproved of some of his later activities but loved him dearly, as did all who knew him, for he was the kindest and most lovable of men. I am glad to

18

say that his son, Keith, who is now a very active theatre entrepreneur, has inherited most of his good qualities and, as far as I know, none of the others! His daughter Loretta is very happily married with three delightful daughters and his widow, Evelyn, is, shall we say, a law unto herself but as likeable as ever and more astute than people realise. Her *bon mots* are famous and extremely comprehensive. One of my favourites was her remark on seeing a photograph of me attired in morning suit and my family dressed to match. It was taken when I received my O.B.E. and showed in the background Buckingham Palace, which she immediately identified as North Pier, Blackpool!

Reggie, three years my junior, speaks, stands and looks (although I am glad to say slightly more bald) so much like me, that after his appearances on Panorama and Nationwide, I received so many congratulations on "my" performance that I eventually decided to accept them! He has recently retired as director of the Salisbury Playhouse but his retirement is a very partial one for he is still closely associated with that theatre, spending much time dealing with their financial matters and advising in many directions only when called upon to do so, which is quite frequently.

He also sits on no less than seven committees, which include two theatre boards, the Arts Council Drama Panel and the newly formed Theatre Trust, of which Lord Goodman is Chairman and Harold Wilson one of its distinguished members. Several years ago he was deservedly awarded the O.B.E. for his services to the theatre.

I consider he was the best theatre manager of his type in the country, and he raised the Salisbury Playhouse from a mediocre twice-nightly repertory theatre to one acclaimed nationally, and was largely responsible for getting their lovely new theatre built several months ahead of schedule. As a tribute to his wonderful work there, the Studio Theatre has been named after him.

I can only recall one quarrel with him. When he was about five, we decided one night, when we were sharing a bedroom, that we would each make up a story. His was about a county cricket match, a game to which he is only slightly less devoted than I, in which he kept referring to a batsman scoring 'boundary two's'. I pointed out that boundaries counted either four or six which he hotly disputed, insisting that he had seen many boundary two's scored. This caused such a violent quarrel between us that we had to be forcibly separated! The only other 'dispute' was a friendly but recurring one during the period when I was at Clifton and he had not yet gone there. I was keen on boxing and, inspired by the triangular boxing tournament then held between Clifton, Malvern and Marlborough, we regularly boxed each other in a simulated tournament. I was, of course, **always Clifton and poor Reggie, then physically much less developed than I, was either Malvern or Marlborough and,** needless to say, always received a good hiding! He broke all family traditions, for which we never quite forgave him, by successfully passing his law degree at Oxford, where he played excellent rugger, once even scoring two tries against the Greyhounds, the University's second XV. He was playing for Moseley when war broke out and interrupted what promised to be an outstanding career.

Although articled to a solicitor just before the war, he entered the theatre after it was over. Before settling down at Salisbury, he went through repertory companies as some people go through pocket handkerchiefs. His first venture was at Kettering and, initially, it was so successful that foolishly, not then realising this was only a post-war boom, Stanley, he and I bought the theatre which eventually, along with a similar venture when we bought the Empire Theatre, Penge, involved us in a loss of several thousand pounds thus contributing considerably to my later financial problems. Soon after we had bought Kettering, Stanley telephoned Reggie to enquire how things were going. He replied despondently that they had only played to £8 on Monday and £12 on Tuesday; Stanley then asked what the advance was, and on being told £14 said in disgust he was going to ring off. My cousin, Myer, a great humourist, who was standing at his side, said: "Don't do that — reverse the charges and send him bankrupt!"

One good thing certainly emerged for Reggie from his Kettering venture, for he engaged in the company an actress named Noreen Craven*, a most delightful and talented person whom he married and who has been a most splendid addition to

*See footnote * on opposite page.

20

our family. I see her all too rarely but always look forward to doing so. They have two absolutely charming daughters. The younger, Kate, recently visited the Alex with the National Theatre's production of Alan Ayckbourn's "Bedroom Farce" as she is a member of their stage management staff. Jane, the older one, also a stage manager until her marriage, being of mixed religious parentage, opted for Christianity and was confirmed.** She later fell in love with and married a very clever Jewish actor from an orthodox family, had to start all over again to become Jewish (it took two years), and is now so orthodox herself that every time poor Jack fancies a piece of bacon he has to steal out of the house to the nearest cafe, under cover of darkness.

At the age of six I went to Chigwell House School, then administered by a most terrifying headmistress, Miss Leigh, of whom masters and boys alike stood in awe. I thoroughly enjoyed my time there, although I was very backward at work.

But I became (after the departure of a really outstanding boy) their star footballer (soccer) and always won the 100 yards. Many years later, when I was invited to present the prizes, I ran in, and won, the Old Boys' Race; it was my only victory that day for the prize giving was not too well organised and such was the confusion that half the younger winners were in tears as they had received those intended for another age group and one very small West Indian boy threatened me with a black eye for giving him the wrong and totally unsuitable prize!

Happily, I was rather more successful when I presented the prizes at a school situated only a short distance away from the house in which we then lived. I understand that a remark I made then has become part of the school's history. I congratulated the pupils on the fact that my wife always said that she could not possibly wish to be jostled out of the bus queue by a nicer set of boys!

*She brought with her an additional bonus in the person of her mother, Lady Anna Craven. A delightful, but somewhat eccentric lady, who would elegantly serve her guests with tea from a lovely china tea-pot. The table would be covered with a beautiful lace tea-cloth and the floor with somewhat ancient dog excreta.

**In the Jewish faith the children are considered to be of their mother's religion.

I took the common entrance exam. for Clifton and, as Miss Leigh said, "If Salberg passes it must mean that standards have fallen to an unbelievable level". Unfortunately, they hadn't. So I had some extra coaching and, to everyone's surprise, passed at the second attempt. Thus in 1926 I went to Clifton. I know it is now not fashionable to uphold the public school system, and no celebrity writing his memoirs ever appears to have anything good to say about it, but for myself I loved life at Clifton. I am positive that although it has faults, it is the best possible training for life, and if only more youngsters could have the opportunities of this type of education and the discipline it imposes, then much of today's hooliganism would be eradicated. In saying that I was happy at Clifton I realise that I was a very normal youngster and that the public school system, as indeed that of any boarding school, may not be suited to everyone. It was in a way surprising that I was so happy — firstly because I was terrible at work* and still feel that the immense amount of time spent on Latin, which I could not master, was wasted. Secondly, because Clifton, and this was a reflection of its broad thinking, was the only public school to contain a Jewish house (Harrow, Cheltenham and Perse had by then abandoned theirs); but I am not a believer in segregation and much as I admired Clifton, I doubt whether I would, therefore, have sent a boy of mine there. For youngsters can be the cruellest as well as the kindest of companions and the pupils of the Jewish House — Polacks — were, naturally, fair game and anyone of a sensitive nature, such as I possessed, suffered at first. But any taunts were not deep-rooted and, in any case, I feel that Jewish people, like all minorities, tend to look for offence where none is intended. I remember when my elder daughter Judith, then rather backward but later quite clever, failed her exam. to the Edgbaston Church of England School, a Jewish friend asked me if I thought it might be because of anti-Semitism? I replied that it might, but on the other hand it could be because she was unable to read or write!

I made very many friendships outside as well as inside my house, many of which I retain to this day. A particular one was with an extrovert, not very good at work but a first class

*At least I never had a paper returned, as did one boy, marked nought out of ten — improving!

22

athlete, called T. Howard Smith. After leaving school and trying several jobs he became an actor and I went to see him in his first part, a small one in "French Without Tears". Afterwards I went backstage and told him I doubted whether he had the necessary talent to make a success of a stage career. He is now known to millions as Trevor Howard! Although we rarely meet nowadays, we regularly send each other messages, especially on the occasions when his lovely wife, Helen Cherry, plays the Alex. About our cricketing association......more later.

Looking back I do not know why I was so bad at work, although I did have some good subjects, but an ability to draw graphs, for example, only held out limited prospects for a successful future! I was, however, mad keen on games and although rather above average at most, did not reach the pinnacle in any, usually failing just when it appeared to be in sight. At boxing I was beaten at my weight in the finals, as I was in the final of the under sixteen and a half Fives competition; never won the 100 yards, but beat the school's fastest runner in the house relay competition. My cricket failed me in what should have been my peak term when I suddenly lost the ability to turn the ball and retain any sort of accuracy and only achieved the school Under-16½ team. I had been hailed as something of an infant prodigy with my leg breaks when in my first term I got into the house team and, in my first over in a house match, clean bowled the school captain, who had already received a trial for Devon, and then ran through the rest of the side. Like all members of Polacks House, I was handicapped by the fact that we were not permitted to play games on Saturday, a rule I am glad to know is no longer in force. At rugger I made the house XV in my first year and a great future was predicted for me which never materialised, possibly partly because of the Saturday exclusion. Actually my biggest claim to fame occurred when I accidentally shot the sergeant major in a very awkward place, at the miniature range, and so went down to 'posteriority'. Up till then he had not liked me; afterwards he positively hated me and always said that "if there is anything that can be done wrong, that there SEDBERGH does it."

I took no part in the school plays and only twice spoke in house debates as public speaking terrified me, something which in future years I had to conquer. I suppose since then I have made thousands of speeches, ranging from talks on the theatre, prize-givings, first and last nights, etc. and am probably not too bad. I still recall my first public announcement on the stage of the Alex when, as house manager, I had to inform the public of a change of cast. I was standing nervously waiting to "go on" when the front doorman came up to me, saluted smartly and said, "Excuse me sir, but I believe the theatre is on fire". Luckily it wasn't, but it didn't help to soothe my nerves. As stated, my scholastic achievements had been few and far between and I was not entirely surprised when, at the age of 16½, my house-master, a wonderful man whom I still see occasionally at Lords and hope to meet at the centenary celebration of Polacks House, sent for me. He said that although I was a popular member of the house and well liked in the school, my work showed little progress and although quite good at games, I would not get a blue (the understatement of the year) in the unlikely event of ever getting into the University, so he really felt there was little point in my staying on at Clifton. I had to communicate this as tactfully as possible to my father who was not particularly pleased, or surprised. So my school days ended.

After leaving I did not go straight into the theatre, much as I wanted to, for there were one or two problems. First of all my father never completely wished me to do so because, much as he loved the theatre, he was never really a theatrical type at heart and would much rather have seen me follow a profession. Whilst I was at school he brought down, on different occasions, a leading Birmingham estate agent and an underwriter at Lloyds, in the hope that they might interest me in their particular profession. Furthermore, he was, at that time, very worried about the future of the theatre which was undergoing a very severe recession. He also feared that if I entered the business his brothers-in-law, to whom he was attached outside business but with whom he had little patience inside, would consider that their children were as entitled as I to become part of the firm and this would create an impossible situation. This, I feel, was an unjustified fear and in fact his newphew, Basil, did work for him when, as recounted elsewhere, he started his repertory company at the Grand Theatre, Wolverhampton. However, a compromise was reached and I joined the firm, then named Agar, Bates, Neal, King & Co., who were the theatre's account-

FOUR GUVNORS

William Coutts 1901-1902

Lester Collingwood 1902-1910

Leon Salberg 1911-1937

Derek Salberg 1937-1977

The Auditorium as viewed from the stage

Exterior of the Theatre circa 1903
(Extended in 1913 and demolished in 1936 when the theatre was re-built)

The front of the present building, with the author in the foreground.

Two outstanding repertory favourites
Above: Eileen Draycott
Below: Betty Bowden

Repertory season 1964: The Tulip Tree
L to R: Beryl Johnstone, Brian Kent, Anthony Howard and
William Avenell
(Also presented at Coventry Belgrade Theatre)

Repertory season 1969: Alfie
Noelle Finch and Adam Faith
(Also presented at the Malvern Festival Theatre)

Repertory season 1953: The Noble Spaniard

L to R: Leslie Sands, Jeanette Hutchinson, Eileen Draycott, Edward Mulhare, C.B. Pulman, Joan Blake, Peter Vaughan and Tilsa Page

Repertory season 1966: What about Stanley?
Rosamund Burne and Peggy Mount

Repertory season 1967: Waiting for Gillian
Anthony Howard, Rosemary Leach and Jack Watling
(This play opened our interchange with the Grand Theatre, Leeds)

Repertory season 1965: Teahouse of the August Moon
Centre: David Daker as Sakini
*(The Alex and Belgrade Theatre, Coventry joined forces for this production
which was presented at both theatres)*

Les Dawson and friend in "Robinson Crusoe", 1971-72

ants. It was tacitly agreed that I should spend eighteen months there and at the end of that period the matter would be reviewed. I was attached to a senior clerk one of whose jobs was to prepare the weekly statement of income and expenditure for the Alex and for the Theatre Royal, Wolverhampton, which was then owned by my father, thus giving me an insight into theatre accountancy.

My time there was very happy but my chief achievements were confined mostly to the sports field as we started a football team soon after I joined, and I was considered to be a more than useful centre forward. I also did well in the annual cricket match, played on the County ground, against Sharp Parsons, our deadly rivals, who audited the Warwickshire Cricket Club accounts. I recall that on the occasion of my first appearance in this match I was not out at lunchtime, but was bowled immediately afterwards attempting to play one of three balls which I could dimly see, as a result of the excellent lunch which always accompanied the event.

My other major achievements were to spill a bottle of ink all over the Private Ledger on the first audit on which I was sent; and when, in harness with the son of one of the partners, we checked the annual balances at a branch of the Municipal Bank (for which we received pay from the bank), we completed the job in absolute record time. Next day we boasted loudly about this and our achievement astonished everybody. Unfortunately, however, it was then discovered that we had omitted to check the last of the four columns and two other clerks were sent to do it all again, which did not make us too popular with our betters.

I was the originator of a rumour which started early one morning when my friend, Bernard Duffy, and I were joined by a most gullible member of the staff who said it seemed very quiet and he wondered where everybody was. For want of something better to say, I remarked that they were probably buying tickets for the Bull Fight which was to take place in Birmingham that day. He was most excited about this and subsequent arrivals who had been primed took up the joke and soon he rushed off to the then junior partner, Edmund King, (now the Alex's chairman), to ask permission to take the afternoon off. So enthusiastic and convincing was he that Edmund not only gave him the afternoon off but decided to do likewise in order not to miss this most unusual event. The Bull Fight is still, I am told, recalled by a few older people. Edmund obviously forgave me for he has been a lifelong friend and one of the people I most admire, especially as he has always been of great assistance to me whenever I have turned to him for advice. However, much as I had enjoyed my period at Agar Bates, I still felt that only a career in the theatre would satisfy me.

So, late in 1932, by which time, like all the staff, I had eaten hundreds of Pattisons farthing buns, I left but not before giving, at the old Central restaurant, a "booze up" for the staff and other friends I had made during my time there. Only recently I ran into the gentleman who served us on that occasion and he told me he still remembers it well. In those days alcohol was very cheap!

Thus I commenced my theatrical career, doing all sorts of jobs such as taking over some of the book-keeping, checking the bill sites, trying to persuade schools to attend the forthcoming visit of the Alexander Marsh Shakespeare Company, and works party organisers to book for the pantomime, a job I undertook for several years. Mostly though I was learning about the theatre under the stern eye of my father and with the help of various members of the staff, all of whom readily accepted, and never resented, "the guvnor's son". In fact they often shielded me when they felt my father was being over-critical of me, for he was, quite rightly, determined that no one should ever feel that he was showing me any favouritism.

I was known as Mr. Derek*, and to the end of my career this title was used by a large percentage of the staff. Feudal, perhaps, but I found it delightful and typical of the family atmosphere of the Alex.

*I was also known as Mr. Salberg, Dad, Father, Guvnor, D.S., and sometimes, I have no doubt, as 'that bloody old fool'!

CHAPTER 6

MOMENTOUS YEARS FOR THE ALEX AND FOR ME

Naturally 1933 was a very important milestone in my life
representing as it did my first full year in the theatre. For the
Alex it was an even more important one for on it hung the
future of the theatre as, after the failure of repertory the
previous year, it was vital that the theatre's fortunes and reputation should be restored.

Fully aware of this, my father, characteristically, realised
that only by being ambitious and not playing for safety lay
hope of achieving this, so for his pantomime "Red Riding Hood"
he engaged a ready-made star, 'Wee' Georgie Wood (now George
Wood, O.B.E., and still working). Previously many artistes such
as Sandy Powell and Billy Danvers had headed the cast of his
pantomimes, but they were then on their way to stardom,
whereas Georgie was already established as one of England's
foremost music-hall and pantomime performers, although he
himself later said that, at that time, nobody wanted him.

The supporting cast was first class and easily the most costly
to date. The assistant stage manager was named on the programme as Derek Clifton, in reality — myself — as for some
reason my father did not want to use my correct name.
I thoroughly enjoyed my period on stage management, for the
production and creative aspect of the theatre have always made
the strongest appeal to me, although I found all departments of
the theatre fascinating.

It was an ideal pantomime with which to begin one's
apprenticeship, for George was, shall we say, a trifle temperamental, thus giving me my first opportunity to test whether I
had any ability in handling artistes. At the same time this past-
master of the art of pantomime taught me many things which
were to stand me in good stead in the future. I must confess

though that my mind, that season, was sometimes not entirely on my job, for I became rather attracted to a female member of the cast (I stress the word 'female', as in this day and age and particularly in the theatre, you never know!). My father was, I know, particularly worried as he realised that the temptations and opportunities open to a young man were even more numerous in the theatre than elsewhere. Looking back I think I can say (with regret?) that I have kept my head pretty well. In addition to my stage management duties I understudied the second comedian, Hal Bryan, but mercifully for the audience he was never 'off'.

The following year I understudied again, this time the wicked uncle in "Babes in the Wood". When he was taken ill, my father cut out the part, not a very large one, rather than risk my performance. I considered that to be a great insult at the time, but on mature reflection feel sure that he was right.

When the pantomime finished in mid-March it had done a great deal to restore the theatre's finances and, at the same time, the morale of my father and those around him. But the question we were all asking ourselves was, naturally, how would the rest of the year fare? After all, the previous one had seen repertory fail, non-stop variety crack and tours, with so much opposition from the major theatres, offering no solution. Why should repertory, which appeared to be the only course open, succeed when it had failed before? Therefore, with much anxiety and misgivings, my father set about engaging a company to follow pantomime and another repertory season was announced.

It was, however, to be a repertory season with a difference. Still twice nightly, but everyone was to play as cast; no longer was there to be a leading man and leading woman. No one was to receive as high a salary as the fantastic one of £40 a week paid to the last leading man, but would be more evenly distributed. An excellent cast was assembled which included Betty Bowden who was to stay for several years and to become (along with Eileen Draycott later) the most popular female artiste to appear in any repertory company at the Alex. Equally popular were Phil Ray and John Morley in a company which worked as a team during the season which opened in mid-March with Ian Hay's "Middle Watch". At the first house on the Monday the takings were exactly £20. 6s. 0d (exclusive of

Entertainment Tax) and the second house was £16. 17s. 0d — the week totalling £355, which would now just about pay a week's wages for two pantomime musicians. The takings for the next six plays fell below that figure but in May, with "Mary Rose" by Sir James Barrie, always, and rather unexpectedly, a favourite with the Alex audiences of those days, the takings rose considerably, only to drop again in early June. I still recall with pleasure, the night when the second house was entirely full and our wonderful secretary of those days, Dolly Smith[*], a household name in Birmingham, and I went 'on the town' to celebrate, which we could not do at the theatre as it was not licensed until years later.

This peak was not maintained but suddenly, in mid-July, possibly because we were the only theatre open in the City (it is often forgotten that a recess during the summer was the normal practice), the takings rose to £439. The play was "Young Woodley" and prior to it the producer approached my father saying that he felt there was no actor in the company suitable for the part of Woodley, the public schoolboy who falls in love with the housemaster's wife, a daring theme in those days. This was before the days when one frequently went outside the company to cast and he suggested that I should play the part. After much discussion my father finally vetoed the idea. How right, what a disaster I would have been! In fact the actor, George Roche, who did play the part was very good and drew a large fan mail.

From then onwards the season became firmly established. Noel Coward's "The Vortex", another daring play in its time but how tame it seemed when I saw a recent revival, played to excellent figures and again Barrie succeeded, this time with "The Little Minister" which took over £600. Admittedly this was exceptional and the average receipts from a play were more usually in the region of £350 — £400 on the week.

Towards the end of the season, Sydney Pease, a very efficient producer of the 'old school', was tragically killed in

---

* I recently received a letter from this remarkable lady, now living in Jersey. She said she had just been on a cruise on the Canberra, won the national pairs Bridge Tournament and bought a new car. She was also working as a company secretary to a jewellers from 9.30 to 12.30. She is 86!

a car crash and George Owen, much more imaginative and ambitious, took over for the remainder of the season which, when it ended, had not been a riot but, after a very poor start, had held its own. We all drew a huge sigh of relief.

So the 1934 season opened on a much more optimistic note and George Owen was soon able to impress his stamp on the productions. He raised the artistic standards considerably and also brought with him several actors who were to become great favourites with audiences for years to come — notably Anthony Viccars who was idolised by the female element in the audience. Play selection was more ambitious and in this he had my full support as, from my earliest days, my father, appreciating my interest in this area of the theatre, had allowed me to join with the producer in selecting plays for the final list which was submitted to him. That year they included Elmer Rice's "Street Scene", Shaw's "Candida", Besier's "Barretts of Wimpole Street" and James Bridie's "Sleeping Clergyman", all of which, unfortunately, had to be cut owing to the exigencies of the twice-nightly system, but it must be stressed that, and I know most young actors of today would not easily believe this, standards, although variable, were, for the most part, very high.

On an even more optimistic note ended the last repertory season in the old theatre because my father had taken a decision that the building he loved so dearly was not adequate to meet the demands of the mid-thirties and the years which would follow. He, therefore, decided that it must be re-built. But before the demolishers moved in he staged an equally successful last pantomime, "Dick Whittington". The star was Clarkson Rose, one of England's leading pantomime dames. However, my father wanted him to play 'Alderman Fitzwarren' which greatly surprised Clarky who said, "but Guvnor, Fitzwarren doesn't even sail to Morocco with the rest of the cast". "At the money I'm paying you, he does" was the reply. This terminated the discussion and he made a great success in the part, in a pantomime which was worthy to end the life of the old theatre.

CHAPTER 7

JOAN

Just as 1933 had been a momentous one for me, the one which followed was even more so because that was the year in which I met Joan who, with Marjorie her sister, had made a great success for my father at Hull and was re-engaged to play pantomime at Birmingham. They came to the theatre mainly for a discussion about their music and dances with David Cochran, the producer for, unlike other artistes, they only had to visit the wardrobe briefly as they made and designed all their own stage clothes. They stayed over to see the evening performance and were waiting at the box office to obtain tickets as I walked down the stairs, resplendent in evening dress and, although I say so myself, not bad looking in those days.

Joan told me much later that she made up her mind there and then to marry me although she already had an 'understanding' with someone, and many years later, on an anniversary of our wedding, she wrote me a most moving poem recalling her feelings at that moment. We fell deeply in love during that pantomime season and remained in love until she died in 1972, just before Christmas and the day after the opening of our "Jack and the Beanstalk" pantomime — but a lot was to happen before then.

We continued to see each other as often as possible after the pantomime season ended and when the Alex was being rebuilt in 1935, I obtained a job at Llandudno as assistant manager for the pier and company manager for the summer show entitled "Bright Times", in which Joan and Marjorie were appearing. We spent every possible moment together.

Then, in 1936, my father, whose illness which caused his death two years later had just started, received a letter written by me to Joan, re-addressed to him in error. It made my feelings for Joan quite clear and to a comparatively orthodox, though by no means fanatical, Jew the thought of marriage between Joan, a Gentile, and myself was unthinkable.

He insisted that I gave up my relationship with Joan. The conflict with which I was faced was a truly terrible one because I knew my father was a sick man and needed my support, and yet I could not face the deep unhappiness I would cause Joan and myself. Torn in two, I eventually said I would discontinue seeing Joan, a promise which, ultimately, I was unable to keep. This meant that our meetings were furtive which Joan and I both hated and, at a time when we should have been happy, we were miserable and indeed had a feeling of guilt and to this day I believe some of the unhappiness of those years has rubbed off on me. It was not, therefore, until 1938 when my father died that, on the eve of Joan (and Marjorie's) departure to produce the dances and play in pantomime in South Africa, we became engaged. On 18th April 1939 we married quietly at St. Pancras Registry Office followed by a small lunch at the Savoy Hotel, which my father's half-brother, Uncle Louis, a man beloved by all, and not least by Joan and myself, refused to attend. I think he would have accepted had Joan become Jewish, but I saw no more reason for her to do so than for me to adopt the Christian religion. Hilda, her mother, would have been extremely unhappy if Joan had changed faith and I doubt whether she was ever entirely happy about the marriage; Joan's Granny, on the other hand, a marvellous old lady, stone deaf but very aware of everything, was devoted to me, as I was to her, was delighted. Nearly 90 when she died, it was her proud boast that she did not possess a false tooth in her head, but always omitted to mention that, in fact, she only possessed one tooth of any kind! In later years Joan said she would like to marry me again — this time in a synagogue, but I never particularly encouraged her; we were so happy as it was and to me it almost smacked of the odious football transfer system! I know it is argued that it creates difficulties for the children but we never found this.

Uncle Louis cut me out of his will (Reggie only qualified by a few years!) and an Aunt of mine said she would prefer me not to visit her house until her two children were safely married (into the faith of course). She later relented, attended the wedding and became extremely fond of Joan, for to know her was to love her. Looking back now over the years, in these more enlightened times, it seems quite unbelievable that such an attitude should have been adopted by so many people. But my brother and cousins (especially Basil) and very many others were completely understanding and a tower of strength to me.

But how far removed was the attitude of some from that of a Jew who, after hearing Cardinal Heenan in 1954, when Mass was celebrated for the first time on television, was prompted to write to him as follows — "The service must surely be the means of bringing home to mankind just how beautiful life can be, if people would only accept faith, whatever the denomination". After all, if people of different creeds cannot agree, what hope is there for nations. Not that I would expect the Chief Rabbi to become the next Pope, although he may have received some encouragement from the recent appointment, as Bishop of Birmingham, of Canon Montefiore, who comes from one of the most distinguished Jewish families.

Joan and I had many years of happiness together. We shared most of the same interests; she was even a mild cricket fan, a game to which, as a child, she had regularly been taken by her father.

We possessed the same love of travel staying in all levels of accommodation (but never luxury or even near) and sometimes ending up at very strange places. On one of our motoring holidays in France, totally unable to obtain accommodation, we were eventually directed to what we afterwards discovered to be a brothel. In the morning on being confronted with an enormous bill, I said that I didn't so much mind the high price of the room, but did object to paying 'corkage'. Joan was amused for one of her greatest qualities was her sense of humour which complemented a most lovable and exuberant personality. In fact our only real difference lay in the fact that whereas she was a brilliant dancer, I was quite hopeless. She used to say that (this was in the days when one had partners.....) I should ask a lady to be not 'my partner' in the next dance, but 'my opponent'......

Together we developed a love of gardening, but whereas I am only a jobbing gardener, she was very knowledgeable and was second to none in her ability to arrange flowers.

She possessed many accomplishments, which included

cooking (improvised!), the ability to paper walls and ceilings and generally to make up for my own deficiencies as a handyman. She could create a hat suitable for the smartest of weddings, in a very short time and at a cost of only a few shillings. She made first and last night presents for female artistes (always an Alex tradition) look so beautiful that they hardly liked to open them.

She and Marjorie were a superb act but only became dancers because they wished to remain together, which was not unnatural for two identical and devoted (although occasionally quarrelsome) twins, but their first love was really straight acting at which Joan, in particular, had gained very high (in fact top) honours at drama school. After we married and Joan left the stage, Marjorie turned to the straight theatre and was appearing with Winston Churchill's daughter, Sarah, at the London Coliseum when war broke out.

As recalled elsewhere, she and Joan played Viola and Sebastian in "Twelfth Night" during one of Joan's very occasional returns to the stage and the fact that they were identical twins added a new depth to the parts and never have Antonio's lines "How have you made division of yourself? An apple cleft in twain is not more twin" have sounded more apt. Joan's only other appearance, until she and Marjorie went overseas with ENSA from 1943 to 1946, was as Puck in "A Midsummer Night's Dream" in a production at Wolverhampton during the early days of the war, which was referred to by a patron, in a recent letter to me, as the best portrayal of the part she had seen.

When I joined the forces she took over the management of our Hereford Company until it closed, and then became assistant to Basil at Wolverhampton where, as at Hereford, she showed tremendous flair for castings and for discovering and communicating with actors and patrons, but management was not really her forte as organisation was not one of her strong points, neither was spelling or adding up; two fields in which my daughters also fail to excel. As Judith once wrote to us early in her school career "Auntie", as they called their headmistress (I wonder what would have happened if I had called my Headmaster at Clifton, "Uncle!"), "says I am doing well but my spelling is a brute."

34

Joan's big contribution to the Alex came when Oliver Gordon persuaded me to let her design the costumes for the 1948 pantomime in place of the previous very expensive designer. They were outstanding and she continued to design them as well as stunning head-dresses, which she also made, until the year of her death. For many years she was also responsible for the design on the programme cover for each pantomime. I was afraid the staff might feel I was pushing her forward, but I need have had no misgivings because everyone loved her and most of all they appreciated her genius (an overworked word but fully justified).

Her relationship with the Alex eventually became a somewhat love-hate one. Desperately fond of it and never resenting, for herself, the amount of my time it occupied, and accepting the financial and other worries it caused us in later years, she was saddened by their detrimental effect which, after the worst was over, resulted in my suffering a mild and happily short lived nervous illness, during which she coped with me wonderfully. Joan, however, found it difficult to accept the fact that in 1968, on the sale of the Alex to the City, it ceased to be a 'family' theatre, although I pointed out that this was the only way in which it could continue, and it was really an achievement to have made this possible at a time when so many theatres were closing. I also said, and this was proved by letters at the time and most certainly subsequently, that in the public's mind it was still a Salberg theatre. But to no avail, she continued to fret and for the last part of her life became seriously depressed. I spent as much time with her as my duties would permit and although everyone was very kind I always felt that her great friend Iris Crosthwaite would have been a great comfort to her, had she still been living in Bimringham. When she died I was heart-broken and things have never been the same since, but I have been very lucky indeed in having a host of good friends who have been a tremendous help to me. Most of all though, I have my two daughters, Judith and Joanna, for after eleven years of marriage (including some years when we did not meet during the war) and after discussing adoption, Judith was born followed shortly by Joanna.

Joan and I were overjoyed and I can only say that no father could have received more kindness and affection from his daughters than I have from mine. Neither has adopted the theatre as a career; Judith works at a London Branch of Brook Street Bureau and Joey at Heathrow Airport in the Medical Department, and as a result she gets wonderful concession flights which in recent years have made possible many exciting holidays. She also, at one time, possessed but alas has now lost, the ability to dream annually the name of the Grand National winner.

They are as different as chalk from cheese; whereas Judith goes raving mad on half a glass of wine, Joey, a rather diminutive figure, can, and has, drunk strong men under the table. She gave up serious drinking though after her second birthday, on which occasion, unknown to us of course, having drained the guests glasses in another room, she returned, made for the door, gave a beatific smile on reaching it and, with a wave of her hand, passed out – and had to be carried upstairs!

I do not know what I would have done without them and now in the family I have Judith's husband, Simon, of whom I heartily approve and whose knowledge of the theatre is, under Judith's guidance, developing as quickly as her knowledge of rugger (which he plays for the Old Merchant Taylors). He is a sports fanatic and although Judith is also quite an enthusiast she was a little annoyed that on their honeymoon night he booked a room on the understanding that it had TV as he wanted to watch 'Match of the Day'. I have it on good authority, however, that to avoid instant divorce he consummated the marriage during the B.B.C.'s equivalent of the commercial break!

I have a great deal for which to be thankful.

CHAPTER 8

CURTAIN DOWN FOR THE OLD ALEX
UP FOR THE NEW

Just as my father had realised in 1926 that the Alex must change its image, so had he sensed for some time that the old Alex, friendly and full of atmosphere though it was, with its old fashioned gallery, cramped seating arrangements and not very modern technical equipment, would in time be unable to challenge the competition of the plush new cinemas then being built to cater for a public who were becoming increasingly demanding in their requirements for comfort. Yet, at the time the decision was taken to re-build, the Alex was flourishing and in fact the 1934 repertory season had been the most successful one to date, and had been preceded by an equally successful pantomime, "Babes in the Wood".

Therefore, it needed tremendous foresight and courage to take this decision, but there is no doubt that had he not done so, with war following so quickly, making building impossible, the Alex would have been totally unable to survive in the present day climate.

On April 6th, 1935, on the last night of the "Dick Whittington" pantomime which, in keeping with the Alex's tradition, was England's longest running pantomime, my father, not a demonstrative man, when making his traditional last night speech, broke down as he said "I ought to be a happy man.... but I'm not. This is the last time I shall face you in this building, which is very near and dear to my heart. I...." then he could not go on. During that evening he brought me on the stage saying "In the new theatre, one day he will be taking my place" (a statement which, sadly, I cannot make, for after sixty six years the name Salberg no longer appears on the notepaper). Clarkson Rose then spoke the 'tag' lines and said "Whatever is put into the New Theatre, do build into it the traditions of the Old". The Company and audience then joined together in singing "Olde Lang Syne", after which the curtain fell for the last time on the old Alex.

The following day the builders moved in, and by the time the next pantomime was due to rehearse in December it had been re-built at a cost of £40,000.

When the theatre re-opened I was made General Manager and Billy Guest remained as house manager. Dolly Smith, that most marvellous of theatre secretaries, stayed initially but was soon to leave in order to get married and be greatly missed by everyone, most of all by my father, for she had been in many ways his right hand man and close confidante. A greatly increased front of house staff waited to greet patrons on Monday 23rd December when the theatre re-opened with a gala performance of that year's pantomime, the cast of which was headed by Wee Georgie Wood and Clarkson Rose. Avril Angers*, now such an outstanding comedienne, who played the part of 'Cinderella', looked beautiful but was really totally unsuited to the part which she could never take seriously. Even when trying on the slipper, she would 'send it up' under her breath! Joan and Marjorie were the hit of the show with their mirror and marionette dances. These, along with their shadow dance of another year, are still remembered with pleasure by many older patrons.

The Gala performance was, in fact, something of a disaster; the new ventilating system did not work properly, speeches were too long, as was the pantomime, which ran for well over four hours.

It was not, in any case, one of our better pantomimes although it received very good notices (critics were, I think, a 'kinder' breed in those days), and was for the most part rather dull. I sometimes felt that one of the ponies expressed his opinion of it at most performances in a very visual manner whilst waiting to take Cinderella to the ball!

Neither was it a very happy one, for George and Clarky, who both admired each other, did not work well in unison and eventually were at loggerheads. Later, in order to quell the very

*I recently saw Avril give a brilliant performance as a comedy fairy in "Jack and the Beanstalk" at Richmond.

true rumours of their disunity, they had a photograph taken together. Seeing it at home years later, Judith, my elder daughter then aged four, said to me, "Daddy, they didn't like each other, did they?" My daughters possess, as did Joan, a tremendous instinct for sensing these things which often made it very difficult for the only man in the house. George and Clarky became great friends again after the pantomime; they were two great pantomime artistes......but not together!

At the end of the pantomime the theatre closed for five days, one of which was Good Friday on which, in those days, theatres, unlike now, were not permitted to open. But we never did so as a mark of respect on the part of a Jewish management who felt that surely this day should be held sacred, as did Sir Barry Jackson at the Birmingham Repertory Theatre.

On Saturday, April 11th, the first repertory season in the new theatre opened with "Hyde Park Corner" and the company included Wilfred Babbage who had already played Clive in "Clive of India" in London, a performance which he repeated later in the season, and Linden Travers, a great beauty who was to achieve considerable success in the West End soon afterwards. But without wishing to be invidious, I would select as the outstanding actor in that, or arguably any repertory company, Brefni O'Rorke. A slightly mad Irishman, easy to rouse, a hard drinker, great wit and very good friend.

He was an extraordinary man in many ways. Brefni received a splendid offer at much higher money whilst working for me, and I said of course I would release him. He replied that this was the one thing he didn't want me to do as he was very happy at the Alex. Happiness, not fame, was his aim in life.* The family brilliance is continued by that fine actor, Cyril Cusack.

The season was very successful and, at prices ranging from 2/3d to 6d, the opening production played to £780 (including one extra performance on Bank Holiday), whereas the first play when repertory re-opened in 1931 only took £355; the plays which followed — "The Late Christopher Bean", "Living Dangerously" and "Laburnum Grove" all played to excellent takings which continued throughout the season.

There was no doubt that the decision to re-build the Alex was paying dividends.

*He died just as he was at last receiving his just due in films.

39

CHAPTER 9

OUR ASSOCIATION WITH
THE GRAND THEATRE, WOLVERHAMPTON

A development which was to have a considerable effect on both repertory and pantomime at the Alex occurred in 1936 when our long association with the lovely Grand Theatre, Wolverhampton commenced. It created a pool of actors because the two cities are very close to each other and from time to time the two companies interchanged their productions.

This extension to our activities came about in the most casual manner. P.J. Purdey, the general manager of the Grand, where they were unsuccessfully running a short season of repertory at the time, came over to Birmingham to see a play with a view to its inclusion there.

Mr. Purdey, a delightful, elderly gentleman, rarely left Wolverhampton to travel even as far as Birmingham and when, on his arrival, he found the play only contained four parts, he decided to return home forthwith. On his way he ran into my father and told him about the appalling business they were doing. My father rather rashly, or so it seemed at the time, offered to put in a company there during the height of the summer for a trial period of four weeks, with the option to continue for a further period if it succeeded.

Mr. Purdey agreed and so, on the 1st June, 1936, the curtain rang up on 'Hyde Park Corner' with a very strong company which soon became extremely popular. The trial four weeks was extended to twenty at the end of which arrangements were made for the following year with Mr. Purdey, who was most helpful at all times but rather eccentric and apt to get irritable. Our first manager, David Manderson, who did so much to launch the company successfully, remembers an occasion when a patron spent a long time talking to him whilst Mr. Purdey was

40

obviously anxious to do likewise. Thoroughly frustrated by the time the patron entered the theatre, Mr. Purdey said, "That chap's a damned nuisance — comes here every week." David swears it's true.

The company included an actor called Gerald Cuff, to whom Kenneth More referred in his book as "one of the best actors with whom I ever worked and from whom I learnt so much", Kenny had joined the company a year or two later and I recall that on his marriage to a member of the company I raised his weekly salary from £9 to £12!

During the years Wolverhampton nurtured many artistes who were to become stars; notably, apart from Kenneth More, Barbara Mitchell, Peggy Mount, Rosamund John, Peter Vaughan, John Barron, Vanda Godsell, Nicholas Selby, Pauline Yates, Gwen Berryman (Doris Archer in "The Archers") and Leonard Rossiter, to name but a few. It included too, many fine actors who never became stars but were the backbone of companies like Wolverhampton, such as Aletha Orr, Lee Fox, Tommy Raynor and Penelope Shaw; a list which I could extend over several pages.

With repertory now firmly entrenched, in 1938 we presented our first pantomime there, "Red Riding Hood", with Wee Georgie Wood as the star, thus spreading the Alex's financial load considerably. My father did not live to see it unfortunately, and died unaware of its tremendous success, which was to be the first of many.

We continued to present repertory there until 1966 when, as a result of falling takings and also, I must admit, of falling standards, the theatre decided to put in another (and cheaper) company with fair results in the first year but disastrous ones afterwards. Repertory then ceased there entirely until much later when an unsuccessful effort was made to revive it. Our pantomimes continued until the end of 1971 and were still at their financial peak when Humphrey Stanbury, the theatre's most excellent director, and his chairman, Anthony Southall, took the decision to produce their own; a policy which has brought the Grand substantial rewards and has indeed entirely revitalised their finances.

Our relationship was at all times a most happy one and each successive manager gave us complete co-operation, not least

Peter Marwoode who originally worked for me as a singer, became our company manager until engaged by the theatre as their general manager. He had the strongest personality of any manager I have ever met, closely followed by that of a later manager, who worked so often as an actor for Reggie and myself, Kenneth Keeling. The staff were magnificent. In Tom Latham Snr. they had the best resident stage manager one could meet (along with Dick Turner at the Alex); he, like Dick, could obtain any item asked for, however obscure, in a matter of minutes.

When he retired he was replaced by another outstanding person, Hughie Coleman, whose wife Ida was loved by all pantomime artistes for whom, apart from acting as wardrobe mistress, she supplied magnificent teas. Typical of the splendid staff was the highly popular Miss Price who presided over the dress circle bar for so many years. These are but a few of the many who helped to make the Grand such an efficient and friendly theatre, but no list would be complete without the name of Tom Latham Jnr. who joined on the electric staff, later became assistant manager and is now house manager. I know of no better or more loyal person. (He is mentioned in a later chapter on cricket, which he loves only slightly less than his beloved Grand Theatre.)

The theatre was owned by a prominent Roman Catholic family, the Myatts, with whom neither my father before me, nor I, ever had a contract, during which time a close relationship was forged between our two families.

My closest associations were with Dr. Constance Myatt (Dr. Connie, as she is known) the chairman of the company, her brother Frank, who could spot a spelling mistake from a distance of many miles, and her sister, Mrs. Taylor. I did, of course, meet other members of the family, but less frequently, and had a high regard for them and for Walter Nelson, the theatre's secretary, and his wife Annie, with all of whom I spent many happy hours.

A big tribute must be paid to all the family who, faced with the decision of either selling the site commercially and making a profit or selling to the Corporation at a lower figure, to their eternal credit took the latter step. In fact the City needed a lot of convincing to buy the theatre and there is little doubt that it was the drive of the man who was to become the theatre's chairman under the new regime, Anthony Southall, a local solicitor and chairman of the Grand Theatre Club (among his many activities) which persuaded them after protracted negotiations. Wolverhampton owes a great debt of gratitude to Tony.

For many years David Forder, as manager, who is a splendid theatre person, and Olga Richards, a tower of strength as stage director, did yeoman service for our management. They have for many years now formed a wonderful team at Colchester where the new Mercury Theatre is, along with Salisbury Playhouse, probably the best new theatre to be built in this country.

One name I have not mentioned so far is that of my cousin, Basil Thomas, who took over the reins from David Manderson when he left to become the manager of the Prince of Wales Theatre, Birmingham.

Basil's influence on our association with the Grand cannot be over-estimated. He became, in due course, one of Wolverhampton's leading personalities and deserves a chapter to himself.

CHAPTER 10

BASIL

Basil was my first cousin and remained one of my very closest friends until he died at a tragically early age, at the Savage Club, on the very day on which I was being inaugurated as a member.

Described by Arthur Askey, in a recent letter to me, as "that lovable and witty man", he possessed one of the best senses of humour I have ever known but was quite unable to control himself when anything struck him as being funny.

A great fan of the Marx Brothers, soon after one of their films started he had to be literally carried out of the cinema in a state of convulsion. When he went to see one of his great favourites, a comic named Billy Bennett ('almost a gentleman') at the local Empire Theatre, he laughed so much in gleeful anticipation that as soon as his number went up on the side of the proscenium arch (an artiste's number corresponding with the one in the programme was indicated in this way), he had to be helped out of the theatre before Billy Bennett actually appeared!

He was often embarrrassed, as were his friends, by a nervous trait which caused him to laugh on the most serious occasions. The silence observed on Armistice Day was an ordeal for him and he had to stay indoors during that period. I recall an occasion at the County Ground when we stood in silence as a tribute to Cecil Parkin, the famous cricketer, who had just died; a silence broken only by Basil's hearty laughter of which he was, of course, thoroughly ashamed. My younger daughter, Joey, is similarly afflicted whenever she enters a church and usually has to be rushed out of the building. On one occasion, when she found herself in the middle of a funeral procession at Rheims Cathedral, her uncontrolled mirth almost caused a riot.

Basil was a brilliant writer. Some of his best known plays

were "Shooting Star", "Book of the Month", "Two of Every-thing", "This Blessed Plot", "The Lovebirds", "Springtime", most of which enjoyed substantial London runs. His songs, written with Barbara Gordon* and usually with music by Harry Parr Davis, included Beatrice Lillie's "Wind Round My Heart"; "When I hear Music", featured in C.B. Cochran's last revue; the theme song for the stage version of "No Orchids for Miss Blandish"; and various songs for films starring Vera Lynn, George Formby and David Niven. Together, with music by Robert Gordon, they wrote many of Arthur Askey's songs, such as "The Budgerigar" and "The Pixie". Also, with Manning Sherwin supplying the music, they wrote the musical "The Kid from Stratford" which ran for eighteen months at the Princes Theatre, starring Arthur Askey. They supplied material for Tommy Trinder, Sid Field and a number of sketches and songs for the Palladium and Prince of Wales Theatres.

He was the author of several pantomime scripts for the Palladium and the Alex. However, he was not very fond of panto-mime and I do not think he had a real feeling for it, with the result that this was never a field in which he excelled. But he was probably most proud of the fact that he had a poem printed in *The Cricketer* about a bowler who always bowled 'just short of a length' and who, when he died, was buried 'just short of a length'; for his great passion outside the theatre, his wife Hedi, and his daughter Susan, was cricket. I am convinced he would rather have made fifty than have written any of his plays or songs, but this ambition was to be denied him for he was a very indifferent performer who could spend half an hour describing an innings he had played the previous Saturday at the end of which, it transpired, he had made 'three, not out'. He once asked me, at the end of a cricket tour, why his batting had failed so consistently: "Basil", I said, rather cruelly, "I think you took your eye off the ball earlier than usual." He also loved soccer and was a fervent fan of Aston Villa and was quite unable to eat on the occasions when they lost. Had he been alive during the years when they dropped from Division One to Division Three, he would have gone extremely hungry, or even

*Now living in Portugal. In correspondence with me during the writing of this book, she entirely endorsed Arthur Askey's assessment of Basil who she describes as "easily the funniest and wittiest man I have ever known."

45

worse, he might have been born in Rochdale — and starved!

He was an outstandingly intelligent person who developed a great knowledge of all matters theatrical which stood him in good stead when later he took over the Wolverhampton company completely and directed the fortunes of the Alex when I joined the Army. Above all he was a modest and utterly honest person, completely devoid of any guile and incapable of a mean action.

Two years ago, Joey and I visited his widow, Hedi, in America where she lives, now happily re-married to a splendid man. We talked a lot about Basil and revived memories, if indeed they required reviving, of a fine person whose friendship and loyalty I will never forget.

CHAPTER 11

PASSING OF AN ERA - MY FATHER DIES

My father had become increasingly unwell since 1936, and by the late summer of 1937 his health deteriorated further and, although only just over sixty, he was finding life physically difficult.

On doctor's advice he went on one of his much loved cruises for relaxation, but any improvement was only temporary and on September 27th, 1938, after playing bridge at the Press Club, he returned to the theatre where I recall standing with him in the foyer as the first house 'went in', and laughing with him at the antics of our diminutive pageboy. He then went to his office where, during the course of the first performance of "Devonshire Cream", he collapsed.

I was sent for and had the ordeal of going in front of the curtain, which had been lowered, to ask if there was a doctor in the house. Some of the audience thought this was a gag, but two doctors answered the request and his own doctor and a heart specialist were sent for, but it was too late — he had died, as he would have wished, in harness.

He was a much beloved man both in and out of the theatre. As M.F.K. Fraser wrote in his book, "Though his true monument is the Alexandra Theatre and the work it is so efficiently and prosperously doing, his memory lives also in a bed named for him at the Royal Cripples Hospital at Bromsgrove, where children (with whom he was often more perfectly at ease than with adults) are converted from twisted shapes into active young citizens.

His funeral brought together thousands of people of all types and creeds; in fact such scenes had never previously been seen at the Jewish Cemetery at Witton where he was buried alongside his wife, whom he never ceased to adore."

The following year the Rocket Club installed a plaque in the (now old) foyer of the theatre. It is above the spot where he stood so often to welcome friends and patrons. It is in bronze with an embossed portrait of my father and an appropriate inscription which reads

"Leon Salberg 1875 — 1937
Erected on the scene of his life's work.
Under the auspices of the Rocket Club on behalf of
his friends in tribute to his memory"

I had a light placed over it and it shines whenever the theatre is open.

The Rocket Club issued, at the same time, a booklet entitled "Leon Salberg — Past President", containing the names of all the subscribers to the plaque, who numbered many hundred. It has a short preface about my father and included a number of tributes of which I quote just a few:

"The fineness of his character, the charm of his personality, and the splendid principles which guided his everyday living, made Leon Salberg's life one of beauty.......He was, in fact, an ambassador of goodwill between Jew and Gentile."
Dr. A. Cohen, Minister of the Birmingham Jewish Congregation

"Mr. Salberg was not only a master but a friend......."
W.T. Guest (for many years the Theatre's loyal manager)

"If I say he was the kindest, most sincere, most loyal and generous friend imaginable, I state the plain truth. Throughout the profession his integrity and his generosity were household words, and what he was in business he was in private friendship."
MF in the Birmingham Weekly Post.

"The charm of his singularly modest personality, the ability he displayed in a difficult profession, and the dignity with which he upheld the highest traditions of his race, made him a popular and respected figure.........Like Maurice Perlmutter, he was a great gentleman."
Birmingham Mail.

"My friend Leon was one of the greatest men of the theatre I have worked for. He was a man first, a manager second, with a tolerance for the actor's faults, and an appreciation of his qualities that endeared him to me. Although a powerful man

in his business, it was his innate simplicity which mattered, and which will make him remembered."
Clarkson Rose.

"When I heard of Leon's death, my thoughts were: "How I'm going to miss his forgiveness and understanding, and that unique loyalty towards those he believed in, which I shared as friend and player."
Georgie Wood.

At the unveiling the then President of the Rocket Club, Eli Davis, recalled much of his charity work and added-

"A contribution will be made to a Jewish charity in token of the fact that he was ever an apostle of friendship, understanding and mutual respect between Jew and Gentile."

So there is a lasting monument to him in the theatre which was his pride, but not his love, for his heart always remained in the old Alex, which was his home whenever he entered it and again to quote M.F.K. Fraser, "When they pulled down the old house, they pulled something from his heart."

He was a great man and I would be happy to feel that he would not have been entirely dissatisfied with my efforts to assume his mantle and to uphold a name which he had made synonymous with integrity and love towards his fellow man.

CHAPTER 12

THE THEATRE & SPORT - - MOSTLY CRICKET

In 1938 the inter-theatres' pantomime charity football match, which had long been discarded, was resumed. The venue was Villa Park and the sides were the Theatre Royal versus the combined Alex and Prince of Wales casts and staff. Evelyn Laye, the loveliest of principal boys, playing at the Theatre Royal that year, kicked off and Elsie and Doris Waters re-started the second half. Our side included Tommy Trinder, later to become the Fulham chairman. He was a better chairman than footballer! The Royal had Bunny Doyle, a first class 'dame' and an excellent footballer, who had played for Grimsby Reserves and Blyth Spartans and there were several other good players on both sides and many not such good ones!

We won 3–2 and I recall with shame that, perhaps because I had been unwell during the morning, after collecting the ball at about the half-way line and running for what felt miles (I had never played on such a large field), I scored the first of my two goals and was then promptly sick in front of at least three thousand spectators.

The same year the inter-theatre pantomime sports were resumed. I won the 100 yards but, as I was rather proud of my running, was a little shocked to find the manager of Aston Hippodrome ahead of me and the winning post only a few yards away. To my great relief he fell when in reach of victory. The Ladies 100 yards was won easily by Carol Hinsley, a member of our company, who was to remain with us for years as a solo dancer and, in due course, first class choreographer. I think, with training, she would have become a first class sprinter as well.

But these were only by way of sidelines, and no book about the Alex would be complete without mention of our cricket activities. Based on our repertory companies, we called ourselves 'The Reptiles' and took over the mantle of Sir Frank Benson who, it is said, once advertised for a "Laertes capable of keeping wicket". It was always rumoured that Basil and I did not interview male artistes, but instead put the nets down in Shaftesbury Avenue. Certainly an actor once wrote to me saying he was a juvenile, 6' 2" and a first rate fast bowler — had I any vacancies? I replied that at the moment our acting strength was indifferent, but our cricket team excellent; when things reversed themselves I would get in touch with him.

Our first cricket match took place in May 1939 when the combined Wolverhampton and Birmingham companies played the "I Can Take It" company, then appearing at the Birmingham Theatre Royal. Their side was captained by Sonnie Hale, a mad keen cricketer whose wife, Jessie Matthews, attended the match which was in aid of the Actors' Benevolent Fund. To quote from the *Birmingham Mail*, "The match attracted well over 1,000 spectators and was won by the combined Repertory Companies who scored 72. Derek Salberg, an enthusiastic cricketer who has several times played for the Warwickshire Club and Ground, was the highest scorer, hitting 32 not out. Sonnie Hale captained the Theatre Royal team taking three wickets and scoring 9 runs."

Our next match was against Northampton Repertory Company and again (being very conceited about my cricket triumphs, which were not all that numerous), I quote a paper, *The Stage* of June 1939, "An all-day match took place on Sunday between the combined Derek Salberg repertory companies on the one side and the Northampton Repertory Theatre on the other. An outstanding feature of the game, which the Salberg companies won by seven wickets, was the spin bowling of Derek Salberg who took, in all, 13 wickets for 37. The scores were Salberg companies 169 and 28 for three wickets; Northampton 63 and 128." For someone who had once taken 1 for 130 in a house match at school, this performance was rather better than 'par for the course'.

Our last game before war intervened took place in July. The *Birmingham Post* reported " The Derek Salberg repertory companies met the Stratford-on-Avon Festival Company in a day match at the Manders sports ground, Wolverhampton, yesterday. Stratford-on-Avon was successful. In the first innings the Festival Company made 79 (R. Wordsworth 49 not out, Gerald Cuff 3 for 35, J. Weaver 3 for 2). The Salberg side, after making 52 for the loss of two wickets, was all out for 76. (N Melrose 42, T. Howard 5 for 33). In the second innings the Stratford players obtained 172 (J. McCallum 46, T. Howard 40, G. Kenton 58; D. Salberg 6 for 38).

The Salberg company was disposed of a second time for 78 (N. Melrose 40)". The J. McCallum referred to is the excellent actor John McCallum, married to Googie Withers, and T. Howard — Trevor Howard — so he and I were able to resume the school rivalry of the days when we played against each other in House matches. He was a fine cricketer who played for Clifton and greatly distinguished himself at Lords in our, then, annual match there against Tonbridge, and afterwards for the Public Schools team at Lords. Soon after the war, on a much more serious level, for some possibly too serious, we resumed our cricket activities and compiled a very formidable fixture list as we were able to call on many fine players. Outstanding was Oliver Gordon, then producing repertory at Wolverhampton. Under his real name, Oliver Battcock, he captained Bucks., habitually topping the minor counties bowling averages, and taking the summer off to play cricket. He was described by Jim Swanton in his recent book as 'the best cricketer who never played first class cricket.' That great athlete, Peter Cranmer, an ex-Warwickshire captain, maintains he was one of the finest bowlers with a new ball he ever played against. He did a great deal to help my bowling average as, when I was 'on' at the other end, batsmen were so relieved to get away from him that they played wild strokes at my bowling which was mainly composed of rather erratic slow leg breaks, similar to those of Sir James Barrie, who said that his deliveries were so slow and rose so high that if he didn't like the look of one he could run after it and bring it back! Equally outstanding, but not such regular members, were Peter Powell, our Birmingham producer who played for Middlesex when only 17, and John Sykes who produced at Wolverhampton for a period and had played for Surrey. Our Secretary, Clifford Wooldridge, played for Stourbridge in the Birmingham League; Anthony Sagar, a splendid actor who died prematurely when on the threshold of big

52

things, had played for Lancashire 2nd XI, and Geoffrey Chater, now one of TV's outstanding actors, was a splendid cricketer as befits a member of the Robinson family who, each year, played a match against the Edrich family. He joined us soon after making 100 against us at Datchet on one of the cricket tours — about which, more later. Several members of the company, such as Peter Vaughan and Tony Steedman, were excellent players and well up to good Club standard, as was Leslie Dunn, regularly to be seen on TV (for the past 23 years Paul Johnson in "The Archers"), and for many years a valued member of our repertory company. We had, as permanent 'guest', Cecil Addleman who played for Moseley in the Birmingham League, eventually captaining them; he was an outstanding all-round athlete and a cricketer of very nearly county standard and a great man to have in a team. One of the keenest members was Tom Latham, now house manager of the Grand Theatre, Wolverhampton, who gets a special mention later in the chapter.

We had several players at varying cricketing levels and, as is inevitable with such teams, the standard often dropped dramatically at the end of the scale. I remember Edward Mulhare, a delightful Irishman then in the Birmingham company (and later to make such a tremendous success as Higgins in "My Fair Lady" in New York that he stayed there and is now one of the idols of Broadway), playing his one and only game for us and being discovered shaving in the dressing room when, owing to a sudden fall of wickets, he was due to bat as last man. There was hardly time to explain to him that if either batsman hit the ball out of reach of a fieldsman he could run. He didn't seem to comprehend, but it hardly mattered as he was out first ball!

When it was agreed that the Wolverhampton company would take a summer break, we decided, with Oliver Gordon's help, to organise a cricket tour to the lovely area around Windsor where he lived. The tour was an enormous success; we played Datchet, Wraysbury (on the Eton College ground), Chalfont St. Peter, Gerrards Cross and Slough. We continued to play these teams for many years to come, with the exception of Slough whose ground was rather 'towny' for a tour such as ours, and substituted a fixture against the Stage Cricket XI.

The team on tour, naturally, included some outsiders, such as Trevor Howard, who played one match, made a duck, missed

a catch and then had to rush off early for his evening performance in the West End! My great army chum, Bob Key, and our
mutual friend, Arthur Coulthard, a great athlete and first class
rugger player, normally joined us, as did R.D. Smith who had
played cricket for Birmingham University and was, until recently,
a top BBC Drama Director. I remember with joy his performance
in a match against Gerrards Cross who always picked a team
largely composed of public school boys, most of whom were in
their school XI. On this occasion they included R.V.C. Robins,
direct from his triumph for Eton v. Harrow at Lords, where he
had bowled out the opposition almost single handed. He soon
dismissed our early batsmen but Reggie Smith and Tom Latham,
who would not claim to be a great batsman and had never
heard of Robins, came together and carted him all over the field
and we won handsomely. Others to accompany us either
regularly or occasionally, included my brother, Reggie, a first
class rugger player but moderate cricketer who invariably
appeared in a different, spendidly coloured cap, which greatly
impressed the opposition who were not to know that he had
won them, not on the cricket field, but for drinking during his
days at Oxford! My cousin, Myer Thomas, no cricketer, but a
splendid person to take on tour, and Brian Harvey (who received
his colours at King Edward's School and was theatre and cricket
correspondent at that time for the *Birmingham Despatch*) often
joined us. A great asset to the side, both on and off the field
(particularly off), was Mike Green, author of *Coarse Fishing,
Coarse Rugger*, etc., who rather fancied his bowling. During
one match, when I was captain, he kept turning his arm over,
making it obvious that he felt it was time that he had a bowl.
I continued to disregard his obvious hints until eventually a ball
was hit into an adjoining field where it landed in some cow
dung. On its return I threw it to him and, to his disgust, said,
"You have a go now, Mike, you're used to bowling shit!"

In an article in *Cricket 1976* he recalled an occasion when
we played Gerrards Cross who, as usual, were composed largely
of public school boys, many of whom had on the back of their
bats such inscriptions as '120 v. Harrow', '70 not out v. Charter-
house' etc. This irritated Basil, not, as already stated, a very
good batsman, so in the tea interval he wrote on his bat '2 not
out v. the Co-op' and '4 v. Woolworths'.

54

In later years I played a lot of cricket with Mike for Harborne and I recall a match when I was captaining the "A" team in the absence of the regular skipper (a delightful man, but no great captain, who had the ability to snatch defeat from the very jaws of victory), soon after a financially disastrous production of 'Twelfth Night' at the Alex. We could not get the opposition out so, eventually, Mike came up to me pointing to one of the several youngsters who were brought in during their school holidays and said, "Why don't you put Shakespeare on?" "Not bloody likely," I said, "last time I did it cost me over £1,000." Umpiring in that match, as he also did for our theatre matches, was Cecil Mumford who went everywhere with us, was most enthusiastic, and a grand person to have around, his only failings as an Umpire being an inability to see or hear!

They were very happy days and I believe did a lot of good for company morale, especially as most of the female members of the casts attended. This, added to our capacity for drinking beer, made us very popular wherever we went! But, like all good things, our cricketing days had to come to an end. Basil, who was so much part of them, died and somehow no longer did there seem to be an influx of staff or actors interested in the game. But whenever those of us who remember those days meet, we soon start to reminisce about them. Sometimes, we even talk about the Theatre!

CHAPTER 13

I BECOME THE NEW 'GUVNOR' — THEN WAR COMES

When my father died in September 1937, I became, at the age of twenty-six, England's youngest theatre director. Looking back I cannot imagine why I was not more daunted by the heavy responsibility of running the Alex and its outside interests which were mostly, at that time, centred round the Grand Theatre, Wolverhampton. I was certainly helped by my partners — my two uncles, who might easily have shown a lack of confidence in my ability to succeed my father but, in fact, gave me every co-operation.

They knew that I had received a very good grounding during the previous five years, especially the past two when, in view of my father's ill health, I had taken on added responsibilities. My biggest asset probably lay in my youth and the confidence that goes with it, allied to any amount of enthusiasm, for I was naturally brimming over with ideas. What young man isn't? But I had the sense to make my first objective that of keeping the theatre on an even keel and trying to avoid the necessity for that dreaded expression "Things aren't what they used to be". In this I had wonderful assistance from Dolly Smith, Billy Guest, David Cochran and Gladys Lutman, and in fact the whole staff, all of whom were prepared to give "Mr. Derek" every chance to prove his worth.

My father's death had answered my overwhelming personal problem, for on the day before she and Marjorie sailed to South Africa to appear in pantomime and produce the dances, Joan and I became engaged. This naturally enabled me to tackle my task in a much happier state of mind. Fortunately there were few immediate problems as repertory continued to thrive and the forthcoming pantomime, 'Aladdin', had already been cast by my father, with David Cochran once again producing, designing costumes and conducting the orchestra. It ran (as did most Alex pantomimes in those days) until Easter Saturday, and at the final performance, in my (first) last night speech, I announced that the next pantomime would be 'Robinson Crusoe' with George Robey, one of the most famous names in the British Theatre, playing the part of Mrs. Crusoe. He was far and away the biggest star yet to be booked, for I was very aware that, with the introduction of glittering 'names' by Emile Littler in his splendid pantomimes at the Prince of Wales, and Moss Empires following suit at the Theatre Royal, we might, in spite of our high reputation, find ourselves getting left behind. The trials and tribulations which followed this booking, I recount in the later chapter on pantomime.

The repertory season which followed was very successful and achieved splendid acting standards and attendance figures which, up to that date, had never been equalled. The choice of play was perhaps unexciting although I recall with particular pleasure performances of Eugene O'Neill's "Anna Christie" and J.B. Priestley's "Time and the Conways". The season also served to introduce a Birmingham playwright, John Taylor, who was discovered by that brilliant, eccentric and lovable producer, George Owen. John wrote many plays for the Alex but, perhaps because they were often a little localised, he never achieved a wider audience.

It had been a very encouraging opening to my regime and I was ambitious to develop the activities of the theatre even further.

With this in mind, at the beginning of 1939, I decided to extend our area of operations to include companies at Hereford and Cheltenham. There were two main reasons: firstly I felt they could act, initially, as a nursery for the Birmingham and Wolverhampton companies. Secondly, that eventually they might make it possible to perform every play for a week in each of the four towns (an extension of the system we had already tried out on occasions with our Birmingham and Wolverhampton companies), for I was dissatisfied with the limitations imposed by weekly repertory and the strain it imposed on actors and staff. But it was never possible to develop this idea, as war came too quickly after the launching of these two companies.

After the war a similar system was tried, with Arts Council

support, by a few companies but for very many reasons it failed, as I now feel it was bound to have done with us. In any case, only Hereford warmed to the idea of repertory as Cheltenham did not, and although later I was to make one more effort there, I did not persevere. However, after the war, I presented the first production in the theatre when it was taken over by the local authority — "Dear Charles" with Jessie Matthews.

Cheltenham has always been a difficult theatre town, but the Everyman Theatre (once named the Opera House), under the direction of one of our best administrators, Rae Hammond, who spent a long time as a trainee with Reggie and myself, has had a splendid record in recent years. Many of its producers, including the present one, Malcolm Farquhar, have come under the Salberg banner, as has Carol Evans, who started at the Alex then went to the Everyman where she has remained for twelve years and is now stage director. So I feel I have done a little to help maintain this delightful theatre. In view of future events it was probably a pity that Hereford did start so well, for after the war Basil and I, perhaps influenced by our fondness for Hereford and its quaint theatre, persuaded the board, against the advice of our chairman, Julius Thomas, a shrewd man, to purchase the theatre. At first our judgement appeared to be correct and business boomed but, with cast changes and a small population on which to draw, business fell away and eventually we leased and finally sold it to Myles Byrne, who did all in his power to continue its life as a theatre, but failed. Reluctantly he turned it into a cinema, then even more reluctantly into a club, and now it is no more. The operation had unfortunately proved to be a costly one.

At the Alex the season was progressing extremely well. We had a very popular company which included Beryl Johnstone, who had long been with our Wolverhampton company, Robert Ginns, one of the most popular of Alex repertory actors, Kathleen St. John, Sheila Brownrigg, Peter Rosser, Anne Pichon, Stanley Illsley and, by no means least, Betty Bowden and Anthony Viccars, idols of the Alex public who, in those days, and I believe equally today, demanded that their actors should also be personalities; something which drama schools cannot teach and is perhaps not always appreciated by producers.

Two other names which were to become famous appeared on the programmes that year. Kenneth More, on loan for a couple of weeks from our Wolverhampton company, and Noel Johnson, later 'Dick Barton — special agent', making his first stage appearance in one of the plays.

All seemed set fair when, in September, as had long seemed inevitable to any thinking person, war came.*

Later in the year permission was granted, in spite of strong opposition from the Lord's Day Observance Society, for theatres to open on Sundays. In anticipation of this I had already made arrangements to present, every Sunday, a Variety Show entitled "Musical Moments" with Cyril Fletcher, then at the very zenith of his fame, as resident compere; a large orchestra and different acts each week. We were thus, somewhat to his chagrin, ahead of Emile Littler who for once, and perhaps the only time in his life, was 'left at the post' as he had no scheme ready for the Prince of Wales Theatre. On the first Sunday there were queues all round the theatre and for some weeks business continued to be excellent, but eventually the difficulty of obtaining artistes, and the similarity of the fare offered, caused a dropping off in attendances and the shows were finally abandoned. Meantime, they had given a much needed boost to the theatre and, I think, to public morale. However, mine wavered slightly after a conversation I had, at the end of one of the performances, with the writer of the war's most patriotic song which proclaimed that, whatever happened, there would always be an England. He argued forcibly that we had no possible chance of winning the war!

Another innovation was to drop the Monday repertory performance and substitute recitals by such famous pianists as Poushinoff, Moseiwitch, Solomon and the violinist Albert Sammons, which were well supported, although a military band played to only about seventy people.

That year's pantomime was "Dick Whittington" and performances, which were timed to beat the black-out, included three morning performances. At the end of that pantomime

*It had perhaps not seemed quite so inevitable to two elderly M.C.C. members who, during the last first class game at Lords, watched silently as workmen removed the marble bust of W.G. Grace from the Long Room. Eventually one of them spoke. "Mark my words," he said, "this means war."

there was an event which was to influence the future of the theatre, a visit by the Ballet Rambert, the first outside company since 1931. It materialised through a suggestion from my friend Joan Levi (now Joan Sohn-Rethel) to Peggy Van Praagh, the famous ballerina, who was a member of the company. She put the idea to Madame Rambert who was extremely enthusiastic.

The visit was a great success which reinforced my resolve that, after the war (all being well), my policy would include some tours. Madame Rambert stayed with us that week and was a most entertaining guest. Happily she is still very active*, but I doubt whether she would now wish to turn a cartwheel on our stage as she did one day for the benefit of Joan and myself, although even then this wonderful lady was no youngster.

The black-out was inhibiting many would-be patrons from coming to the theatre, but it performed one good deed for us as, of necessity, it enforced a decision to present each play not twice but once nightly. This had the added advantage of widening the play selection, and the season included productions of "Merchant of Venice", Ibsen's "Ghosts" and a moving but rarely performed play, "Cradle Song", in which my sister-in-law Marjorie, a member of the company that year, gave a lovely performance, as did Kathleen St. John and all the cast.

In view of the fact that I would shortly be joining the army, Bill Dobson had joined the staff. He was a manager of great personality and remained for many years after the war, and was to prove a great asset, not only to the Alex, but to the social life of Birmingham.

Knowing that he had been a Sergeant Major in World War I, I told him that I had been totally inadequate at arms drill in my OTC days at Clifton. So he kindly drilled me in my office each day, with a walking stick substituted for a rifle. We used to lock the office door as we should have looked extremely foolish if anyone had walked in. Heaven knows what deep dark plots the staff would have thought we were hatching!

Soon I entered the army but, being stationed near home, was able to continue to take an active interest in the theatre. However, during 1942 Basil was taking greatly increased control, in conjunction with Bill Dobson, and they were largely responsible

---

*She is now ninety.

for the success of the repertory season in which the Wolverhampton and Birmingham companies pooled their resources to a greater degree than ever before. This helped to maintain the standard in a difficult period, especially with the shortage of manpower.

CHAPTER 14

MY YEARS IN UNIFORM

I wish I could say that my war service had been valiant and distinguished, but this would not be true, although I had early on (unknown to Joan) volunteered for the R.A.F. As there was then no manpower shortage, I was told to come back later, but never did, a merciful release for both the country and myself. How I came to do this I am uncertain to this day as flying, to me, is only an unpleasant necessity. It was probably because I wanted, at all costs, to avoid continual parades which, at that time, was my (wrong) concept of the army. Instead, I eventually joined the Royal Corps of Signals and was posted locally to Wylde Green where I reported to the Company Office and had my details taken down by one, Sidney Smith, who has remained a great friend to this day, as has his delightful wife, Florence.

On instructions from the Quartermaster, Jim Connor, who has also remained a good friend of mine, I was kept waiting for two hours to be kitted out for, as he told me later, I was to be held firmly in my place whether I owned a theatre or not! (Little did he know how apprehensive I felt.) Next day I was detailed to haul coal around with a fabulous character, Ted da Costa, who, until war broke out, had been the musical director at the Empire, Birmingham. He occupied the next bed to me and, although immaculate in tails, was about the scruffiest person imaginable at all other times. My next duty was latrine fatigue and I suggested to my mate that our slogan might, with the slight alteration of the second word, bear a strong resemblance to the nightly statement of our theatre doorman who used to call out "Good seats in all parts."

Soon I was found a much more congenial task when I was detailed to work in the sergeants' mess. In charge was a splendid man, Fred Fellows, and my mate was a young man, Bob Key, who was to become a lifelong friend, as have all the members of his family.* In order to impress Fred I took him to the theatre to show him round but when I came to the top circle, it was manned by a newcomer who did not know me and would not let me in. I remonstrated mildly and finally, in desperation, said "Actually I am Derek Salberg" to which he replied "I don't care if your are bloody Winston Churchill, you're not coming in here without a ticket." Fred was not all that impressed!

I had a similar experience last year when I took Eric Morecambe to the Warwickshire County Cricket Ground. When we arrived at the entrance to the committee room the new doorman would not admit me, for although I had been a committee member for very many years, my card was not marked 'official'. I pleaded, feeling rather foolish, but to no avail; but he then recognised Eric, asked for his autograph, and we were in!

However, this was in the future and interrupts the tale of my army career.

Eventually I was transferred to the line section where, apart from an ability to climb a pole, I was useless and was usually given a hole to dig where I could do no harm until it was time to help the driver 'brew up'. Each morning we would call at a transport cafe on the way to the job and eventually we called at the job on the way to the transport cafe! I loved it.

I used to organise concerts and was able to get many famous artistes down to the unit, and I imagine this, plus the fact that against a rather weak R.A.F. unit I performed the hat-trick, was the reason that my O.C., a very keen cricketer, gave me two (unpaid, local acting!) stripes. It was certainly not for my ability as a soldier.

After just over a year, Greatrex Newman (of 'Fol-de-Rol' and lyric writing fame), who held the rank of Colonel, applied for my transfer to RASCA/EFI which embraced the military side of ENSA (Entertainments National Service Association). In due course the application came through and I had to report to my O.C. for an interview which bore a strong similarity to the

* He and his wife Anne now run the excellent Gerrans Bay Hotel at Portscatho in Cornwall where I usually spend a few delightful days each year.

one which, as already described, I had undergone many years earlier with my housemaster. Briefly he said, "We shall be sorry to lose you, you're a nice chap, but as signals potential— bloody hopeless!" (we were a friendly unit!). I had arranged a concert, so my O.C. applied for my departure to be delayed until it was over, and at the end of it occurred one of the nicest things that has ever happened to me. To thank me, I suppose, for organising the concerts and for making theatre tickets available, I was presented with an engraved whisky flask which I cherish to this day. I had immensely enjoyed my time with No. 2 Company and made a number of friendships, apart from those already mentiond, many of which still endure. Reg Brewer in particular has remained a close friend, as has Tom Fahy (fellow member of the Rocket Club and cricket enthusiast), and Alf Pursall who read one of the earlier manuscripts of this book and made many constructive comments (as did Liz Stern*). I attend the annual reunion and can never understand why everyone has aged except me (and Jim Connor, who never does — which I find most irritating).

So, in January 1943, I went on an officers' course where my deficiencies soon became known. People came from miles to see me march.........always just slightly out of step......and to watch my arms drill which, in spite of the earlier practice with the walking stick, had not improved since my OTC days. I was told later that my efforts to dismantle and re-assemble a sten gun was the talk of all future courses! My only good marks were obtained in throwing a hand grenade, which I did with a leg break action, and on the morning runs when I came in ahead of the rest of the course, and not far behind the fanatically fit instructor. They were spendid people on the course, but I was delighted when it was over.

My experiences with the sten gun were typical of my complete inadequacy at anything even remotely mechanical. On my first attempt, for example, at using a self service petrol pump I took an age to remove the pump, could not get it properly into my tank and then had great difficulty in replacing it. Altogether I spent about ten minutes, during which time dozens of cars had lined up behind me or had moved on in despair, inevitably

*Once a stage-manager with our Wolverhampton company and now a stalwart of the "Crossroads" stage-management staff.

64

losing the garage several pounds. Eventually I proceeded to the office to pay, said "Pump No. 5 — how much please." She gave me a scornful look before replying acidly — "4½p!" I have never returned to that petrol station.

I am equally unsuccessful as a photographer. Once, however, I was delighted with a picture I had taken of the Leaning Tower of Pisa, but my pride was short lived when I discovered that every picture on the roll showed a building or a view at exactly the same angle as the Leaning Tower!

There was a delay before my commission came through and as I had been posted overseas I travelled with the rank of S.Q.M.S. (Sgt. Major) on a voyage round the Cape.

Although it was at the height of submarine warfare, the voyage was comparatively uneventful, but some of the convoy, who left us after Freetown to take the shorter route which had just opened up, were not so lucky and tragically many of those ships went down. Our next stop was Capetown where we all wore topees (a form of headgear long discarded) on a route march, getting laughs Morecambe and Wise would have envied.

We arrived in Egypt after about seven weeks, then to the transit camp at Geneifa before proceeding to report to Cairo for posting to Tripoli where 10 Corps, which included the famous 'desert rats', were resting, with their entertainment a high priority. I travelled there by sea from Alexandria and en route developed a temperature of over 103°. We were told to stand by for an air attack which did not materialise, nevertheless, the threat did not help my temperature. On arrival in Tripoli the virus returned and I went into hospital a day or two before the King was due to pass by.

On the day of his visit we were rushed into beds and placed outside the hospital so that he could see us as he went by. The King undoubtedly thought he was looking at a lot of heroes, whereas most of us were only suffering from advanced Gyppy tummy, body ailments brought on by profuse sweating, or some other comparatively minor complaint. Afterwards we learnt that the King, who looked extremely unhappy, was himself suffering from Gyppy tummy.

I stayed in Tripoli for some time, subsisting for much of it on corned beef, so much so that to this day I cannot look it in the face. Soon after my arrival there I was told that acting as a

Post Corporal in an R.A.F. station was someone vaguely connected with the theatre. His name was Leslie Grade and I was able to be of some help to him which neither he, nor his brother Lew, ever forgot. Both, particularly Leslie, were of tremendous assistance to me over the years and, as related later, when the Alex was facing a very severe crisis, they aided the theatre financially.

My next move was to Sicily, long after it had ceased to be of military importance. I have only a few recollections of this period, chiefly of an evening spent with Emlyn Williams when we talked until the early hours, and of a week's visit by Billy Russell ('Only a Working Man'), the erstwhile famous Black Country character comedian, with whom I had many nostalgic talks about Birmingham.

I was officer-in-charge of entertainment for No. 1 District, which later operated just behind rear 8th Army, and I moved with them from Sicily to Italy to a small, much bombed town called Foligno. While we were there I spent a few days leave in Rome, which had just fallen, and attended one of the Pope's earlier audiences when he blessed the troops. It was strange to realise that, only a few weeks earlier, he had been doing the same for the German troops.

The Alex repertory company arrived in Naples at a time when I had to report for a conference there, so we had a very joyful reunion and later, when I routed them in my own area, spent many convivial evenings with them, receiving first hand news about the Alex and Birmingham. In charge of the party was that consistently useful producer and actor, Philip Stainton, helped by World War I veteran, Vernon Fortescue who, even in E.N.S.A. uniform, resembled a general!

From Foligno, to rear 8th Army, to a field in a place called Poggibonsi near Florence, where I had been assigned to requisition theatres and cinemas and prepare to receive ENSA shows when the town was captured. But in the event it took so long to fall that I was posted back to No. 1 district and stayed with them until their move to Padua, by which time the war was over. I only learnt this a day later as I was travelling around, visiting small units, with Alex Jackson the famous England footballer, then a welfare officer.

I was then ordered to report home for posting to Germany

but was sent instead to Cairo where, because the officer who was being flown out to act as O/IC Middle East Forces entertainment was injured in a plane crash, I became temporary officer in charge, an appointment later ratified. This was a difficult time as the British were very unwelcome and it was unwise to go out in the streets in uniform. On one occasion the car in which I was travelling was surrounded by a howling mob (and believe me an Egyptian mob can howl!), and only the skill of the Arab driver made our escape possible. I thought I was about to suffer the fate of some soldiers who had been surrounded and murdered in Alexandria the previous week.

I was then due for demobilisation but suffered a spontaneous pneumothorax (collapsed lung) and was removed to hospital, then back to England in an old and very inadequate Italian hospital ship which was totally unable to cope with the troops' distress caused by severe gales and rolling seas.

On arrival in England we were taken to a hospital up North and I can still recall my frustration when we stopped for a while in New Street Station within sight of the Alex. Then to Birminham's Queen Elizabeth Hospital for a few days where, after signing a document stating that I would not claim a pension, I was demobbed.

This is not a history of ENSA, about which much has been written, mostly critical, and much of it unfair. One complaint was that ENSA shows did not go sufficiently near the front line, but in fact they went wherever they were sent and, at one time, Joan and Marjorie had to be hastily evacuated from the unit they were playing in view of an imminent German counter attack. But more often they would be playing to troops who were nowhere near a battle zone, but nevertheless suffering from excessive boredom and very much in need of entertainment.

Another criticism was that the standards were often very low. This was true but it must be borne in mind that ENSA was faced with the impossible task of covering a massive area and frankly there were not enough good artistes to go round. But there were some wonderful shows and performers, and the sight of an ENSA female, even if she was not specially attractive, meant a lot to troops who, particularly in the early days, hardly ever saw an English girl.

Admittedly, although most ENSA artistes were very hard working, some were there for what they could get out of it, mostly those who had never 'had it so good' and would have found it difficult to obtain a job in the theatre in peace time. Just a few of the big stars who came out for only a few weeks were very demanding, but most of them, such as the legendary Vera Lynn, Gracie Fields, Vivien Leigh, Beatrice Lillie, George Formby and Will Fyffe, to name but a few, did a splendid job. Incidentally, when Will Fyffe was playing in my area we had occasion to visit the field latrines together. I can now claim to be one of the few Englishmen who knows what a Scotsman wears underneath his kilt....but I promised not to tell!

On the whole I think ENSA did a good job and I feel it was an insult when, after the war, its head, Basil Dean, admittedly an autocratic and often difficult man, did not receive a knighthood.

During all these years my thoughts naturally kept turning to the Alex where much had been happening during my absence.

CHAPTER 15

1943–1946 BASIL AT THE HELM

Naturally when I went overseas my already greatly diminished association with the theatre ceased, but my partners, and this was much appreciated by me, continued to use the expression "Derek Salberg presents" on posters, programmes, etc., but Basil's name rightly appeared alongside mine as presenting the Wolverhampton company.

When I left these shores repertory was in a very healthy state, and soon a decision (one I had always hoped to take) was made to present each repertory production for two weeks instead of one. The advantages were manifold, and the Alex was ahead of its time in discarding a system which is now virtually extinct. This was made possible largely because, with excellent war news, virtual freedom from raids (and no TV in those days), the theatre was flourishing and full houses were the order of the day. A less happy event, caused by war circumstances, was the departure from tradition of presenting the pantomime, "Little Miss Muffet", in conjunction with another management for the first time since the Coutts regime in 1902 and which was not to happen again until 1976. The book, however, was home made as it was written by Philip Garston Jones who had regularly appeared with our repertory company, and simultaneously in "The Archers", in which he has for long played Jack Woolley.

The following year (1944) was a golden one for, with the war news becoming ever better and the raids over (in the Midlands at least), theatres throughout the country were doing marvellous business. It was felt that this was a good time to turn the theatre into a limited company under the very able chairmanship of my uncle Julius, who was Basil's father. The remainder of the board was composed of my aunt, Sarah

Thomas (whose husband was one of the original purchasers), Charles Keeling (for so long our solicitor), G.C. King (our accountant and father of Edmund our present chairman) and, of course, Basil. Cliff Wooldridge, who had recently joined the company, was secretary. Cliff cared deeply for the theatre and eventually guided it through very difficult times, and it was very sad that when he left, many years later, it was in an atmosphere of acrimony.

All continued to go well in 1945, which was the year when "Worm's Eye View" was discovered by Basil after a number of managements had turned it down. He presented it first at Wolverhampton and then at Birmingham, and in due course it found its way to London and ran for years earning us substantial royalties. Our financial rewards, excellent though they were, could have been much greater for H.J. Barlow, a Wednesbury industrialist, who saw the play at Wolverhampton, bought the touring rights in conjunction with ourselves, but unfortunately the tour failed dismally.

But with the confidence of one completely unversed in the theatre, he decided, against all the portents, to present it at the Whitehall Theatre in London where, in spite of a very unfavourable contract with that theatre, he made a small fortune. But, after the losses sustained on tour, our board had decided not to make any further investment, a decision I feel sure I would have endorsed had I been in charge. Such is show business.

1946 saw, in embryo, the step which was to be a pattern for the future and with which I was in full agreement, for I had felt even before the war that, however successful, a policy of repertory was not the entire fulfilment for a theatre such as the Alex. But at that time the Royal and Prince of Wales (destroyed in one of Birmingham's earliest raids in 1940) could call on the cream of the touring productions. By 1946, however, the situation had changed; there were a large number of productions available and only the Theatre Royal now in opposition as a top touring theatre. So Basil, realising this, decided to include some tours prior to the repertory season. The first, Leslie Banks and Hermione Baddeley in a thriller, "Grand National Night", played to excellent business, as did those which followed. They set the scene for the regular Spring and Autumn touring seasons which, from 1947 onwards, were to continue and eventually, from 1974 (with the exception of Pantomime), were to occupy the complete year.

1946 also saw two other events. One was the retirement of Billy Guest who had served the theatre since 1907 in various managerial capacities, and who had been of invaluable help to my father, especially in his earlier days. He belonged to the Old School of manager and was always resplendent in tails, adorned by a carnation and an opera hat (which I disliked intensely but never had the heart to tell him). He was a true and loyal servant and a well liked Birmingham character.

The other was my return late in the year to resume a reign which had been an extremely disjointed one. During my years overseas much fine work had been accomplished by the repertory company, which had included many artistes who were to achieve wider fame, such as Joan Miller, Robin Bailey, Alec McCowen, Larry Noble, Vanda Godsall, Andrew Osborn, Maxine Audley and Hugh Kelly, to name but a few. Plays had covered a wide field and had embraced many first productions, which is a very important part of the function of any repertory company. They balanced a programme which had usually included a number of interesting plays, some 'run of the mill' ones, and regularly the annual Shakespeare production. In brief the Alex had been worthily upholding the best traditions of the British repertory movement.

Nevertheless, on my return I was a little disappointed by the productions, possibly because the recently appointed and excellent producer was dividing his time (by arrangement) between the Alex and another theatre of which he was a director. This is not really satisfactory (the Birmingham Rep. had a similar problem more recently with the brilliant Peter Dews), and I was told that the standard that year was a little below the level of previous ones.

Too many actors were employed, but not engaged in enough productions. I recall running into an actor in London whom I had seen in the first play on my return to the theatre several weeks before. I asked him what he was doing. "Working for you" he replied. I could not think of a really suitable reply, so with a nod and a smile walked on!

I was recently reminded of a similar incident by John Crocker, the actor and author of many excellent pantomime scripts, who recalled a telegram I once sent him saying, "Can offer you a part in Vanity Fair at the Alex, rehearsing July 20th. Are you doing anything?" He replied in due course, "Would be delighted to accept. Am playing for you at Hereford." Ah well!

The pantomime which followed, "Simple Simon", was made memorable for me by an outstanding performance by Wendy Toye and splendid direction by Hastings Mann, a brilliant producer who later died in a fire. Tragically, his first wife perished in the same way in a dressing room in Glasgow, since when his biggest dread had always been fire.

To my way of thinking, although superbly artistic, it was not in the true tradition of Alex pantomimes, and the comedy, usually an Alex strong point, was lamentable although Naughton and Gold then, admittedly, past their best, did their utmost to infuse it with some life.

There is no doubt that a wonderful job had been done during those years and a tremendous debt was owed to Basil, Bill Dobson and those around them, not forgetting the wise chairman — Julius.

When they were young
The author's daughters, Joanna (left) and Judith as bridesmaids

**Toasting Judith and Simon on the occasion of their wedding
in 1976**
L to R: Arthur Lowe, John Le Mesurier, Judith, Simon,
Leslie Sands and the author

The author with the Warwickshire Cricket Colts XI, which he captained for several years

(On the right is Edmund King, then Warwickshire Chairman, and still the Alex Chairman, and on his left, Derief Taylor, a wonderful coach, much loved by his 'boys')

Our Cricket Team on tour
Standing: C. Addleman, M. Thomas, J. Sykes, G. Chater, R. Salberg,
J. Jowett, R. Key, A Coulthard, T. Howard
Seated: C. Mumford, C. Woolridge, D. Salberg, A. Sagar,
B. Thomas, T. Latham

The Author's Signals Hut-mates
Bob Key, Corporal Downes, Dennis Mills, Harry Mason
and the author

On an outing with the Box Office Staff
L to R: Sal, Lorna, the author, Joan, Selema and Elsa

1965: Triumph Productions' "An Ideal Husband"
The picture includes: Margaret Lockwood (at the door),
Michael Dennison, Dulcie Gray, Ursula Jeans, Roger Livesey
and Richard Todd

Pantomime Dress Rehearsal — production staff take a tea break
William Avenell, the author, Roy Astley

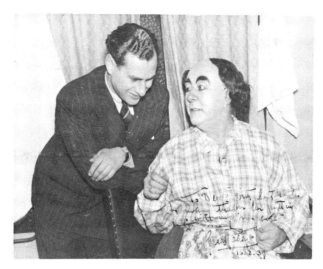

The author chatting to George Robey on February 13th, 1939
(The night Robey returned to the Pantomime, "Robinson Crusoe", after injuries sustained falling off the stage)

Joan and Marjories's famous Mirror Dance
(Joan is inside the mirror)

The Lord Mayor, Councillor Neville Bosworth, opening the bridge extension in 1968

The recently retired Bishop of Birmingham,
The Rt. Rev. Laurence Brown, with some of the dancers during
his annual pantomime rehearsal visit

The author's cousin, Basil

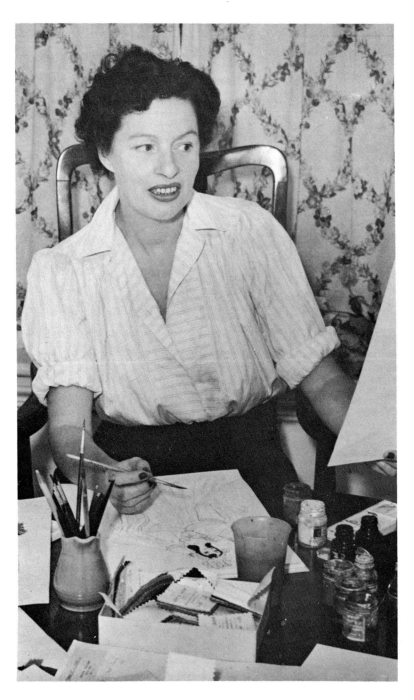

Joan working on her costume and head-dress designs

CHAPTER 16

BACK IN HARNESS

On my return I at first sat back so that I could pick up the threads again as a great deal had changed during my long absence, but by the end of the year I was ready and enthusiastic to get fully to work.

My first action of consequence was to extend the Spring and Autumn touring seasons, although I knew it would not be easy to obtain attractions because we were only just becoming recognised as a touring theatre and of course the Theatre Royal was very clearly Birmingham's leading theatre. I candidly think that had that theatre been under personal and local management as in the days of Philip Rodway, or of Emile Littler (whose Prince of Wales Theatre had made such an impact during his relatively short reign), we would have found it very difficult to compete.

But luckily I was able to obtain some very good productions and opened with the Old Vic Company's "Taming of the Shrew" with Trevor Howard and Patricia Burke. Trevor stayed with us and I had a hectic week. It was perhaps fortunate for me (but not for the box office) that the play's run was restricted to six days as, had it been for longer, I doubt whether any insurance company would have accepted me as a fair risk. The breweries on the other hand would have been delighted!

Other outstanding attractions in my very encouraging first full year were Benjamin Britten's "Beggars Opera" and Eileen Herlie whose performance in "The Eagle has Two Heads" had galvanised audiences throughout England.

For that year's repertory season I promoted John Gabriel, from associate producer as his predecessor had returned full time to his own theatre. John, who I had first met in the army, was a spendid actor and sensitive producer.

Newcomers to the company, most of whom remained for several seasons, included Raymond Francis, later to become a national figure in TV's "No Hiding Place"; Larry Noble, afterwards a leading member of the Whitehall Farce team; and Pauline Williams, who was to meet her future husband, Leslie Sands, at the Alex when he joined the company in 1949. Leslie married one of the nicest persons I ever met in the theatre, and I am glad to say I have met very many.

Strangely enough, although I have had very few serious differences of opinion with artistes, one was with Leslie when he disagreed with my producer, Peter Powell, and myself when we did not give Pauline the part he considered she should have played in Terence Rattigan's "Separate Tables". He felt so strongly about this that he said he would wish to leave if we did not agree to the change. As a result he left and, as a loyal wife, Pauline accompanied him. These two great favourites were a big loss, but we parted on entirely friendly terms, having agreed to differ. A year later we jointly sent out (in conjunction with Leslie Grade) a tour of his play "Beside the Seaside" with George Formby. That, coupled with the fact that they were both, to our delight, able to attend my elder daughter's recent wedding, is proof, if proof be needed, of our continuing friendship.

The company (inevitably) included Eileen Draycott, that great Alex favourite — a splendid actress and lovely person with whom, in all her years with me, I only had one disagreement. Because she felt she could no longer tackle some of the parts she used to play, she insisted on receiving a smaller salary — to which I could not agree. A beautifully vague person, she once wrote me a very long letter which I waded through until, at the end, I came to the one line it was all about. It read...."PS — this means I shan't be able to join the company until the second day of rehearsal." There are many wonderful stories about her. I particularly like the one told by Roy Astley, our stage director for so many years (and now one of the top stage directors in London's musical comedy scene). Apparently an appalling driver, she backed into someone's car but luckily did absolutely no damage. Nevertheless he got out of his car in a rage and ranted at her for several minutes. She stood it for as long as she could and then, with all the dignity at her command (and

74

she had plenty!), and raising herself to her full five foot nothing, said "Sir, if I weren't a perfect lady, I'd tell you to f . . k off!" Eileen was never very good at remembering names, either on or off the stage and, as Philip Garston Jones reminded me, in a scene from "Towards Zero" she married off two girls, but with such authority that the audience hardly noticed. She should have become a big star but I doubt whether she would have been any happier.

The company was further enhanced, although only for a limited number of productions, by Elspeth Duxbury who would have appeared more often had she not always put her husband, John Waterhouse, the *Birmingham Post's* music critic, and her large family, before her stage career. Elspeth was one of the best actresses of her day (her hilarious performance with Jimmy Edwards and Eric Sykes in "Big Bad Mouse" will never be forgotten by anyone who saw it either on the stage or TV). She also made a great success in the film "Make Mine Mink", based on "Breath of Spring", playing the part she had originated at its first production at the Alex under the direction of Allan Davis.

The seasons two biggest successes were J.B. Priestley's "An Inspector Calls" and Ben Travers' "Thark". There was only one flop — "Captain Brassbound's Conversion" by Shaw. It was, admittedly, boomtime in the theatre but more important, the standard was excellent.

At the end of the season, through John Gabriel's connections in that country, the company paid their second visit to Newfoundland where they again received a great reception. This visit was unfortunately marred by the fact that a member of the company, writing to a theatre critic in Birmingham, made one or two indiscreet remarks which were published. We did not visit Newfoundland again!

That year's pantomime, "Babes in the Wood", introduced to the Alex as Director — Oliver Gordon. His organisation of pantomime, which he loved, was fantastic, and I learnt a lot from him which stood me in good stead when eventually I produced the pantomimes myself. In later years he was responsible for the pantomimes for Reggie at Salisbury, where his enormous experience was of great help to repertory actors. A great producer of farce, he did not claim to understand

75

Chekhov and was only on nodding terms with Shakespeare! His cricket, which was his great love, along with the theatre and about five wives (no one knows exactly how many), has been referred to in another chapter. He was a memorable character and a man my daughters, Joan and I loved dearly.

When he died, his funeral was attended by a host of friends and my brother, who gave one of the two addresses, ended with one of Oliver's favourite expressions, "Well....cheerio cock" — somehow it was very moving. We then all repaired to the pub, as Oliver would have wished.

Tours in 1948 continued to do well, although it was not really a vintage year as far as calibre was concerned. They included Clive Brook in "The Gloconda Smile"; Basil Dean's production of "The School for Scandal" with Evelyn Laye; and the first of several visits by the Young Vic Company. We were the largest theatre they played and it was gratifying that performances were always packed with parties of young people, largely organised by Yolande Bird who has remained a great friend of mine although nowadays we meet all too rarely, usually at the National Theatre where she is assistant secretary to the board. These visits also commenced my friendship with Stephen Arlen, the manager of the company, which lasted until he died so prematurely and who, as related later, became the first administrator of the National Theatre on his secondment from Sadlers Wells where he held a similar post.

Repertory flourished again that year with "The Amazing Dr. Clitterhouse" in which Raymond Francis excelled as the Doctor, and "Pygmalion" with Pauline Williams as Eliza Doolittle, the two most successful box office productions.

The highlight in the Spring of 1949 was Christopher Fry's "The Lady's not for Burning" with Pamela Brown, John Gielgud and Claire Bloom as members of an all star cast which also included Richard Leech, who had only recently left our Hereford company, and a comparatively unknown actor, Richard Burton. A new play by Ronald Duncan, "Stratton" with Clive Brook, which no one, including Clive Brook*, understood; John Clements and Kay Hammond in the "Beaux Stratagem" and Fay Compton in "Mary Bonaventure", were other interesting events.

*Or, according to Clive, the author himself!

When the repertory season opened, Peter Powell was the new producer. Peter, who had recently directed at the Arts Theatre in London, was also a playwright of great promise about whom Ivor Brown had written, when reviewing his first play, "Running Wild", "we look to him for important things." He was a fine producer who stayed for several seasons and put a very definite stamp on his productions. During these years we established a close relationship both inside and outside the theatre. If he had a fault as a producer it was that he sometimes found it difficult to put his heart completely into a 'bread and butter' play when he had a more challenging one in prospect. He was also a pantomime devotee and produced several for me at Belfast and Wolverhampton with great success.

He was helped in his first season by a very strong cast which numbered amongst its newcomers, Leslie Sands (who joined soon after it opened), and John Le Mesurier who gave probably the best performance of the season as the failed schoolmaster, Andrew Crocker Harris, in Rattigan's "The Browning Version". (Incidentally, his co-partner-to-be in "Dad's Army", Arthur Lowe, had been a recent member of our Hereford company.) Other high spots were "Deep are the Roots" with two excellent West Indian artistes, Ida Shepley and Earl Cameron, playing the leads; a moving new play, "Flowers for the Living", and "Present Laughter" by Noel Coward in which Peter Vaughan was hilarious as Roland Maule, giving the best of many excellent portrayals of the part I have seen (although Richard Briers, who later played it on tour at the Alex, ran him close).

Tony Steedman who was to make such a deep impression for many years to come, joined the company in 1950, a season which contained, arguably, the best individual performance I can recall.

The play was Arthur Miller's "Death of a Salesman", the production by Peter Powell and the performance by Colin Laurence, who very sadly died in a car crash on the last night of a repertory season three years later.

I still remember the telephone ringing about five in the morning and Joan, who had an almost frightening sixth sense, saying "I'm afraid that will be about Colin". She told me she felt sure when he left the office after the farewell party that night that something terrible would happen. She had wanted to warn him not to go in the car, but felt she could not do so without appearing to be foolish and alarmist.

It was particularly sad that the season should have ended so tragically as it had been a very successful one with many interesting plays, amongst them, Pinero's "The Magistrate"; "Whiteoaks" with Eileen Draycott superb as Granny; "St. Joan" with Ingrid Burke making an extremely good 'shot' at the part; "Pride and Prejudice; and "The Smooth Faced Gentleman" by Peter Powell which just failed to 'come off' but served to give, in a very tiny part, the first introduction to the stage of a local girl, Zena Walker.

Tours which were not outstanding included Evelyn Laye and Frank Lawton in "September Tide" by Daphne du Maurier and "Madam Tic Tac" which starred the famous French actress Francoise Rosay. She was a volatile and rather temperamental lady, who told me she would not be playing the Saturday matinee, but would appear for the evening performance. I told her she would play both or neither. She played both. I did not learn until later that this great actress had left her country because she hated the collaborators. "The Green Bay Tree" with Hugh Williams and Jack Watling could only hint at the homosexual undertones for, unlike now, it was an almost forbidden subject, and it is doubtful whether the Alex audience of those days even understood them.

The following year was to be our Jubilee Year, so I will devote a chapter to it.

CHAPTER 17

1951 – THE ALEX GOLDEN JUBILEE YEAR

The Golden Jubilee occurred in May and almost the first message of goodwill came from the first proprietor, William Coutts who, somehow, none of us had imagined was still alive. There were a number of special events to mark the occasion beginning with a charity performance of the current production, Sheridan's "School for Scandal", as a result of which the sum of £275 was handed over to the Lord Mayor to be donated to the funds of the Playing Fields Association, which was the charity of his choice. The audience included a number of friends of the theatre, many of whom had travelled from afar, and acclaimed a magnificent production, directed by Peter Powell with a prologue written by him and beautifully spoken by David Dodimead. Altogether it was a measure of the distance we had advanced from those early repertory days. At the end of the performance, when I came on stage to make a speech, an office chair was lowered from the 'flies', a present from the staff to me. In thanking them, I said that I hoped I would not have to start my day's work by that method!

Next day there was a luncheon at the Queen's Hotel, chaired by Trevor Howard who made a splendid speech, after which another presentation was made to me by the Lord Mayor. "The Stage" was proposed by T.C. Kemp, then the illustrious critic of the *Birmingham Post* and one of the most delightful of men. (His wife is still very much 'alive and kicking' and his daughter, Shelagh, is a regular visitor to the theatre). This toast was replied to first by Helen Cherry, Trevor's lovely and talented wife, and then by Sir Barry Jackson. This I took as a great compliment, as he was always very reticent about making speeches; Herbert Dunkerly, who then controlled the BBC in the region, proposed the Chairman and, at the end, everyone agreed that it had been a wonderful occasion.

79

There was only one slightly discordant note — the main dish was ham — possibly a little tactless on the part of the organisers, considering that the theatre was owned by a Jewish family! As always, I ate mine with relish, but I believe some of the more elderly of my relations had to persuade themselves that it was beef, and Kosher at that!!

In November, John Clements, who was appearing in "Man and Superman" with that superb artiste, Kay Hammond (his wife), unveiled, in the presence of the Lord Mayor and Lady Mayoress, a beautiful clock presented by well wishers to the theatre, and at the same time gave me an album containing the names of subscribers to the presentation.

The clock, an outstanding example of 18th century French craftsmanship (a similar one was sold for £1,700 in 1863), was mounted over the Box Office in the old foyer. On the addition of the new foyer it was moved there and stood elegantly above the staircase until, in March 1977, tragedy struck when, unbelievably, it was stolen early one morning and has never been seen since, in spite of every possible effort on the part of the police. So now the beauty of the clock, reflecting the kindness of so many friends who wished to show their feelings for the theatre which, in different ways, had served the city for fifty years, no longer adorns the theatre.

The plays that season were worthy of the Jubilee and included, as our contribution to the Festival of Britain, a joint production with Northampton repertory theatre of "The Beggar's Opera". A link with the early repertory days was the inclusion in the company of Vernon Fortescue, a member of the second company in 1928 and for many years our producer at Hereford.

There were some very exciting touring productions, notably Peter Ustinov's "Love of Four Colonels" with Peter Ustinov and Moira Lister and a wonderful all-round cast; and a first production of "Waters of the Moon" with Edith Evans, Sybil Thorndike, Kathleen Harrison and Wendy Hiller; "The Wedding of Electra" with Peggy Ashcroft, Catherine Lacy and Robert Eddison; Eric Portman in Peter Ustinov's "Moment of Truth"; Yvonne Arnaud and Joyce Redman in Annouilh's "Colombe", Ruth Draper who, as always, drew packed houses; and the Old Vic's "Clandestine Marriage" with Donald Wolfit. Donald did more than almost any actor to keep the provincial theatre alive, calling forth a remark from Noel Coward who, when discussing the rival merits of John Gielgud and Donald, said that the main difference was that John Gielgud was a 'tour de force' and Donald Wolfit was 'forced to tour'. Unkind, but typically Coward. An uneasy week this, for Donald, always ready for a quarrel if he felt he had a grievance, had fallen out with the Old Vic and indeed, as far as one could tell, with the rest of the company.

The only fly in the ointment of a memorable year was the sad event which occurred in our "Sleeping Beauty" pantomime, which I relate in the later chapter on pantomime.

CHAPTER 18

AUDIENCES

No theatre is better served by its audience than the Alex, which has always possessed a strong regular following. I got to know very many of them extremely well and always looked forward to a chat with them on their way in, and maybe a drink in the interval or after the show with as many as possible.

The pattern for the week was set each Monday when I greeted, at the bridge coffee bar, the ever smiling Bells and Willis's who, in order to park their cars, always arrived early. It continued in similar fashion throughout the week which usually ended with a chat with Margaret and Mrs. Palmer (sometimes accompanied by Joan and Vic Oliver), and drinks with Harry Simmonds and Audrey.*

To me, communication with patrons was one of the great joys of running a theatre and I know that to many of them visiting the Alex was not just the act of going to a theatre, but almost a way of life. As a member of the Birmingham (Alexandra) Theatre Club said to me at the termination of a recent panel on which I had sat at one of their meetings, "You know, going to the Alex has always been a hobby to me", and letters to the local papers, published on the announcement of my retirement, reflected a deep affection, such as the one from Angela Wright which referred to "the dear old Alex".

Many written to me at that time and following my actual retirement, included such phrases as "our theatre", "the many years of pleasure in the friendly Alex", "to attend the Alex, since I came to Birmingham many years ago, has been one of the greatest pleasures of my life", "we, as a family, have always

*Last year I spent a lovely week-end with them alongside one of the finest stretches of river in the country, during which Harry unsuccessfully tried to initiate me into the skills of fishing.

had great love for your theatre" and, "the Alex has claimed a good part of our lives". One wrote that a friend of hers had emigrated to New Zealand in 1943 but still writes to say how much she misses the Alex and wants to know all about it, and another, "I have been a patron for years and have never missed an Alex pantomime since I was 7; if it closed I would miss my haven of great joy".

These are only a very few quotations, but they reflect the feeling for the Alex as accurately as a remark made to me recently at the Annual Dinner of the Dudley Little Theatre (a flourishing amateur organisation who *do* support the professional theatre), by a member who said, "I go to many theatres, but nowhere do I get the same atmosphere as at the Alex". Just before I retired a patron said to me in the foyer, with a beaming smile on his face, "I hear its bloody awful tonight", and then went cheerfully into the auditorium; for, to him, as to many people, a visit to the Alex meant more than just seeing a play. It is not easy to define what has created this feeling for the Alex, both in the City and further afield, and not only amongst its regular patrons, but also amongst people who possibly rarely visit it. The very abbreviation Alex (or Alec) in itself suggests affection.

It is almost certainly the most liked of Birmingham's three theatres, and yet as a building it has many faults. It is, from necessity, too wide but fortunately, as it has the closest dress circle to the stage of any theatre in the country, it has retained intimacy. Its seats are decidedly uncomfortable and with 1,562 of them, at a present day cost of over £25 a seat, heaven alone knows when they will be replaced. Its ventilation leaves a lot to be desired and its cloakroom facilities, although greatly improved in recent years, could be better. It lacks stage depth— not directly noticeable to the public, but partly responsible for the loss of the Ballet and Opera companies to the Hippodrome.

In this connection it is tragic to recall that in 1966 Charles Simpson, then Chairman of the Works and Building Committee, (later to become Lord Mayor, and now a City representative on our Council of Management), informed me that the land behind our backstage wall would soon become available. This would have meant a complete revolution in our stage and other facilities, but I had to tell him that the theatre was entirely without capital and was having a great struggle even to exist. It is now part of the new telephone exchange.

What, therefore, is the reason for the affection in which the Alex is held?

I think the answer lies in its special atmosphere, for it has been greatly loved by everyone connected with it, a characteristic required by a building as much as by people. As John Gielgud said in a recent interview on TV, "It doesn't matter how shabby a theatre is, so long as it has got atmosphere", a slight exaggeration perhaps, but only a slight one.

Naturally, atmosphere and love are not in themselves sufficient as it is what happens on the stage that really counts, but they can at least help considerably to mitigate the disappointment when, as must sometimes happen, one has not enjoyed a performance. In any case, atmosphere is very much a matter of personal reaction and will affect each audience differently, for although a strong hard core remains constant, there is a big difference between the audience for, say, an Agatha Christie thriller and that of "Godspell", D'Oyly Carte or Ibsen. But all have one characteristic in common — they always include a number of late-comers. I sympathise with many of them, realising as I do, the problems of parking, traffic jams, the late arrival of baby-sitters and many other hazards. Nevertheless, I am sure that, with a little extra effort, many latecomers could arrive on time, for when we advanced the starting time from 7.15p.m. to 7.30p.m. it was fascinating to stand in the foyer watching people who used to come rushing in madly at 7.18p.m. now rushing in madly at 7.33.

I must confess, though, to not extending this sympathy to people who cannot resist eating for the limited duration of an act and who take the curtain rise as a cue to pass the chocolate box down the row where, invariably, it stops at the lady in front of one, who tries those noisy, crinkly chocolates one by one, at last makes her choice and then possibly drops the whole damn lot on the floor.

I still recall, with mixed feelings, a pantomime performance to which Smiths Crisps brought a large party of children and they, being a most generous firm, gave to each child a packet of Smiths Crisps. However, they say it's an ill wind, and I was told that quite a number of people came a second time...... in

84

order to hear the pantomime!

Audiences contain a myriad of types and our regulars at one time included two of my great favourites—both delightful, rather zany ladies, and great fans of Ivor Novello who they had got to know very well. Unfortunately, owing to illness, they were unable to see his new musical on its prior-to-London run at the Theatre Royal. They wrote and told him this, whereupon he sent them two tickets for a performance soon after it opened in London, first class tickets on the train and booked them, also at his expense, into a good hotel—all of which was typical of that most kind man. They duly saw the show, went round by invitation to his dressing room afterwards and sat down. "Well?" said Ivor Novello, enquiringly. "Didn't like it, Ivor" was all they said. A bit hard after all he had done, and that expression was used by Joan and myself ever afterwards whenever anything displeased us, and even now by my sister-in-law Marjorie and myself.

I treasure this and many other comments, such as the one from a lady sitting in front of me at the Royal Shakespeare Theatre recently, who enquired of her companion whether that evening's production, "Salad Days", had been written by Shakespeare. Another special favourite of mine occurred when I visited Aston Hippodrome (now a bingo hall) to see a ballet company in that theatre which usually housed nude revues. I went in to the nearby Barton Arms in the second interval where I overhead the following conversation between two men who were obviously supporters of the revues, but had decided to give the ballet a chance. "What do you think of the show this week—this 'ere ballet?" "Not bad," came the reply, "But it has been on for over an hour and they haven't spoken a bloody word yet."

I also like the story of Philip Rodway who, hearing a patron arguing with one of his box office staff at the old Theatre Royal Birmingham, intervened to ask what the problem was. The patron said he wanted seats in the Dress Circle for Saturday's performance, and had been told there weren't any. Philip Rodway assured him this was so, whereupon the intending patron said in that case he would have stalls. On being told that in fact there weren't any seats available anywhere as the theatre was completely sold out, he stalked out saying "Well, I call that damn bad management".

But, whatever their idiosyncracies, these patrons *did* support the theatre, whereas thousands only come on the occasion when there is a big TV name heading the cast or, as they put it, "to be entertained". No harm in that, and quite natural too in these days of stress, but then what is 'entertainment', and might they not escape equally through a serious, well-written play as opposed to, say, a slight comedy.

But if we are to persuade the public to take a chance, we have to gain their confidence, and in order to do so must first create some recognisable policy giving our theatre its particular identity.

And this, I admit, is getting more difficult these days, with the shortage of productions. But at least a manager, in evening dress, can make them welcome as they arrive and listen to any complaints or answer queries. Such as the one from a lady who asked Norman Wood* whether we had in our lost property an item mislaid by her young son during a performance of "Oliver" the previous week. Norman's enquiry as to the precise nature of the article elicited the information that it was a hampster. He should always refund their money if "auntie was at the last moment prevented from coming to the theatre".** This costs little in hard cash, but gains much in goodwill and is a policy I have always laid down, but with which our devoted box office manageress, Joan Vaughton, (a worthy successor to Mrs. Bramham, killed in an air raid, and Mrs. Siddons, a famous Alex figure who devoted her life to the theatre), did not always entirely agree. On the card signed by all the box office staff just before my Gala Performance (of which more later) she jokingly wrote, "I refused to refund money for your Gala Night. Should I have done?" But she knows that, for audiences, the evening starts at the Box Office, and it is Joan and her staff who set the pattern for their entertainment because the very act of buying a ticket can, in itself, be an ordeal or a pleasure. I know it is sometimes difficult, under pressure, not to become impatient or make mistakes (at the peak time of the year the staff are handling over 200,000 tickets), but there can never be any excuse for discourtesy.

After buying one's ticket the next port of call may well be

*The theatre's house-manager.
**Even though the ticket states that no refund can be made.

86

the bridge bar (adorned by Barbara, surely the most beautiful of bar staff) where we try to avoid the 11th Commandment of most theatre bars — "Thou shalt not get served", and where, I hope, none of our patrons receive the reply given to me on a visit to a theatre to see an artiste I knew was getting over £2,000 a week. I was ruminating, on the way to the shabby bar, what a very high salary that was. On arrival, I ordered a gin and tonic with ice and a slice of lemon; the barmaid replied that they did not possess any lemon, which seemed absurd (certainly taken in relation to the salary of that artiste), and I said so, whereupon her face lit up and she recalled that, in fact, they did have one last week, but it had gone bad! In my opinion—not the way to run a bar, and this can reflect on the way a theatre, all too often, is administered. As an alternative to having a drink or going straight into the auditorium, the patron may visit the coffee bar where Essie*, assisted by Lily, serves coffee, sandwiches and cakes. At this point the recorded voice of Charles Kraus (the son of Otakar Kraus, the famous opera singer), once our manager but now manager of the London Coliseum, will be heard announcing that it is now time to enter the auditorium. Here it is part of Doreen's** job to ensure that the usherettes are alert, helpful and, hopefully, ready with a smile to sell a programme which will contain some useful information and at the same time not be overpriced. (I once paid 25p at a theatre just to discover, in a two handed play, which was Flora Robson—and the man had a beard anyway!)

It is here where the real magic of the theatre should begin in anticipation of the moment when the house lights dim, the

* Essie is a great Alex character who exemplified for me the attitude of our staff when, after three capacity performances in one day (there had been a morning show for youngsters), she said, "We were on our knees but we loved it because it meant we were doing well." A similar remark was made to me as I walked through the stalls early one morning and asked Christine, our head cleaner, why she looked so glum. She replied that recently there had not been enough work to do, which meant that 'our' theatre was not doing well.

** Doreen, with whom I always had an excellent relationship, has long been a loyal and conscientious member of the staff. She can be seen shedding tears in the picture of the finale of my Gala Performance, which she assured me were not tears of joy!

strains of music die away, and the curtain, preferably a claret coloured one, rises — for to me, this still holds out the promise of an enchanted world. But so frequently nowadays, and often for no good reason, the curtain is permanently up and the set visible but unlit. The strains of music are only taped, thus tending to lose that human contact which is one of the theatre's essentials, and the reason we have always retained a first class pianist — nowadays Arthur Roberts, who has had distinguished predecessors in Maurice Udloff and Tony Davidson. At one time we employed a seven piece orchestra, but modern economics now make this totally impossible.

I realise that all this sounds extremely idealistic and regrettably does not always happen quite like that, but it is absolutely essential, if a theatre is to survive, that patrons are greeted as friends and not, as sometimes, almost as intruders.

This is especially true if we are to attract potential, but apathetic, patrons such as my Rotarian friend, Norman, about whom I wrote an article many years ago in the Birmingham Repertory Theatre's house magazine *Proscenium*, on the invitation of Humphrey Stanbury, then that theatre's manager and now the extremely able director of the Grand Theatre, Wolverhampton. I feel if only we could persuade the Normans of this world to visit the theatre, we would have achieved a resounding victory. With permission, I reproduce that article.

"THE FAILURE OF A NORMAN CONQUEST"

"Whenever I arrive in a town I always enjoy talking to the locals who invariably tell me that 'we're very funny people here'; usually this is said in the tone adopted by any member of most families when assuring you that the rest of the family is slightly mad. If, in conversation, it transpires that I work in the theatre, they either rack their brains to recollect where they have heard the word 'theatre' before, or else they assure one that they are very keen theatre-goers. If, as often happens, it transpires that their last visit to the theatre was to see 'Peter Pan' two years ago then I place them in the same category as my friend Norman, who told me to my great joy, about five years ago, that he was an avid theatre-goer.

I must admit that on learning how enthusiastic Norman was, I was a little surprised to find that this enthusiasm did not go as far as translating itself into actually visiting the theatre, but the reason he gave me for this non-attendance was that he and his wife always liked a meal after the show and in Birmingham this was not possible. As this was five years' ago, I accepted this, although I did not feel that even then this was correct. However, the next season I pointed out to him that now it was easy to eat as not only had an hotel opened, but there were two other restaurants within a stone's throw of the theatre. He was delighted about this and said he was sure he would now be coming. I saw him again later and asked him whether he had now been to the theatre, but he said as a matter of fact that he had not, because 7.15 was a very difficult time for him. I accepted this too, but knowing how enthusiastic he was, I was delighted to be able to tell him the year afterwards that our opening nights were now at 7.45; Saturdays were at 5p.m. and 8p.m.; Wednesday matinees at 2.30p.m. and every other night at 7.15p.m. This, I felt must give him a wide range of performance times. I was somewhat surprised some months later, therefore, when he told me he was still a 'non-attender' for he went on to say 'You see, Derek, the trouble is you can't park your bloody car.' The fascinating thing is that Norman apparently managed to solve all his problems for the recent visit of the National Theatre Company when Albert Finney was appearing in 'A Flea in Her Ear'. Doubtless, however, they will arise again during our forthcoming repertory season!

But the aforesaid citizens may be part of that 3% of the public who visit the theatre regularly, love it, criticise it and enable provincial theatres to remain open, however precariously.

But whatever the town, always the question is asked 'Why are we in this city so badly off for theatres, when every other town is overflowing with them, or more advanced in its civic outlook.' For example, a correspondent in last week's Guardian writing about Manchester's very small Library Theatre, compares its grant unfavourably with that of four other cities (yes, he included Birmingham) and finishes his letter with the plaintive plea — 'Cannot Manchester make an effort to be best instead of cheapest?' When in Newcastle recently, I read a letter in a local paper, irately asking why Newcastle's only commercial theatre had just closed for a fortnight — (the reason was, of course, that it was having the utmost difficulty in obtaining suitable tours. This week for example The Stage only lists eighteen productions as being on tour). Gloucester rightly complains that it has no theatre at all, neither has Exeter. Liverpool and Sheffield they say are 'very difficult'; Coventry's Belgrade says that it has not yet found a regular audience, and so one could go on indefinitely.

In fact everyone really feels everbody else is doing pretty well theatrically. Birmingham is, of course, no exception and as becomes the second city it is very critical of itself, although

I often feel we, as citizens, whilst aware of the debit side of the balance sheet, do not always look at the credit side.

The fact is that the situation is much the same throughout the country because the theatrical pattern has changed entirely during the last twenty years and now only three provincial cities in England have more than one commercial theatre (including Birmingham) and none more than two. The reason for this is not just, as many people feel it is, the advent of TV, but it goes a very great deal deeper than this; which, however, would be the subject of another article."

N.B. As this was written in 1966 much, of course, has changed, but not the attitude of Norman and other similar theatre 'lovers'.

CHAPTER 19

COMMITTEES -- THEATRE AND OTHERS

Although I have probably served on more committees than most people, I do not consider myself to be a particularly good committee man, although possibly a reasonably efficient chairman, which is a somewhat different function. My first theatre committee was in 1947, when I was invited to join the Drama Panel of the Arts Council, of which I remained a member until 1960, re-joining from 1965-73.

The invitation was a great compliment to the Alex as it was, at that time, very unusual to include a representative of the commercial theatre. The members were drawn from many spheres and included many actors of whom I recall, at random, Alec Guinness, Peggy Ashcroft, John Clements, a tower of strength, as was Constance Cummings and her husband, Benn Levy. Noel Coward, who was a member for a time, attended a meeting at which the future of the Old Vic was discussed. A representative of that theatre made an impassioned plea for better seats in the gallery where, he said, "school children had to sit on hard wooden seats", which prompted Coward to comment in his dry, clipped speech, "Serve them right — little beasts." This was the only remark he made during the meeting and was thus the only one he ever made as, to the best of my knowledge, he never attended another!

Peter Ustinov, whilst a member, as could be anticipated, made memorable and extremely witty contributions to discussions.

Another actor-member was John Gielgud and I was reminded by Jo Hodgkinson, one-time drama director of the Arts Council, who succeeded three stalwarts of the theatre, John Moody, Llewellyn Rees and Charles Landstone*, of a remark he made

*See * footnote on following page.

after a discussion during which some people criticised the Reps for tending to overplay the popular pieces, but one, at any rate, was proposing to put on "Hamlet". Whereupon he raised his head from his papers and said, with a gay twinkle, "Well.... *that's* a popular piece."

The panel was by no means composed entirely of actors, who were, in fact, in the minority. One of many outstanding non-actors was Hugh Willatt who later became Secretary General of the Arts Council and was deservedly knighted.

The Arts Council is often criticised, but whilst some of their decisions have inevitably been wrong, they have, for the most part, done a difficult job extremely well and none could have shown more devotion than their permanent staff. It must also be remembered that never have they had sufficient money and have always had to decide whether to 'raise' or 'spread'. Things are now easier, but in those early days the amount of money at their disposal was derisory. I recall the panel having to refuse the Rep. at Barrow-in-Furness the paltry sum of (I think) £250, feeling, rightly or wrongly, that it was insufficient to be of real help and could be more usefully employed elsewhere. It is interesting to note that the Birmingham Repertory Theatre's first grant (in 1954) was £500 and in 1977, £238,000.

The Alex was, in fact, the first commercial theatre to receive any grant from the Arts Council but I must say, whilst duly grateful, I feel the sum of £16,500 is paltry compared, for example, with £98,000 for the Belgrade, Coventry, £69,750 for Derby Playhouse and £42,740 for the diminutive Chester Gateway Theatre. I know only too well that there are many factors to be taken into consideration when deciding both upon the level and urgency for a subsidy, and I do not begrudge these theatres their grants, but surely there is considerable inconsistency in these comparisons.

I also served on the committee formed by the Arts Council to enquire into price structure of seats, a complete waste of time, as no sort of standardisation is possible. Later I was a

---

*Jo recalls a memorial service for a famous actor during which he noticed Charles, at one time a theatre manager, was continually twisting his neck. He turned to his companion, then in charge of the box office at the Old Vic, and said, "Why is Charles looking over his shoulder so much?" — like a flash she said, "He's counting the house, he can't help it."

member of a committee set up by the Arts Council, and magnificently chaired by J.W. Lambert of the *Sunday Times*, to enquire into the whole future of the provincial theatre and I presented the first paper. We sat for several months and, I think, came up with some very good recommendations, not many of which have been implemented! But, as a result, the Theatre Investment Fund, a somewhat complicated fund which would make money available for productions, thus helping to supply product, has been set up and is at last in being. It was through the Arts Council that I received a grant from a fund created by the then Minister for the Arts, Jennie Lee, which enabled me to make a short visit to Russia to study the theatre there. The story of this visit would occupy an entire book, suffice it to say I found it enthralling but although the International Theatre Institute, through Kenneth Rae, had made the arrangements for my visit with their counterpart in Russia, through some lack of communication their end, these never materialised and I had to fend for myself as best I could.

However, I was asked by the *Moscow News* to give my impressions, which were mostly favourable but included one or two minor criticisms, which may account for the fact that the article never appeared. Owing to special circumstances, Joan and I did not travel with a group and although normally I much prefer to go individually, I would strongly advise anyone visiting Russia to do so as part of an organised party, otherwise the amount of time wasted dealing with Intourist is immense. Also, having a guide permanently enables one to learn a great deal more during the limited time at one's disposal. It was a great and fascinating, though frustrating, experience.

During my earlier years on the Arts Council Drama Panel, I also served on the Sadler's Wells Theatre Trust. Not being well versed in opera, I found the insight into that world very fascinating and was delighted to be re-elected after my first term of office had expired. Perhaps they never discovered that I cannot sing a note! I met some delightful people, including the present Minister for the Arts — Lord Donaldson, to whom I am ever grateful for introducing me to a firm who make wonderful Cheddar cheese. Another happy relationship was with the extremely efficient secretary to the Board, Pat Bancroft, daughter of that most respected man, Jack Bancroft who owned

93

the Embassy Theatre, Peterborough, and sister of Judith, for a long time my excellent secretary. She succeeded Valerie who I was delighted to meet again recently after I had given a talk to the English speaking Union, where she had met her busband, although we all felt she would never meet anyone to match up to her standards!

During these periods I was also on the board of the Council of Managements of the Theatre Managers' Association, whose members were mostly connected with the commercial theatre, and it was fascinating to listen to the completely different approach of people working in that field. Today, of course, commercial and non-commercial theatre activities have become so entwined that the gulf has largely disappeared. On my retirement I was made a life member and look upon this as a great honour.

In 1961 to my astonishment (and to that of one of the National newspapers who, on learning that I produced pantomimes, assumed that I was probably semi-literate) came an invitation to join the Board of the National Theatre which was about to be formed. The chairman was Viscount Chandos, who sadly never lived to see the National Theatre move from the Old Vic to the South Bank, especially as it was largely his drive, added to that of Kenneth Rae, that really pressurised the building of the National Theatre. The other board members were Hugh ('Binkie') Beaumont, the leading and most enlightened of West End Theatre managers; Kenneth Clark, best known to the public through his television lectures; his namesake (but no relation), Sir Ashley Clarke, our ambassador to Rome for many years and a BBC governor; Mrs. Freda Corbett, a barrister-at-law and at that time, chairman of the LCC General Purposes Committee; Sir William Keswick, Director of the Bank of England; Sir Douglas Logan, Principal of the University of London, a governor of the Old Vic and director of the Old Vic Trust, as was Lord Wilmott who was also a director of Glyndebourne; and Henry Moore, the famous sculptor, next to whom I invariably sat, hoping he would not destroy the 'doodles' he always drew during meetings, but he always did. He was an excellent member of the Board and bore out the words written about him by Donald Hall in *The Life and Work of a Great Sculptor* — "Not always does he do his homework, but he is invaluable in discussion." He is one of the most delightful and modest men one could meet.

I already had the privilege of knowing that great man, Laurence Olivier who, artistically, was the creator in chief of the National Theatre Company. I suspect he was not really very fond of committees and has said publicly that the only thing he had in common with Viscount Chandos was that they shared the burning desire to see the National Theatre built. My admiration for him increased even further as time went on.

One of the first tasks of the Board was to find an administrator and I was immensely flattered to be invited to accept that appointment. I had been offered a similar one with the Old Vic a year or so earlier and before it became the temporary home of the National Theatre, but whilst very grateful and appreciative, I had declined. This was, of course, a different matter, and the prospect of becoming the administrator of the most prestigious theatre in England at such an exciting moment, and at a salary infinitely higher than I was receiving, required very deep consideration. I asked for a few days to think it over, and meantime Sir Emrys Williams and Jo Hodgkinson, both of the Arts Council, pressed me to accept.

I discussed it fully with Joan, pointing out that it would solve our financial problems which were by no means few, but acceptance would, of course, entail moving to London and to severing my connection with the Alex, other than in a consultancy capacity. Joan knew that my heart would always remain in Birmingham and with the Alex and that, in spite of the financial and other advantages, I would not want to leave, although we both realised the future of the Alex was in the balance. Ultimately, she made the decision easy for me by saying that she knew that I would never really be happy away from the Alex, so I told Viscount Chandos and wrote a letter to the Board, who were most understanding.

In the event, they engaged Stephen Arlen, a Birmingham man and, as mentioned previously, a great friend of mine. He was very much better suited to the job than I would have been and they never had any regrets.

Soon afterwards, I was invited to join the Board of the Birmingham Repertory Theatre, a great compliment, not just to me but to the Alex, that a theatre should appoint to their

Board one of the 'opposition'. I served on that Board for six years and thought I had got problems until I heard theirs! I have since re-joined the Board and hope I can be of some assistance at a difficult time in their affairs, as I am very fond of, and greatly admire that theatre. But my heart must always belong to the Alex; and I have not accepted offers to serve on other theatre boards outside Birmingham.

In 1969 CORT* decided to appoint, in addition to their permanent chairman, on a yearly basis, one to preside at their conferences. I was chosen to be the first such chairman which, too, was a compliment, as the Alex was at one time ineligible for membership because it was then a commercial theatre (i.e. not in receipt of a subsidy and thus entitled to keep profits, if it could make any). The first conference at which I presided was held at the Festival Hall in London and our guest of honour was, somewhat to our surprise and delight, HRH the Prince of Wales, who had been invited by Phyllis Leggatt (the indefatigable secretary of CORT since its inception) more, I think, in hope than expectation. My job was to meet him (along with Viscount Chandos, the Mayor and other dignitaries), introduce him to as many people as possible and sit with him at lunch. I was full of trepidation beforehand, especially as I had to make a speech at the luncheon and act as toastmaster (which I had not been told until the last moment) before a most distinguished gathering. But so charming and unpretentious is this delightful young man, that it was not long before all nerves left me and we conversed freely on a wide range of subjects which included our mutual belief that the most important thing in life is the family. He made a splendid speech in which he said his family ought to go in more for amateur dramatics as 'they had plenty of room at home'. By the time I escorted him to his car I only just prevented myself from saying "If you're ever in Birmingham anytime, sir, do look me up!"

Apart from my membership of the Birmingham Rep. Board I serve on the West Midlands Arts Association committee, and the council of the Midlands Arts Centre, a wonderful undertaking which will be ever linked with the names of John English and Mollie Randle, for whom no praise is high enough. They have been faced with many problems but have remained confident

* Council of Regional Theatres

about the future of the fine work which they started and of their utter belief in it.

Apart from sitting as a magistrate, I am on several committees, in particular, the Royal Commonwealth Society for the Blind, three Warwickshire cricket committees, and the Warwickshire Cricket Supporters Association, of which I am one of the two remaining original members. The other is my great friend Edgar Hiley (to whom I am frequently as rude as he is to me, but without malice on either side). Edgar has many assets but undeniably the greatest is Ingrid, his most delightful wife. He has done a grand job as chairman and appreciates, as much as I, and indeed everyone connected with the Association, the wonderful work done by Winnie and David Blakemore and, at its inception, by Ray Hitchcock. As a result cricket and, to a lesser degree, hospitals have benefited greatly. I was President of Central Area, St. John Ambulance for several years and became a Serving Brother of the Order.

I always felt strongly that, to be part of the life of a city and contribute towards making the theatre one served part of that life, such involvement was essential. More important, I hoped I was doing some good.

CHAPTER 20

1952—1963
HALCYON YEARS FOR REPERTORY AND TOURS

REPERTORY

The year following our Golden Jubilee was to be the first of a number of successful years.

When the repertory season opened the company contained a number of artistes from the Jubilee season, among them Colin Laurence, Eileen Draycott and Tony Steedman, with newcomers Pauline Williams, Edward Mulhare, Leslie Dunn, Anthony Sagar, Ronald Radd, Joan Blake and Tilsa Page. There were many fine productions, notably Steinbeck's "Of Mice and Men" (which followed an equally bad one, "The Scarlet Pimpernel") in which Tony Steedman and Ronald Radd gave magnificent performances as Lennie and George, receiving excellent support from Leslie Sands, Leslie Dunn and Joan Blake. Artistically, Ibsen's "An Enemy of the People" ran it close with Ronald Radd, a fine actor who died prematurely when bound for stardom, again outstanding. Neither play, understandably, was a box office success, nor was "Ring Round the Moon" in which Joan Blake and Edward Mulhare excelled. However, Ivor Novello's "I Lived with You", which included Billie Whitelaw, and Agatha Christie's "Ten Little Niggers" (as we were permitted to call it in those days, but has now been re-named "Ten Little Indians"), both played to excellent houses.

The following year was Coronation Year and, with much the same company but joined by that brilliant actor Peter Vaughan and Jeannette Hutchinson, later Jack Warner's leading lady in "Dixon of Dock Green", we celebrated the event with a special production of "Twelfth Night". It did not attract audiences and as we felt we could no longer compete with

Stratford or the Birmingham Rep., who were achieving fame with their "Henry" cycle, we decided to discontinue repertory productions of Shakespeare's plays. An excellent performance of Oscar Wilde's "An Ideal Husband" coincided with the City of London's recognition of his existence when they erected on the wall of his house a plaque bearing the inscription "Oscar Wilde — dramatist and wit lived here". "Worms Eye View" was revived but now seemed hopelessly 'dated' — such is the passage of time.

The 1954 season was very successful at the box office but contained only few plays of note. Charles Morgan's "The Flashing Stream" and "She Stoops to Conquer" were outstanding, and the first presentation of "Because I am Black" only a near miss. "Rookery Nook", in which Rex Garner, a newcomer, and Leslie Sands, both great farceurs and all round actors, excelled and, unexpectedly, a very slight play, "For Better, For Worse", were the most successful box office plays.

In 1955 we achieved one of our best repertory productions, although it failed at the box office — Chekov's "The Cherry Orchard", of which C.L.W. in the *Birmingham Mail* wrote "......the company have never done better than this." (One must, of course, bear in mind when making comparisons that fine plays bring out the best in the actors.) I recall particularly, among many excellent performances, those of Elspeth Duxbury, Leslie Sands, Pauline Williams, Julia Lang (of "Listen with Mother" fame), Jeannette Hutchinson, Ward Williams, Robert Chetwyn, now one of England's top producers, and Michael Barrington*. (Michael was a great person to have in a company and, like me, a mild hypochondriac; whenever either of us met and enquired after the other's health, back would come the reply, accompanied by a sad shake of the head, "very seedy".) "The Cat and the Canary", "Love's a Luxury" and "Alibi" with Leslie French as Poirot, all played to excellent houses, but Eugene O'Neill's "Ah Wilderness", another excellent production, failed to draw.

That season the name of Ursula O'Leary, who had been a member of our Wolverhampton company, appeared for the first time. Her stage appearances have been severely rationed because of family demands, but I rank her as one of the best

*Best known to audiences as the harassed governor in "Porridge".

actresses who never became a star.

1956 contained few outstanding plays, although "My Three Angels" was beautifully acted and we were one of the few reps. to succeed with it. Another new play by Leslie Sands, "For Pete's Sake", not as good as "Beside the Seaside", was excellent entertainment nevertheless. In spite of few highlights, the season broke all box office records with an excellent company which included two very attractive newcomers, Delena Kidd and Maureen Beck.

The 1957 company was enhanced by the inclusion of Georgine Anderson, a lovely sensitive actress, and Bryan Pringle who not only frequently set the audiences alight, but almost did likewise to the theatre when, after one of the Alex's famous 'offices' (when we entertained the company to drinks at a social gathering at the end of the week), he repaired to his dressing room and fell asleep with a lighted cigarette in his mouth. The cigarette slipped on to his armchair and was smouldering when discovered just in time by the theatre fireman. The appearance of Bernard Hepton, then the director of the Birmingham Rep., and now surely one of our finest actors, demonstrated the very close links which have always existed between the two theatres; his wife, Nancie Jackson, a frequent member of the Birmingham Repertory Company, also played on a number of occasions. She was a much loved and talented person and her recent death was a great sorrow to all of us. Harold Pinter, then known as David Baron, was a member of the company and gave some excellent performances. A now famous name to appear in the cast list of "Hay Fever" was that of Vivien Merchant. Before the engagement I had wanted to meet her, but neither of us could find a mutually convenient date. Eventually, the only possible one coincided with a Test Match at Lords, so we arranged to meet outside the main gates and the interview duly took place in the midst of a milling mass of people. She recalled this when she played the Alex recently, and said it was quite her most unusual interview. I told her it was not mine, as I once interviewed Diana Dors, who was due to appear for me in pantomime at Bournemouth, in the lavatory of the club she was playing at the time — as it was the only available accommodation owing to re-building.

Another meeting which, if not quite as unusual as the other

100

two, remains vividly in my memory. It took place on a morning when I had omitted to bring my spectacles and as I was due to interview an actor I had never met, I knew I would wish to make some notes. I therefore asked Joyce Pegg (that wonderful lady to whom I refer later in the book) to rummage amongst the lost property, which has even been known to include false teeth, to try and find a pair which I could use. She succeeded, and I hurriedly put them on as she brought in the actor, who gave me some very peculiar looks during the interview and once or twice, to my surprise, appeared to me to be smiling at me for no good reason. I discovered the reason as soon as he left when, on removing the spectacles I realised, to my horror, that they were adorned on each side by diamante studded wings.

In September we presented, in association with Allan Davis who directed it, the first production of "Breath of Spring" which started an association similar to the later one with Peter Bridge. It was eventually produced in London where it had a very successful run with four of the cast who had appeared in it at the Alex and was later filmed under the title "Make Mine Mink". The set for the London production was made at the Alex, designed by our Norman Smith and painted by Rosemary Jaynes. As a result of giving the play its first production and providing the set we, as was the normal arrangement, participated in the takings and so reaped financial rewards.

The play which followed was R.C. Sherriff's "The Telescope" which Peter Powell later turned into a musical. Sadly, at its opening night at the Winter Gardens Theatre, London, at which Joan and I were present, it was received with boos. This is a dreadful experience and one I cannot understand; it seems peculiar to the theatre for nobody boos a greengrocer who has sold him an indifferent cauliflower the week before or, much as one would like to do, the bank manager who has refused an overdraft. I suffered this experience again when, under our management, Dulcie Gray's "Love Affair", which had seen the light of day at the Alex, was accorded a similar reception at the Lyric Theatre, Hammersmith.

Among the interesting newcomers to the company in 1958 was John Standing, Kay Hammond's son. I recall telling her that I felt John 'might never be a great actor, but would almost assuredly become a star'. Well he has certainly become a star,

101

and let's face it, there are not many great actors! The outstanding play was "Summer of the Seventeenth Doll" with Derek Royle who had just joined the company, and was to become one of the most popular members of all time, showing his versatility. Other outstanding newcomers were Margaret Denyer who had joined us from Salisbury (Maggie is married to the actor Arthur Hewlett who has remained one of my closest friends since we met in Tripoli during the war), and Brian Kent (now with the National Theatre Company) who stayed with us for several seasons, became a great favourite and gave many excellent performances.

There were several fine productions that year (apart from "Summer of the Seventeenth Doll) notably Tennessee Williams' "Summer and Smoke" in which my then secretary, Judy Black, a talented actress with the Crescent Theatre, the famous local amateur theatre, gave a lovely performance. The top box office receipts were for "Sailor Beware" and "Doctor in the House", and the least for "Waltz of the Toreadors".

During the following season we forged a very important link with Peter Bridge who had just presented, in London, the play "Any Other Business". He came to our production and was so impressed both by the standard of acting and settings that he entrusted us with the first production of most of his future plays, which afterwards were invariably performed in London, with the sets constructed by Sidney Jones and designed by Norman Smith, bringing us both cash and prestige. Best of all for me though was the close friendship which resulted between Joan, myself, Peter and his most attractive wife, Ros. He is a delightfully extrovert character and, at one time, a first class tennis referee. Ros is in every way his ideal counterpart, and I imagine keeps his exuberance as much in check as possible.

"The Wooden Dish" (which emptied the theatre) and "View from the Bridge" were the outstanding productions. Newcomers were Terry Scully, later magnificent as 'Private Hamp' in the TV play and in the series in which he played Henry VI, Meg Wynn Owen who continues worthily to uphold a famous family stage name, and Ronald Magill who became John Neville's associate producer at the Nottingham Playhouse and is currently so excellent in "Emmerdale Farm". At the end of the season Peter Powell, who wished to concentrate on his writing, decided to leave and received well deserved tributes from management, artistes and members of the public alike, for he had done a magnificent job during his many years with us. I therefore decided to employ guest producers, a system which continued until 1966 and has both its good and bad points. On the credit side, each guest director brings a freshness and enthusiasm to a production and the company, who may consider that a permanent producer has taught them all he knows, often welcome a fresh impetus, especially as, when engaging a guest producer, one does so bearing in mind the type of play which suits him best.

On the debit side, with a guest director it is unlikely that the same team spirit will be built up and, furthermore, it is not easy to engage producers of equal calibre to Peter Powell for example, particularly when the play is not a very exciting one. He is not on the spot for conferences and will have only a limited knowledge of the company's capabilities. At the same time this has its advantages as he will not have preconceived ideas, and actors would find this less limiting. So, on the assumption that a permanent director, who must certainly not direct all the plays, is the right one, as Malcolm Farquhar and Christopher Dunham proved to be later, I come down on the side of employing one. This in fact was a recommendation made to me by the Council of Management who felt, amongst other things, that it would lessen the amount of work I was doing, and I readily agreed that I would abide by it as soon as I could find a suitable director. At the same time they made a recommendation, possibly for a similar reason, that I should discontinue producing pantomime, but with this I could not acquiesce and later events, I am sure, proved that in this I was entirely correct. It was a well meant but unwise suggestion which would, in any case, have involved the theatre in considerable extra expense.

So in 1960, with guest producers, we entered on a new phase with a company which included two splendid new actresses, Helen Dorward and Heather Canning (later to become a member of the Royal Shakespeare Company), who excelled in an outstanding production of Eugene O'Neill's "Desire under the Elms" by Frank Dunlop, at one time the associate director of the National Theatre and later founder director of the National Theatre's Young Vic Company. It was, disappointingly, a box office failure as was Ted Willis's "Hot Summer Night". A new play, "The Long View", did moderately well but never received a London production. Once again, Agatha Christie topped the list with "The Uninvited Guest", closely followed by "The French Mistress" by Sonnie Hale, under the pen name of Robert Munro.

We ran a competition for local authors but, as so often happens, no really outstanding play was unearthed. However, one by a regular patron, Shirley Ann Bates, showed promise and won the award but not a production.

1961 saw the introduction of two outstanding newcomers, Judy Parfitt (now married to Tony Steedman) who had made a guest appearance the previous year. Now acknowledged as one of our finest younger actresses, she was recently nominated for the award of 'Young actress of the year'. The other was Frank Woodfield who became an Alex legend and remained almost continuously until repertory ceased in 1973, and added much distinction during those years.

The link with Peter Bridge was continued with "Guilty Party" (originally named "Refer to Drawer" and changed on my suggestion), which did extremely well afterwards at the St. Martin's Theatre. We were thus connected with two plays, launched by us, running in London at the same time. The season included another new play, "Life Worth Living" by Robert Storey, directed by Basil Dean, at one time England's top director who rates columns in "Who's Who" in the theatre. The play, for which Vanda Godsell joined the company, was described by one of the Birmingham papers as 'the best piece of contemporary theatre for some time' but was not to the liking of our audience and came bottom of the attendance poll, although playing to 9,591 people which, for the least successful play, was a very reasonable figure. "Black Coffee" topped the list attracting 17,612 people, followed by our old friend "Hot and Cold in All Rooms". High on the list came a quite mild saucy American comedy, "Marriage Go Round" with a cast of only four, including Anne Aubrey guesting, and disproving the theory that the public will not support small cast plays.

The average attendance for each play that season was the satisfactory one of over 13,000 people at a top price of only 5/-, scaling down to 1/- at the back of the balcony. But when the

1962 season opened the highest price was increased, with profuse apologies, to 6/-, although the 1/- price still remained. The most successful production was "Salad Days" followed by "Love's a Luxury" with Derek Royle giving an hilarious performance and proving his versatility in a serious part in the following play "Breaking Point", both at the Alex and afterwards when it was presented in London by Peter Bridge. An excellent production of C.P. Snow's "The Affair" rounded off a most successful season, which maintained an audience attendance level only slightly below that of the previous year but which was to drop to just over 11,000 in 1963, which was to be our last successful repertory season.

It opened with "Witness for the Prosecution", and for once, probably because the public were now too familiar with the final denouement, the Agatha Christie magic failed to attract audiences, as did the next play, "Night Season", by a local author, Kenneth Hill, which I had already seen at Birmingham's Crescent Theatre. Although splendidly produced by Michael Finlayson (for two years our producer at Wolverhampton), and with some excellent performances, notably from Rosemary Leach and Janet Whiteside (now with the National Theatre and undoubtedly one of the best actresses to have graced an Alex company), somehow the production did not quite come to life and I found it in many ways less enjoyable than the one at the Crescent. We presented, in association with Peter Bridge, "Difference of Opinion" (another of the plays of George Ross and Campbell Singer), excellently produced as always by Anthony Sharp. It achieved a West End run and, along with all his other plays, brought us in substantial royalties. Derek Royle was a 'scream' in his own farce, "Flat Spin", and there was a most exciting production of "Becket" in contrast, which rather unexpectedly drew excellent houses as did, more predictably, Noel Coward's "Hay Fever" and Agatha Christie's "The Hollow".

Although the season had shown a drop, nonetheless when it finished all looked set reasonably fair for the future but this, as related later, was not to be the case.

TOURS

During this same period the policy of Spring and Autmun touring seasons had become firmly established and we received some fine productions of which, once again, it is only possible to give a brief resume and to pick out some highlights or special events. In 1952 they included Alec Guinness in "Under the Sycamore Tree", Emlyn Williams' magnificent readings of Dickens' "Bleak House" and then as Dickens himself. "The Square Ring", a play about boxing, failed, as has every play I can recall with sport as its theme, such as "Badgers Green", R.C. Sheriff's play about village cricket, and Basil's play, "Shooting Star", about soccer. Possibly this is on account of the high percentage of females in the audience, so perhaps a play about tennis would be a success....... although one about show jumping might be beyond a theatre's resources!

On Monday, 17th November, came the now legendary "The Mousetrap" with Richard Attenborough and Sheila Sim, about which, on leaving the theatre, one OAP was heard to say to another, "Well, this won't run......" Neither did it receive good notices here or at its opening in Nottingham the previous week. At the lunch to celebrate the 25th year of "The Mousetrap", Richard Attenborough recalled that after its initial poor reception, the producer, cast, and Agatha Christie all held a conference. There was much gloom and to dispel it Agatha Christie, then halfway up the stairs on her way to bed, leaned over the bannister and said, "Don't worry children. I'm sure we will get a nice little run out of it."

One who thought it might succeed (but was not wildly enthusiastic about it) was my cousin Victor Saville, once one of England's top film producers with such films as "Goodbye, Mr Chips" and "South Riding", with Ralph Richardson and Ann Todd, to his credit, and who made Jessie Matthews the darling of the British film public. He bought a half share of the film rights for £5,000; there was, however, a proviso in the contract, namely that the film could not be made until the play had terminated its London run. Victor is now eighty-one!

In 1953, Eric Portman and Dorothy Tutin in Graham Greene's "Living Room", John Mills and Joan Greenwood in Mary Hayley-Bell's "The Uninvited Guest", John Clements and

106

Kay Hammond in "Pygmalion", and Peter Ustinov's "No Sign of the Dove" with two ex-Alex repertory actors, Raymond Huntley and Robin Bailey in the cast, were outstanding successes. The following year, whilst not a very exciting one, brought Christopher Fry's "The Dark is Light Enough", with Edith Evans and James Donald, at one time a member of our repertory company at Wolverhampton, "After the Ball", a beautifully mounted musical based on "Lady Windermere's Fan", with Vanessa Lee and Peter Graves, and Sadlers Wells paying one of their most successful visits. This was the year we requested patrons not to smoke in the auditorium whilst the curtain was up, which has now become standard practice in most theatres, but caused resentment from a few patrons at the time.

Spring 1955 caused me some of the unhappiest moments of my entire career. Although it is now a long time ago and I do not enjoy opening old wounds, it is difficult not to refer to the incident.

I booked "Peter Pan" with a lady playing the role who was at that time one of the biggest box office names in the country (as a result of her weekly appearances on a TV panel game), consequently the theatre was sold out at all performances. I went round to see her on the Monday before the evening performance and she thanked me for the flowers which it has always been our custom to give to ladies on first nights, and we had a most pleasant chat. I told her that my two youngsters were looking forward to seeing her at the Saturday afternoon performance; I thought she looked a little blank, but she said nothing. A little later, however, my normally imperturbable manager, Bill Dobson, came into my office with an ashen face to say that the lady said she did not play any of the four matinee performances. I went straight round to see her and she told me this had been the case at each theatre, and an announcement was always made to that effect before the curtain rose. I could not accept this, and said if she persisted in this intention there were bound to be repercussions, but she remained adamant. Not knowing quite what to do, but determined to let as many of the public know as possible, I had the following inserted in our advertisement, "It is regretted that, owing to overwork, Miss .... is restricted in the number of appearances. Should any patron require a refund, will they please apply at the

Box Office."

This might only have caused limited comment, but Claude Westall of the *Birmingham Mail*, a very direct character if ever there was one, wrote an article to which she took strong objection. She demanded an apology from the Editor, and to Claude's dismay, received one. But the gist of it had got into the national press and soon every press reporter in England seemed to converge on the Alex and each day's Nationals gave it enormous coverage. Needless to say, the lady concerned was not very complimentary about me in her interviews, especially as her appearances were often greeted with sporadic boos and her understudy who, of course, had been playing the part throughout the tour at matinees, was, to her surprise, roundly cheered. I found it terribly distasteful to say the least and dreaded reading the papers each morning. I welcomed the end of the week with a huge sigh of relief.

Three weeks later we had a different, but almost equally fraught, experience. A.E. Matthews, who was appearing in "The Manor of Northstead" and who had been completely 'off the bottle' for some time, took to it again as a result of hearing some bad news at the end of the week, so much so that he was almost incoherent at the early Saturday performance, and totally so by the later one, which he played sitting down and without ever giving a single cue to poor Charles Heslop with whom he played his longest scenes and who, by the end of the evening, was in a state bordering on hysteria. Nevertheless Matty decided that he was in a fit state to attend the usual Saturday night drink in my office after the performance — got lost in the stalls en-route — was rescued and finally appeared in the office in complete disarray and with not a fly button done up! He soon collapsed and had to be carried downstairs. What a man! We will certainly never see his like again.

After these events it was good to return to normality, with Moira Shearer in "I am a Camera" and Paul Scofield, Diana Wynyard and Brian Oulton in "Hamlet". The cast also included Ernest Thesiger, a great character who constantly referred to his great friend "Dear Queen Mary", with whom he used to do crochet work. He was very old by the end of his career and enjoyed telling the story of someone who stared hard at him in a tube and eventually said, "Excuse me, but

108

weren't you Ernest Thesiger?" The season abounded with many other big names, Jessie Matthews, Nigel Patrick, David Tomlinson, Michael Denison, Dulcie Gray, Maxine Audley and Jack Warner, to mention but a few.

The most notable event in 1956 was the British premiere of "The Chalk Garden" with an all star cast including Edith Evans, Peggy Ashcroft and Felix Aylmer, produced by John Gielgud. The first night was the most glittering I can remember at the Alex, with an audience which included Laurence Olivier, 'Binkie' Beaumont, under whose management it was presented, Robert Helpman and many other notables. Our rather elderly stage doorkeeper who, after the performance, was simultaneously trying to control autograph hunters, deal with requests for taxis, give advice on restaurants and attend to his normal duties, answered a telephone call. By now distraught, and afraid to leave his stage door unattended, he shouted up the stairs, "Is there an Edith Evans in the theatre? If so, she's wanted on the 'phone!" This would not be possible nowadays with Jim, that doyen of stage-door keepers, or his day-time counterpart, ace photographer, John.

This outstanding season also brought that delightful man, Tyrone Power in "Devil's Disciple", Alec Guinness in a premiere of Feydeau's "Hotel Paradiso", John Clements, Kay Hammond and Margaret Rutherford in "The Way of the World", the funniest portrayal I have seen of Lord Fancourt Babberly in "Charley's Aunt", by Frankie Howerd — an inspired piece of casting, as it is difficult to imagine anyone less likely to have been a titled undergraduate at Oxford, or for that matter any where else, and wound up with Emlyn Williams in his Dylan Thomas readings entitled "A Boy Crying", which held the audience spellbound.

A.E. Matthews visited us again in 1957 with "A Month of Sundays", and was strictly sober throughout the week. Emile Littler presented Basil's newest play "The Lovebird", with Ronald Shiner and Dora Bryan. Basil was depressed by its poor notices here, but it had a very successful London run of which, very sadly, he was unaware as he died just before it opened. In December, after various messages from Moscow saying first that it was 'on' and then that it was 'off', we presented, by arrangement with the British Soviet Friendship Society, the

Urals Ensemble from Sverdlosk. A most disorganised but delightful company.

1958 opened with a visit from D'Oyly Carte followed by our own presentation of Leslie Sands' "Beside the Seaside", with George Formby and Nancy Roberts (older patrons will remember her as Grandma Grove), which was presented in conjunction with Leslie Sands and Leslie Grade. It was not a happy tour as George and Beryl were having their marital troubles which afterwards became public. Brian Rix in "Simple Spymen" and Paul Schofield in the musical "Expresso Bongo" were both very popular.

"The Flowering Cherry", an early production in 1959, with Ralph Richardson and Meriel Forbes, was followed by Vanessa Lee and Peter Graves in a beautifully mounted, but rather unsatisfactory, production of "The Merry Widow". Vanessa had played principal boy at the Alex some years previously under her original name, Ruby Moule (not surprising that she should change it). A not very good new play "Seashell" with Sybil Thorndike and Heather Sears, included a little known actor -- Sean Connery. "The Tunnel of Love", a first production, with Robert Morley, was also rather disappointing.

Although 1960 included some excellent productions, amongst them, as usual, Operas and Ballets, it was not an outstanding year. Noel Coward's "Waiting in the Wings", based on Brinsworth, the last home for so many actors (Noel Coward was for long its very active president), contained superb performances by Lewis Casson, Sybil Thorndike, Marie Lohr and a host of famous actresses. It was not to everyone's taste for, as in London, many people thought it was a sentimental orgy — a sort of Veterans of Variety, but I found it extremely moving.

In 1961 "On the Avenue" received its premiere en-route to London. It was extremely under-rehearsed and on the day it opened, although in a state of chaos, I heard the producer and designer engaged in a heated discussion about the exact position in which a bowl of flowers should be placed! When I went in to Beryl Reid's dressing room before curtain up, to wish her luck, she was so over-wrought that she immediately and understandably burst into tears. Margaret Lockwood filled the theatre with "Signpost to Murder", and the year wound up with "Boeing Boeing" in which David Tomlinson gave a superb

110

comedy performance. Although it did a good week with us, the business on tour had been patchy. I told David, who was a little depressed, that I felt sure it would succeed if it got to London, but the title might keep people out. As is now theatre history, after a break and some re-casting, it opened there and made a small fortune, and continues to make money to this day. But how wrong can one be about a title!

When the Festival Ballet paid their usual visit John Gilpin arrived a few minutes late for the matinee, by which time Dame Beryl Grey, something of a martinet, had authorised an announcement that "due to unfortunate indisposition, John Gilpin will not be dancing this afternoon", and he was not allowed to!

Outstanding in 1962 were "Irma La Douce"; "Ross" with Michael Bryant giving a superb performance as T.E. Lawrence; "Private Eye" and "Public Ear", a double bill by Peter Shaffer which included Maggie Smith, Kenneth Williams and Terry Scully (late of our repertory company). To end the season Agatha Christie's "Rule of Three", three greatly below standard one act plays, did very poor business.

Tours in 1963 included Flora Robson and Griffith Jones in a dull two-handed play, "Close Quarters"; Cicely Courtneidge, Jack Hulbert and Robertson Hare in Agatha Christie's "Spider's Web", a combination which, although Cis was miscast (but as always brilliant), could hardly fail to fill the theatre; Arnold Wesker's "Chips with Everything", then unknown, did very badly, but "Goodnight Mrs. Puffin" with Irene Handl, filled every seat, as did "Rattle of a Simple Man". Sybil Thorndike and Lewis Casson came in "Queen B", a very poor play (as, sadly, was so often the case with that wonderful couple who did so much good for the reputation of the theatre).

These years had been very satisfactory, but increasing costs and the drop in repertory attendances, although small, were beginning to sound a warning note and it was so costly to run a theatre, even in those days, that our profits were very small but achieved without any subsidy.

CHAPTER 21

REPERTORY DECLINES AND ENDS IN 1975

Although in 1963 the average attendance figure for each production had dropped to 11,000, it was not a very dramatic decrease, but in 1964 it was a really alarming one and the figure fell to 9,750. It is an interesting sidelight that this figure, nevertheless, exceeeded that of virtually every weekly touring production. It was, of course, spread over two weeks with much the same patrons attending each production, whereas now, with weekly tours, although attracting a very strong hard core of regular patrons, they are drawn from a much wider circle. Artistically, the season included some fine productions; "Under Milk Wood", (although I feel it is better heard than seen) beautifully directed by Geoffrey Ost, for so long producer for the Sheffield Playhouse; "Tulip Tree" with the older members of the company — Frank Woodfield, Bill Avenell, Beryl Johnstone, and Anthony Howard especially shining in a production we later took to the Belgrade Theatre, Coventry. "Spring and Port Wine" received its first production (in association with Allan Davis who directed it), and although very popular needed considerable revision. Allan subsequently worked very hard on it and it opened in London with three of the original Alex cast, John Alderton, Ray Mort and Jan Carey, who were later joined by Janet Whiteside. It started quietly, but revived after a TV excerpt, and ran for a very long time earning us quite substantial royalties and helping a little to balance our losses on the season, as did "The Reluctant Debutante" with Paul Marklew, a locally born actor, giving one of his best performances. The season was curtailed so that Brian Kent, Beryl Johnstone and Anthony Howard could appear in a new serial which it was hoped might achieve a degree of success — it was called "Crossroads"!

After the decrease in attendances that season we realised

112

that the one which followed would be very vital for the theatre's future. Unfortunately it commenced badly, and of the earlier productions the only popular one was "Betzi", a play about Napoleon by William Douglas Home, receiving its second production (my brother first presented it at Salisbury). It was beautifully played and well directed by Oliver Gordon, who had produced it originally and was, I felt, superior to the one which later ran briefly in London. Peggy Mount appeared with the company in a new play "Did you feel it move" by Edward Caddick, which did not transfer to London but helped our box office enormously. Late in the season came a superb production of "Tea House of the August Moon" which was a joint effort between ourselves and the Belgrade Theatre, Coventry, and contained many fine performances especially from David Daker as Sakini.* Another outstanding production, "The Masters"**, was directed by that excellent producer, Geoffrey Edwards. But whatever the play, the attendance figure usually stayed roughly the same, with Agatha Christie again the exception, when "Peril at End House" played to 11,500 patrons. The perennial "Ghost Train" attracted only slightly fewer people.

For the 1966 season Malcolm Farquhar joined us as producer, and the system of engaging guest producers (except of course for the occasional play) was discontinued. Malcolm, who was at one time an actor at the Birmingham Rep., was a worthy successor to Peter Powell, which is in itself a high compliment, and during the years he was with us did much fine work and we achieved a very happy relationship. It was certainly in no way his fault that the average fortnightly attendance figure dropped for the first time to under 9,000. The only plays to do really well were — a new one, "What about Stanley?" with Peggy

*David, an outstanding member of the company, can probably claim a record as he once received, in the same issue of the *Sunday Times*, rave notices for his performance in a stage play, a TV play and a film.

**Giving an excellent performance in it was Ronald Russell who, with his wife, Peggy Ann Wood, a lovely actress who appeared at the Alex all too rarely, ran the Little Theatre, Bristol until it became part of the Bristol Old Vic Company. At the C.O.R.T. conference in Bristol he made what was probably the best speech I have ever heard. His brother, Sir Lionel, was the Chief Education Officer for Birmingham and, like Ronnie, is a distinguished Old Cliftonian.

Mount again as guest star, Agatha Christie's "Black Coffee", and a slight but delightful comedy, "Two Dozen Red Roses" in which Janet Whiteside gave one of her many first class performances, as did Dennis Spencer, a great Alex stalwart, both as actor and occasional producer — usually of farces. (He is himself the author of many successful ones.) These plays drew from 10,500 to 12,000 patrons, proving that there was still a considerable potential audience. Bill Naughton's "June Evening" received a first production (the Alex's record for new productions was excellent) in which Brian Kent returned to us from "Crossroads". Whilst attracting fair houses it did not achieve the success of "Spring and Port Wine" and never received a London run in spite of the author's considerable reputation. "Gentle Avalanche", a most interesting play although not popular, included in the cast that lovely actress Josephine Tewson who made several appearances during the season.

When the season ended, it had become obvious that if repertory was to continue drastic steps must be taken and so, after much deliberation, a new system was evolved with Henry Sherwood, an important West End manager. By arrangement with John Beaumont, the managing director of the lovely Grand Theatre, Leeds, we were to present jointly, with a greatly enlarged company which included two extremely talented newcomers, Janet Hargreaves and David Simeon, five of that season's productions each playing two weeks at Birmingham and two at Leeds. The plays included guest stars such as Jack Watling, Marius Goring, Naunton Wayne (a very delightful Old Cliftonian), Rosemary Leach, Michael Gwynne, Dermot Walsh and Richard Greene. The figures at Birmingham did improve, but only slightly, and expenses were of course much higher and the Leeds' takings, at a theatre with no repertory background, were very poor. Fortunately we were only to a very limited extent responsible financially for Leeds, but it turned out to be a very costly experiment. Administratively it was almost impossible, and it was all too easy for artistes to be in the wrong town at the right moment or *vice versa*. On one occasion, for example, Dennis Spencer and Jenny McNae, a newcomer the previous season and a great asset during her four years with the company, had to leave Leeds at about five in the morning — an hour unknown to most actors — in order to rehearse in Birmingham

114

for a short time and then return to Leeds for the evening performance.

On the credit side, two of the productions, "According to the Evidence" by Henry Cecil and "The Bells" with Marius Goring, received London productions, the former achieving a reasonable run but, in spite of a tremendous performance by Marius, present day audiences would not accept "The Bells".

Paradoxically, when the experiment ceased and we returned to normality, without stars, "Friends and Neighbours", expertly produced by Dennis Spencer, easily headed the box office attendance figures, playing to nearly 12,000 people.

So, sadly, what might have proved to be a solution failed, and when the 1968 season arrived it was more in hope than expectation that we embarked on it. In fact I was so dubious that I had already decided to further decrease the number of weeks in order to accommodate two more touring attractions. It opened promisingly, however, with "The Odd Couple", which had been given a trial run for a week at the Civic Theatre, Darlington (now magnificently administered by Peter Tod, who received much of his early training at the Alex and with Reggie at Salisbury). The leading roles were played jointly by Barry Lineham, who I booked after seeing him play the part at the Theatre Royal, York, and Raymond Bowers who, during his four years, proved to be one of the best actors to have graced an Alex repertory company. In the cast was a newcomer, Noelle Finch, who remained for several seasons and became a firm favourite. That season she was outstanding in "The French Mistress" which did extremely well, and "The Flowering Cherry", directed by Terence Lodge. Terence was recommended to me by my friend, Dennis Crickmay, then headmaster of Wellesbourne School (of which I was a governor, and now, like so many private schools, is no more). Each year Dennis expertly produced a school play and I saw Terence in "Caesar and Cleopatra" and immediately arranged for him to join the Wolverhampton company when he left school. He later went to the Birmingham Rep. and eventually, with Bernard Hepton, became associate director of the Liverpool Playhouse.

Dennis Spencer's adaptation of "Dracula" with Valentine Dyall as the Count, surprisingly did not draw. "The Farmer's Wife", which achieved fame in the early days at the Birming-

115

ham Rep., was very popular, but the biggest box office success was a revival of "Hot and Cold in All Rooms", which has never been known to fail, and played to 12,450 people, thus helping the average attendance figure to rise. Malcolm Farquhar left at the end of the season and I reverted to the system of guest producers, having been unsuccessful in finding a suitable replacement for this splendid producer.

The season had at least not shown any decrease in attendances compared with its immediate predecessors, and this gave me some encouragement for the next one which produced some box office successes. Notably, Adam Faith as guest star in "Alfie" which also played for four days at the Malvern Festival Theatre; Agatha Christie's "Murder at the Vicarage"; and "The Prime of Miss Jean Brodie" in which Jenny McNae excelled as Miss Brodie in what was, in many ways, the most satisfactory production of the season. An event which held great promise was the premiere of Guy Bolton's "A Man and His Wife" with Emrys Jones joining the company to play Sir Winston Churchill and Sheila Brownrigg, a pre-war Alex favourite, to play Lady Churchill. To everyone's disappointment it did not come up to expectations and never reached London.

Unfortunately, in 1970, the attendance figures dropped once again and the season could claim few real box office successes in spite of some good productions. Especially "Plaza Suite" in which Brian Kent's performance, notably in the last of the three plays, was one of his very best and received excellent support from Helen Dorward, Paul Henry (now so brilliant as Benny in "Crossroads") and Jeanette Tomsett. A newcomer to the company, Adrian Pearson, gave some excellent performances and stayed until repertory ended, also playing in several of our pantomimes and becoming, like so many actors, a close family friend. Other newcomers, all of whom made first class contributions, included Michael Cotterill, Derek Seaton, Kathleen Worth and Amelia Bayntun.

The season wound up with "Full House" by Ivor Novello, with Joan Turner as guest artiste. She had the greatest difficulty in learning the part, never really knew it, grossly overplayed it, but almost acted everyone else off the stage, which took some doing with Ursula O'Leary playing alongside her. It was presented for one week only and played to good houses.

In retrospect, I feel that this was the moment at which I should have made the recommendation to the Council of Management, which I knew they awaited, to discontinue repertory. I was hesitant to do so, not for sentimental reasons, which I did not allow to influence me, but because I realised that, should it not be possible to find enough tours, no other policy was possible and it would almost certainly be the end of the theatre.

So repertory, given another chance, opened with "Not Now Darling", and I was encouraged when WHW in the *Birmingham Mail* referred to it as "the happiest opening to a season I can remember". The cast (as nearly always) included Frank Woodfield, for so many years a tower of strength, and that season celebrated fifty years on the stage. Sue Nicholls joined us soon after leaving "Crossroads" (recently seen on TV in "The Duchess of Duke Street" and as the secretary in "The Rise and Fall of Reginald Perrin" in which, with Leonard Rossiter, John Barron and Brigit Forsyth, she was one of four members to have worked under the Salberg banner). "Not Now Darling" played to rather better than average figures, and for a moment our waning hopes flickered, but only "Rebecca", "The Boy Friend", "Love from a Stranger" and the rather thin "Doctor in the House" were box office successes. "What the Butler Saw" was greatly liked by our younger audience and equally disliked by the majority of the upper age group, a problem which had become increasingly difficult to resolve.

Nevertheless, attendance figures had improved slightly and as this was the first time they had done so for several years, I still hesitated to take the almost inevitable step and embarked, in 1972, on a new season. Christopher Dunham, who had so excellently directed "The Boy Friend" and "All in Good Time" the previous year, became permanent director and proved to be a tower of strength. The company's excellent newcomers included Richard Frost, Lynette Erving, Peter Robert Scott and Christine Edmonds. Barrie's "What Every Woman Knows" with Peter, Christine, Raymond Bowers and Patricia Kerry outstanding, and "Ten Little Indians" (neé "Niggers") did far and away the best business of the season. Once again three cheers for Agatha, whose 25th Anniversary lunch for "The Mousetrap" I recently attended as a guest of Peter Saunders, who I regard as a supreme example of what a theatre director/producer should be.

But attendance figures had declined to around 5,000 — 6,000 a production, therefore I compromised further by not opening the 1973 season until June. Newcomers Michael Sanderson, Liz Norman, Jill Graham and, for some productions, Glyn Worsnip (of Esther Rantzen's "That's Life" fame) all gave good performances. But the writing which had for so long been on the wall, was now there in very large letters. When, on November 3rd, the season ended with a not very good production of "The Ghost Train" (but which the author, Arnold Ridley of "Dad's Army" fame, was good enough to say he had enjoyed), so at the same time did repertory.

This decision was a sad one for me as it spelt the end of so many excellent productions and untold memorable performances — but it had become inevitable. Let us examine some of the reasons which I feel were mainly responsible for its decline.

It would, of course, be easy to say that ever mounting costs was the culprit, but it went deeper than that. For one thing, the public now, as never before, demanded big star names, which of course the repertory system did not provide. Furthermore, when our patrons either died, retired away from Birmingham, or decided that they did not want to venture out at night, they were not being replaced by a sufficient number of new ones. To make matters more difficult, the type of play which our somewhat 'middle of the road' public liked best was not being written and as a result we were including too many revivals. Consequently our programme veered on the 'safe' side, whereas at one time we could take a risk on an average of about one play in four, which is stimulating for audience, director and actor alike. This made the task of attracting good actors who would remain with the company, especially with the ever present lure of TV, increasingly difficult.

A further problem we faced was that not only were our salaries way behind those paid by television but we, who at one time paid the highest repertory salaries in the country, were now finding it difficult even to keep pace with many companies who were receiving reasonable, and in some cases quite high, subsidies. Also, whereas we were once one of the very few repertory companies running its productions for more than a week, a great incentive to artistes, virtually all companies had now increased their run to a minimum of two weeks, and in many cases to three or four, which is not possible in our large auditorium. So one of our big levers for obtaining artistes was lost to us.

Happily, in spite of these problems, we were still able to maintain a strong nucleus of permanent actors, but were, with increasing frequency, having to cast outside the company, sometimes with actors who were not of the standard our audiences had come to expect. For, whenever I wanted an artiste for a particular play, invariably the answer would come back from the agent that 'He' (or 'She'), 'would love to play in your beautiful theatre . . . . . . etc . . . . . . but at the moment is waiting to hear the result of a TV interview, or had decided not to leave London. But please do ask again another time.' If, however, the play was a new one with a possible London future, or one of the now more rare 'challenging' ones, they were usually, miraculously, available. Many actors are, I know, frustrated by this attitude on the part of their agent, feeling that they would rather be working than hanging around London on the off-chance. For after all they came into the profession to work.

So, one way and another, in spite of many splendid actors and productions, there is no doubt that the overall standard had fallen in recent years, even if only imperceptibly.

And that, in the final analysis, was the most important factor of all.

CHAPTER 22

THE BRIDGE EXTENSION

When the theatre was rebuilt it was still on a main road, but with Birmingham's impending redevelopment it would be cut off and relegated into a relative back alley, which was not a happy prospect. But this was circumvented when, after much negotiation, instigated and carried through by Robert Oulsnam, the honorary secretary of the theatre's Council of Management, work was commenced on an extension which stretched across the road and placed our frontage in a prominent position. Completed in 1968, it was opened by the Lord Mayor, Alderman Neville Bosworth, in front of a packed assembly composed mainly of regular patrons and well-wishers of the theatre.

It provided room in the foyer for patrons to move in comfort and for exhibitions to be held, and included a very much improved, but somewhat ill planned, box office. Upstairs was a coffee bar, chocolate kiosk and, initially, a snack bar which was not a success and was also the source of the smell of cooking. As a consequence I intended to substitute a menu containing only soup, hors d'oeuvres, cold food etc. on a help-yourself basis, but the board preferred that the area should be used as a bar to replace the Garrick Bar. I was not enthusiastic about this, partly perhaps because I had a strong affection for that bar, but chiefly because I was afraid it would cause great obstruction when the patrons were going in. In any case I always felt (and still do) that the provision of food in a theatre is essential; futhermore I doubted whether sales would increase to any great extent. But it was decided to build the bar, which opened in 1973, and although the obstruction does occur, it is not usually too severe. Both before and after the show takings have greatly increased, although not necessarily the interval trade. The limited food amenities at the coffee bar could, I feel, be improved but there are, of course, many problems.

Puss in Boots 1966-1967
Des O'Connor and Lynn Wynters

Jack and the Beanstalk 1973-74
George Lacy and Jimmy Tarbuck share a joke at rehearsal

Mother Goose 1962-63
Jack Tripp, Beryl Reid and Ted Rogers in the author's
favourite pantomime

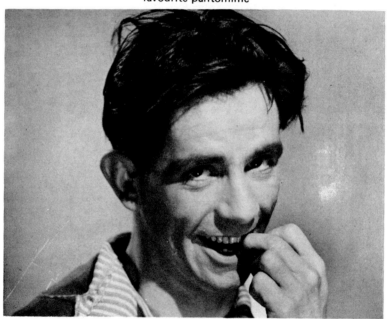

Norman Wisdom in "Robinson Crusoe" 1948-49
His first pantomime for the author

The Island Scene from "Robinson Crusoe" 1938-39
(painted and designed by Roy Cooke)
The first pantomime presented by the author — note in those days there were 32 dancers

The opening scene from "Cinderella" 1970-71
(Designed by Kenneth Turner)
Ronnie Corbett is in the centre

The Ballroom scene from "Cinderella" 1935-36, the first pantomime in the re-built theatre
(Designed by Roy Cooke)

Curries Higland Waterfalls — similar scenes used in many pantomimes

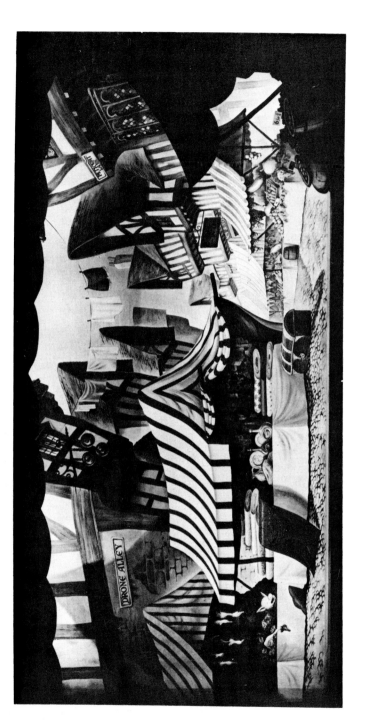

The author's favourite front cloth

(Painted by Rex Spencer for "Dick Whittington" 1952 and always used thereafter)

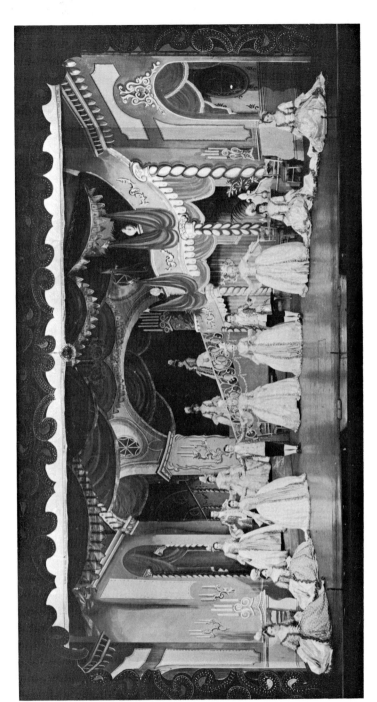

Goody Two Shoes 1967-68 — the Squire's Ballroom
(Designed by Kenneth Turner)

I was certainly wrong, but must admit that, just as my father had never really loved the new Alex as he had the old, neither have I ever really liked the Bridge Bar. For me, and for many people, it is an impersonal area with nothing approaching the atmosphere of the Garrick Bar, for so long in the care of May and Madge who helped to create its special characteristics. Or of the small Leon Bar (on which Eric stamped his personality) and which, owing to its access from backstage, also acts as a 'green room'.

Of the events which led up to the Bridge Extension I quote an article in *Encore* (our House magazine which was published for many years) written by Bob Oulsnam, one of my greatest friends (and to whose wife, Pat, I am devoted). Bob is not always the most tactful of people and I have often likened him to a cat I once owned which I loved dearly, although it continually wet on the carpet!

Certainly it was Bob's drive and initiative which made the extension possible*, at no cost to ourselves except that of furnishing it, and in this we were helped by a donation from the ever helpful Birmingham (Alexandra) Theatre Club and by a grant from the Building and Amenities Department of the Arts Council. The article, headed 'A Pipe Dream Comes True', reads as follows:

"It is very easy to build if you have money, but if you have none it is virtually impossible — or is it? How do you find £74,000 from the sky? It's not so hard when you have a guardian angel and the Alex have 156 of them — the members of our City Council. But it all takes time — in fact over seven years of begging, cajoling, pleading, bargaining, bullying and just plain dreaming. It all started in June 1962 when Derek Salberg told me that he was worried about the future of the theatre if it was to find itself in a backwater should shops be built on the other side of the road fronting Suffolk Ringway. I discussed the matter with the Theatre's Consultant Architects, The John Madin Design Group, and it was agreed that they would prepare a scheme for the comprehensive re-development of the one acre site opposite the theatre up as far as the Albany Hotel, and that I would try and find means whereby the Theatre extension could be built at no cost to the Alex. In March 1963 John Madin presented me with a sketch scheme, and in company with Alderman Teg Bowen, a good friend of

*The internal details were masterminded by Cliff Wooldridge.

the Alex, I went to see Alderman Harry Watton, who was then the chief spokesman of the ruling labour group in the City. Alderman Watton was most helpful and encouraging and said that the City would do all they could to assist the Theatre.

COMPLICATION — Neville Borg, the City Engineer and Surveyor, informed me that the Albany Hotel also wanted the site for a banqueting suite. Could we get together? I had discussions with the Development Company who built the Albany Hotel (Property and General Investments Limited) and I persuaded them that if I could negotiate a lease of the whole site from the City at a preferential rent, they would build the Theatre extension for nothing. In January 1964 in conjunction with John Madin, I submitted to the City a comprehensive scheme to provide for a new Theatre entrance, a banqueting suite, 21 shops and an underground car park, and this was approved in principle by the City Council. The cost of the Theatre extenstion was estimated at £100,000.

ANOTHER COMPLICATION — In July, the Albany Hotel decided that they did not want a banqueting suite, (they have of course now built a magnificent suite complete with squash court, swimming pool, etc.) and as a result the Developers were not so enthusiastic. I suggested a multi storey car park in its place and the Developers agreed, providing the cost of the Theatre extension was substantially reduced, a figure of £50,000 was suggested.

At the end of 1964 I agreed terms with the City for the Developers to lease the site at a Ground Rent of £250 per annum, with the City taking half the rents in excess of £28,000 per annum, providing the Alex had a £79,000 extension for nothing.

AND ANOTHER COMPLICATION — the Developers would only go on if the Theatre cost was reduced to £65,000 plus fees. Plans revised.

YET ANOTHER COMPLICATION — The Theatre cost must be reduced to £65,000 inlcuding fees, and the Developers would welcome someone else taking over the scheme. I invoked the help of Alderman Dennis Thomas, the Chairman of the Public Works Committee, who convened a meeting of all concerned, and as a result the Developers agreed to proceed, provided the Alex accepted a modified scheme.

AND YET ANOTHER COMPLICATION — Protestations from the architects who said it was impossible to provide a satisfactory scheme within the finance allowed. They were of course right, but miracles can happen! In February 1967 the lease was signed but then came the FINAL STRAW. Due to long delay and rising costs the lowest tender for the theatre was over £76,000 and it was obvious that the scheme would not proceed on this basis. I approached Alderman Charles Simpson (now a City representative on our Council of Management) the new Chairman of the Public Works Committee and as a result the City agreed to revise the terms of the lease and in their turn the Developers agreed to spend £74,000 on the theatre, for which, many grateful thanks.

............The scheme finally got underway in January 1967 and was completed in June 1969 thanks, to a large extent, to the architects, the John Madin Design Group.

Then came the problem of finding sufficient money to pay for the furnishings.......but that is another story!

On March 13th, 1963 the final words on my letter to Derek Salberg were — 'Let us keep our fingers crossed in the hope that our pipe dreams will become a reality.'

Lucky 13th. They have!"

CHAPTER 23

1964—1973: TOURING SEASONS

Although, as we have seen, repertory had started to decline and finally ended in 1975, pantomime was again flourishing and tours were more than holding their own, giving excellent and varied entertainment of which, obviously, once again, it is only possible to give a restricted and somewhat random summary.

The first of these years provided one of the great highlights in the theatre's history — the initial performance of the first ever tour by the newly formed National Theatre Company. The play was "Othello" with Laurence Olivier as the 'Moor' and Frank Finlay as 'Iago'. As Olivier had been unwell the production date had been delayed and as J.C. Trewin wrote in the *Birmingham Post*, although giving high praise to Olivier, "Last night's performance can only be taken as an earnest of better things to come", and this proved to be the case when I saw it later in London.

Later in the year we were again visited by the National Theatre who presented "Uncle Vanya" with Laurence Olivier, Michael Redgrave, Joan Plowright and Max Adrian, which I had already seen at Chichester where it was as nearly perfect a performance as I have ever seen.

This was followed at the end of the week by "Hobson's Choice" in which Joan Plowright's performance alone would have made a visit worthwhile. The cast also included Frank Finlay as 'Willie Mossop' and Michael Redgrave as the father, both giving, as one would expect, outstanding performances.

Like Trevor Howard, Michael Redgrave went to Clifton (but had left just before I arrived) — unlike Trevor, who did not even appear in them, he shone in the school plays and his performance as Lady Macbeth, to quote a master, "received favourable comparison with that of Sybil Thorndike". He won the Kadoorie Cup for the best musician in the school, but his

124

main interest lay neither in music nor acting, but in writing. A remarkable man.

Sadlers Wells Opera Company and the major ballet companies included us, as always, until 1974 when they transferred to the larger Hippodrome Theatre where, at great cost, a commodious orchestra pit has been installed and which has a larger seating capacity together with a somewhat bigger stage.

The following year a very 'starry' production of "An Ideal Husband" played to capacity with a cast which included Michael Denison, Dulcie Gray*, Richard Todd, Ursula Jeans and Roger Livesey, but was somewhat disappointing. Nevertheless, after a performance attended by a large party organised by Phyllis Bushill-Matthews (Philip Rodway's daughter) and the Ladies' Committee of the Royal Commonwealth Society for the Blind**, everyone, dazzled by the star names, raved about the production and asked why there were not more attractions of equal calibre seen in Birmingham? Virtually none of them had apparently patronised the equally good, and possibly better, production at the Birmingham Rep. a year or so earlier. This is really 'the story of our life' — knowing how to attract the public to shows which have neither a London success behind them, nor star names in the cast. If we knew the answer the theatre would be much healthier, both financially and artistically, than it is today.

The National Theatre's visit included a premiere of "Juno and the Paycock" at a performance of which Sean O'Casey's widow was present, and "Flea in Her Ear" with Albert Finney. Ballet Rambert danced again after a lapse of many years — but now regularly fill the Birmingham Repertory Theatre in an auditorium probably better suited to their work. In great contrast was a week's variety bill starring Frankie Howerd, the first such presentation in my time at the Alex, which played to delighted audiences who obviously appreciated his humour which is hard to define. A typical example was his appeal to the audience to "Show your teeth. No, *show* your teeth madam,

*Dulcie and Michael, who I am proud to number among my friends, have done a tremendous amount to keep the provincial theatre alive.

**Of which Mary Shellam is the devoted and untiring organising secretary, and for whose work I have unbounded admiration, as has everyone who knows her.

don't hand them round."* Subsequently we have presented two similar bills, one headed by Ken Dodd, the other by Morecambe and Wise, both playing to capacity. A splendid production of "Oh, What a Lovely War" wound up the season playing to enthusiastic audiences.

Early in 1967 Brian Rix packed the theatre, this time with "Stand by your Bedouin". Indeed, only once, on that occasion, with a double bill, did he ever fail to draw near capacity houses, for although, whenever his farces were announced, many regular patrons cancelled, they were always replaced by a considerably bigger number. We played to capacity with "Alibi for a Judge" with Andrew Cruickshank, then fresh from his series "Dr. Finlay's Casebook". The settings were the ones made for the long London run at the Alex by Sidney Jones and designed by Norman Smith. As a result of these links with other managements, Norman, now with ATV, achieved a repuation well beyond the confines of Birmingham, and the Alex was enabled to benefit financially and to gain prestige.

A revival of "Dear Octopus" followed and Jack Hulbert, then in his seventies and in plaster as a result of a fall in the auditorium of a darkened theatre a week earlier, still managed to appear. He, like his wife, Cicely Courtneidge, is a wonderful professional in every sense of the word. They are indeed the salt of the theatrical earth.

The 1968 season commenced with a very funny production, "Not Now Darling", destined for a long London run with that superb actor, Donald Sinden, brilliant as always. The National Theatre brought "Home and Beauty", not one of Somerset Maugham's best plays, but worthwhile if only for Arthur Lowe's performance, which was a joy and gave a much needed lift. They also played four performances of "Rosencrantz and Guildenstein are Dead" to capacity audiences — a large proportion of whom were completely baffled by it.

The annual visit from Sadler's Wells Opera started the 1969 season, followed by a play I greatly admired, "Close the Coalhouse Door". Although it attracted a large number of younger theatre goers, it was not well supported, probably as it contained no star names and the subject held no obvious

*Not very amusing in print, but coming from Frankie Howerd, it sounded hilarious.

126

appeal. A new play, "Birds on the Wing", after opening a few weeks earlier in Edinburgh, came to us direct from Canada (a far cry from the days when companies used to meet each Sunday on Crewe station). Not a great play, it was redeemed by Ian Carmichael who gave his usual brilliant performance. The visit of "Prospect" with Ian McKellan playing the roles of Edward II and Richard II was an exciting event, but the rest of the cast did not provide sufficient support.

The opening play of 1970, "Lady Frederick", including Tony Britton, Margaret Lockwood, Dermot Walsh and Raymond Francis, although not one of Lonsdale's best plays, was, thanks to the cast, a big box office success. Then came a much heralded event, "Abelard and Heloise", in which the two stars, Keith Michell and Diana Rigg, played a nude scene, in those days considered very daring, whereas today hardly an eyebrow is raised even when streakers run across the field at such hallowed venues as Twickenham and Lords. Hayley Mills in "The Wild Duck", which broke into the repertory season, filled the theatre.

Disaster struck in November when Alan Badel who, in spite of illness, had somehow played "Othello" during the early part of the week, was unable to appear for the remaining three days in the scheduled play, "Kean". There was no suitable understudy ready and so, on one of the very rare occasions in its history, the Alex was closed and money refunded for what would have been four packed performances.

The following year included the first of two visits by that superb ensemble, The Little Angels of Korea. Brian Rix continued his annual visits and filled the theatre, as did June Bronhill in an 'economy pack' production of "Glamorous Night", and John Hanson in "A Waltz Dream". The Nottingham Playhouse company's "Cherry Orchard", though containing many fine actors, did not, I felt, compare favourably with Peter Powell's earlier repertory production.

An early play in 1972, Henrik Ibsen's "A Doll's House" with Wendy Craig, was a combination which misled many parents into bringing their children under the misapprehension that this very gloomy play would provide them with a happy evening. Titles can be misleading and I recall that, many years before, a couple walked out in disgust during a performance of Barrie's "Mary Rose", thinking they had come to see the musical "Rose Marie"! It was to happen again in 1976 when Phyllis Calvert and Nigel Patrick starred in "Dear Daddy"; these two artistes, both noted especially for their work in the comedy field, combined with the title, raised visions in the public's mind of an evening of riotous comedy. They laughed uproariously for the first five minutes, but hardly did so again as they found that the play, which later won the award of the Society of West End Managers, was a serious and extremely outspoken one about family life. Another play, entitled "On Monday Next", also, predictably, created great confusion, as did Ivor Novello's "Full House".

Close on the heels of "A Doll's House" came another of Ibsen's plays, one of my favourites, "The Master Builder", which I had last seen beautifully played by the National Theatre Company in their first season at the Old Vic. This production, with Andrew Cruickshank as 'Solness', emptied the theatre — providing a great contrast to his previous appearance in "Alibi for a Judge". This was mostly to be attributed to the name of Ibsen, but nevertheless demonstrated once again how quickly, after a TV series has ceased, an actor's name begins to lose its drawing power.

Opera always filled the theatre with the popular works. Sadlers Wells did so that year with "Orpheus in the Underworld" and "The Marriage of Figaro", but neither "Count Ory" nor "The Coronation of Poppea" attracted good houses.

We thus came to 1973 which was to be the last with separate Spring and Autumn touring periods for, from 1974 onwards, with repertory discontinued, the whole year was to be devoted to tours except, of course, for the pantomime season.

John Hanson in "Lilac Time" filled the theatre, and shortly afterwards "Hatzabarim", the Israeli Dance Company, arguably the worst company of its kind to visit these shores, emptied it. The week was mostly notable for the excellent relationship between them and our backstage staff which, as always, included a number of Arabs; all delightful people. The Royal Ballet, with a repertoire consisting of a series of short ballets, did very moderately, whereas the Scottish Ballet, who brought "Giselle", played to excellent houses for the public infinitely prefer full length ballets. "Sleuth", which aroused mixed opinions, did extremely well, but there was little else of outstanding interest, with one big exception -- the visit of Marlene Dietrich, that marvellous artiste, of whom Anthony Everitt said in the *Birmingham Post*, "The way she takes her bows is alone worth the money", and Mr. McCann wrote in the *Birmingham Mail*, "Seeing her in the flesh was like finding the holy grail". We had been warned that she might be difficult, so I telephoned a friend who knew her well and asked if he had any special tips or advice to give us. He said, "No, just be helpful and tactful." A little later, reading Leslie Frewin's book on Marlene Dietrich, I came across the following: "Marlene was dissatisfied with her appearance in the rushes of one of her films, and said to the cameraman, "I don't understand it; when you were filming 'The Garden of Allah' you made me look gorgeous." "Ah," he replied, "you must remember that *I* was then eight years younger" and apparently this most tactful remark delighted her.

But although she was precise in her demands we found her most accommodating, and no trouble at all. This was partly, I feel, because Mike Bullock and, to a lesser extent, myself gave her every attention from the time we met her on the Sunday, when we were both a little disconcerted to find a rather careworn and travel weary, not so young lady.

The transformation the following day was almost unbelievable and when, later in the week, I sat in her dressing room drinking a cup of tea, whilst she sat on the make-up table dangling her famous legs (clad in trousers), I felt I was with a lady of 30 and not one of well over 70. After her appearance each night she held court to a large audience of fans waiting at the stage door and again outside her hotel, but not before she had meticulously prepared herself to do so.

It is dangerous and perhaps impossible to make comparisons, but just as I would rate Morecambe and Wise the greatest entertainers to appear at the Alex, with Ken Dodd (so much funnier on the stage than on TV) not far behind, Laurence Olivier the finest actor, so undoubtedly Marlene Dietrich was the greatest 'star'.

Unhappily, and probably partly because very many people felt she was 'past her best', Birmingham audiences, and provincial ones in general, did not really respond and with our expenses totalling over £14,000 we were involved in a very heavy loss. It is never pleasant to lose money, but if it can ever be acceptable then this was indeed one of those occasions.

Shortly afterwards, a play with Kenneth More had to be cancelled owing to his sudden illness and was replaced, at the last moment, by "That's No Lady, That's My Husband" with Francis Matthews and Clive Morton (until his death, one of my greatest friends in the theatre). Most patrons who had booked to see Kenneth More retained their tickets — and were well rewarded.

For the most part they had been exciting and successful years, and I would like to pay tribute to that great theatre enthusiast, Renee Stepham, through whom I booked so many of the productions.

Nevertheless, lack of capital, inflation and falling receipts had created a crisis during these years. As a result, as related in the following chapter, during these years the theatre passed out of private ownership.

CHAPTER 24

CRISIS YEARS — WE SURVIVE

As related, the years 1952—1963 were most successful ones during which pantomime takings were restored to the level of the peak years, with the limited touring seasons attracting good houses and repertory continuing to thrive. But overheads were mounting, trends were changing, and soon capital would be required partially to re-seat, re-carpet and re-decorate the theatre. Capital was a commodity of which the theatre had always been very short and, in spite of the apparently healthy situation, I had said in a speech as early as 1957 that the commercial theatre, which included the Alex, had a very hard road ahead and that a large number of theatres might eventually disappear. Sadly, these words have turned out to be prophetic indeed.

In 1965 the renovations became absolutely essential and now included the urgent need for a new switchboard. We just did not possess the money, and to exacerbate the situation, repertory had begun its decline. Therefore, I went to see Alderman Harry Watton, leader of the Labour Party, then in power, and explained the situation, saying that the theatre must have an infusion of capital. He was wonderfully understanding and immediately contacted Alderman Griffin, the leader of the opposition, to whom we explained the position. The result was that shortly a loan of £30,000 was made to the theatre to carry out the necessary work, to be repaid at £2,000 a year; an arrangement which we met the following year but were unable to do in the subsequent one. So I had to go to the City and tell them that the theatre's financial situation had become desperate.

The first published mention of our difficulties came in the *Birmingham Post* dated March 1968, when Gordon Price*, our PRO for so many years, stated in a talk he gave to radio and
*See footnote * on following page.

television dealers, that if some financial help was not forthcoming in a few months time...."You may not have an Alexandra Theatre, Birmingham."

Other papers naturally took this up and as a result they received many letters of support for the Alex, the first of which, from Evelyn Laye, referred to the Alex as:

> "....a highly respected theatre, respected nationally and an integral part of the life of the City of Birmingham, which might well have fallen, like so many others, but for the devotion of the Salberg family."

The City were extremely sympathetic but, to make matters more difficult for them, the Birmingham Repertory Theatre too was currently facing severe financial problems just at the time when they were hoping to build a new theatre. A merger with the Alex was suggested, with money spent to improve the Alex building, but the *Birmingham Post* next day put it succinctly in a leader headed "Surely Not". The idea, of course, was a 'non-starter' and to quote the *Daily Telegraph* dated June 9th, the "suggestion has been rejected out of hand by the Rep." There the idea ended, but was followed by the ridiculous notion of a merger between the Rep. and the Hippodrome, further delaying our fate which hung very much in the balance. Many articles appeared in the papers followed, in 1968, by letters and statements from the Council House. It was reported in the *Birmingham Mail*, for example, that "the Council would come to the rescue of the Alex; a decision not taken by an overwhelming majority, however." Alderman Beaumont Dark said "A theatre which can lose £5,000** on a pantomime can surely lose a frightening amount of money on other things." Later, he was one of the first City representatives on our Council of Management when it was formed, and I thought had come to

*Gordon is a most talented person with an extremely inventive brain. Blessed with a nimble tongue, he was much in demand as a speaker when, no doubt, he included some of his fund of Irish stories. It was his drive which re-kindled enthusiasm for the Playgoers Club when it had dwindled. He now runs a theatrical agency combined with a shop where he derives a large part of his income from selling black face soap to black children! I always greatly look forward to meeting Gordon, especially if he is accompanied by his charming wife, Shirley.

**This was a statement made out of context of the actual facts.

132

understand our problems until I read, recently, that he was reported as saying that some of the Alex City grant should be diverted to the Hippodrome, which would make no significant impact on their finances but would be a step towards the closure of the Alex.

An article in the *Birmingham Post* read:

"While the going was good for provincial theatres, the Salbergs ran the Alex, naturally as a commercial enterprise, but also with a sense of responsibility to the public. It is a Birmingham theatre, personally directed, and has become part of the development planned around it."

One very gratifying feature was that almost unanimously the letters to the Editor were favourable. I quote from a few:

"I have just seen this week's repertory production at the Alexandra Theatre, 'Signpost to Murder'. Congratulations to the company on a first class performance worthy of any West End stage. It seems incredible that there should be any need to beg for support for this survival of old Brum. If you prefer a hard, impersonal approach and just want a comfortable meeting place for smoking, eating and chattering, well, there are other places."
E.N.B., Northfield

"It is not only philistine to suggest that our immensely rich city should not subsidise more than one theatre, it is utterly illogical. Here is an example of the failure to break out of water-tight compartments of thought and to apply imagination to the future developments of our community. Of what long term use will it be to encourage, as we do, an enjoyment of and participation in drama in many of our schools and, to be more particular, rightly to help sustain the work of the Midlands Arts Centre for Young People, if, when those young people mature, there are no theatres left to visit?"
Mrs. B. Ruehl, B'ham 29

"........there is surely a very strong case for public support for the Alex which caters for a wide variety of 'brows' with its season of repertory, touring attractions and pantomime. It now occupies a unique position as the city's one surviving commercial theatre, and this largely because of the extreme non-commercialism of its management, which remained stead-fast in the face of the tide of rising costs until, with the waters at danger mark, it was forced to cry out. (How many of you who profess to love the theatre would have done so much?)

Action is needed today, not tomorrow, for in this context tomorrow is always one day too late."
Marian Jenkinson, Birmingham 14

There was, of course, the occasional letter voicing opposition. J. Brown wrote:

"I suggest that the *Evening Mail* runs a poll similar to those run about immigration to see if the ratepayers wish to support one theatre, let alone two. Surely the people who go to the Theatre should pay the true cost of seeing the show. I feel that in these days of financial hardship, less should be spent on supporting the entertainment of the minority. We have supported the so-called arts for too long already. You never hear of Council grants being given for Villa Park, St. Andrew's or the County Ground."

There were also a number of letters criticising the suggested scheme to combine the Alex and the Birmingham Rep. One from Stephen Thomas, chairman of the Birmingham Repertory Theatre 67 Club, said:

"The Alexandra was built as a touring theatre and, under the expert guidance of Mr. Derek Salberg, has carved a special place for itself in the cultural life of the City, and it would be foolish to destroy Mr. Salberg's achievement by implementing a compromise. In addition, the closure of the 'Rep' as an independent entity would be a bitter blow to the young play-goers movement which is attempting to educate and stimulate the theatre audiences of tomorrow. The fact that Theatre 67 has achieved a membership of over 1,000 is an indication that interest in drama is increasing."

The Birmingham (Alexandra) Theatre Club, which has always been such a great ally, organised a petition and obtained thousands of signatures. They and other friends of the theatre persuaded people to write to Aldermen Griffin and Bosworth (of the party now in power). They both told me later that, although they knew it existed, they were surprised at the tremendous fund of goodwill there was for the Alex.

In August, Fred Norris reported in the *Birmingham Mail* that Alderman Griffin had said the Alexandra 'will certainly be rescued'.

Meanwhile, I was exploring all avenues to infuse capital into the theatre in an endeavour to keep the doors open, as I felt that once they were closed they would remain in that

134

position. Therefore, I approached the Arts Council, although I knew only too well that their powers did not, at that time, extend to assisting commercial enterprises, and that they were already overstretched with demands from the non-profit distributing companies they supported. I went first to my friend Jo Hodgkinson, the drama director, and informed him of our plight, and he persuaded Lord Goodman, then secretary general of the Arts Council, to delay an imminent appointment in another part of London to see me. Most courteously, he did so, and I obtained almost immediately the promise of a cheque for £9,000 which could not, however, be used until we formed a non-profit distributing company. So without delay I visited or telephoned a number of people who might form the Council of Management. Meanwhile, largely owing to the ingenuity of our then business manager, Cliff Wooldridge, a scheme was devised so that by August the theatre could use this £9,000. I also received a cheque from Lew Grade in recognition of the help I had given ATV by releasing artistes when they were about to commence "Crossroads", and from his brother Leslie, a substantial loan with neither interest nor a repayment date attached to it. These measures were, of course, only temporary, but gave us breathing space as I was negotiating with the City at an ever-increasing pace.

I received a sympathetic hearing in many quarters, but none touched me so much as when Dick Turner ("Big Dick")* came to me saying "Guv" (as he always called me), "I know the theatre's in trouble. I've got a few pounds put away, if they would be any help, they're yours." This was a wonderful gesture, the recollection of which still gives me a warm glow.

In September the *Birmingham Post* reported Alderman Bosworth as saying:

> "The feeling is that the public do want to keep the Alexandra, but that it cannot go on as it is, and this means that the City will have to purchase it."

*Dick is one of our two longest serving members, he joined in 1930. The other is that irrepressible character, Ada, who has dressed every (female) principal boy since the thirties. She has an enormous sense of humour and recounts her anecdotes in a rich Birmingham accent, rivalled only by that of another Alex stalwart, Betty (I recently discovered it is really Bettina) Harper.

Not expressed all that enthusiastically, but very encouraging nevertheless.

Then in October came the great news. The Council had agreed to buy the theatre for £85,000, which would put us back 'in the black', but would not give any recompense to any of our shareholders (including, of course, myself as I held about 40% of the shares). The first £28,000 went to the City to pay off the debt we owed them, and a large proportion of the balance to pay off the debenture holders; thus leaving no spare capital, which has bedevilled us ever since.

The City then leased the theatre to a new company run by the Council of Management composed of the people I had invited, all of whom I knew would have something to offer; a supposition which has since proved correct. (I include their names and brief details in an Appendix at the end of the book.)

The City, quite understandably, wanted fair representation on the Council and, although their personnel has changed, never has any of them been less than helpful and sympathetic to our problems for, as Alderman Bosworth said at the time: "We don't want to run their affairs in any way, but if we are providing the purchasing price and a contribution towards running it, I think it is in the interests of the citizens that our voice should be heard. There will be no attempt to dominate it."

Never at any time has the City's attitude changed, but naturally they have expected us to play our part, as I know they feel we have done. In an interview, when asked how I felt about the sale, I said: "Any chap who is drowning hopes to be pulled out of the water, but he would rather not have fallen in, in the first place." I think that summed it up, but I must pay tribute to the local authority, for at one time I feel sure the climate of thinking would not have been in favour of saving a commercial (as it then was) theatre.

And so the Alex was preserved, but they had been harassing times for all of us at the theatre, and I think that an article written after an interview with me, by Leslie Duckworth (and which I include with his permission and that of the *Birmingham Post*) excellently reflected the background and the stresses involved before the sale of the theatre was completed.

The full story of how the Alec was saved —a triumph of faith and friendship . . .

If it had not been for the faith and determination of one man, Birmingham — Britain's second city — would now have only two theatres. The Alexandra, traditional home of pantomime and repertory, the life work of two generations of Salbergs — Leon and his son Derek — would have had to close its doors. Today, for the first time **LESLIE DUCKWORTH** tells the full story of how the theatre was saved and eventually bought for the city, thanks largely to the efforts of Derek Salberg and the generosity of friends.

DEREK SALBERG is 56 now, but if he lives to be 100 he will not forget the night of Friday, May 31, 1968. It was on that hot summer's evening— one of the few there were last year — that the Alexandra Theatre, which has been his life's work, could have died. It did not—thanks to the forbearance of one man.

It all hinged on a telephone call that had to be made to the Administrator of the D'Oyly Carte Opera Company, which was just ending a fortnight's season at the theatre. That night the company was presenting *H M S Pinafore*. The next day was settling day for their share of the second week's takings, 70 per cent. The first week worked out at about £4,000, which was paid, and the second was just under that sum.

What Derek Salberg had to tell the Administrator, Mr. Frederick Lloyd, who was an old friend — which, in one sense, helped to make it worse —was that the amount could not be paid in full. He had to ask him if he would accept £1,500, plus a post-dated cheque until the money to meet the balance, £3,000 or so, had come in from pantomime and other advance bookings. To have paid the D'Oyly Carte's share then would have meant that the theatre's bank overdraft would have exceeded the limit of £10,000.

The dawning of a new hope

The first call was put through to the Savoy Theatre in London, but Mr. Lloyd had left. Then Derek Salberg rang his home and luckily found

137

him in. Better still, he listened to the story of the theatre's difficulties and more important, listened sympathetically. Finally he agreed to wait.

Derek Salberg had other problems on his mind that night—his daughter was unwell, his wife had for some years been sharing his worries over the affairs of the theatre, they couldn't find a star name for the Bournemouth pantomime—but he went home more relieved than he had been for months, though knowing that he had really only bought time and that the money still had to be found in two months.

That night saw, at one and the same time, the nadir of the Alec's fortunes and the dawning of a new hope that it might still be possible to find a way out of the wood. The story had begun more than ten years ago, but—like so many stories that came out after the war—it can be told only now because the theatre has at last been saved by the Corporation of Birmingham's buying it.

It was in 1956, when the post-war boom was over and the touring shows were becoming fewer and fewer, that Derek Salberg first saw the writing on the wall which told him that the position of the commercial theatre as a whole was becoming impossible and that continually rising costs could no longer be offset merely by increasing the price of seats and attracting larger audiences.

"The theatre isn't like the export trade," Mr. Salberg said. "We can't expand; we're bound in by our four walls."

And there's a limit to the prices you can charge for seats. In 1955, for instance, the prices for repertory at the Alec ranged from a shilling in the balcony to 4s 4d in the dress circle. By 1968 they had risen from 2s to 8s 6d. For pantomime the figures went up from 9d to 4s 6d in 1932 to 3s 6d to 13s 6d in 1968-69. For touring shows, the most expensive to put on, the figures were 1s 6d to 7s in 1955 and 2s 6d to 14s in 1968 with an occasional increase for special shows to 17s.

Still, the Alec soldiered on with its traditional policy of pantomime, repertory and touring shows, losing money here and there, until in 1963 the management was faced with providing a new lighting switchboard, new heating and new carpeting and re-decoration all at once.

'The council was sympathetic and helpful'

It was estimated that all this would cost £40,000 to £50,000 and there seemed only one way of paying for it — to ask the corporation for help. So Derek Salberg went to see Ald. Harry Watton, leader of the Labour Group, who then had a majority on the city council, to ask for a loan. The council was sympathetic and helpful to the extent of a loan of £30,000 to be repaid at the rate of £2,000 a year. Well, that paid for the switchboard and what was left went towards the heating but the rest had to come out of the theatre's own resources. There had always been a lack of capital, but up to 1955 it had never been acute. Now it was. The first repayment to the city was made at the appointed time; the second could not be paid.

The council was "very reasonable," but its loan was not the only problem. There were also £25,000 worth of debentures which had to be refloated at a higher percentage, "Most years brought us some stroke of good fortune," Derek Salberg said, "but from the end of the pantomime of 1966-67 nothing particularly good turned up for us. And then we ran into disaster."

For the repertory season of 1967 an interchange arrangement with the Grand Theatre, Leeds, was tried in the hope that pooling resources would help to reduce the costs of productions and enable them to engage better known players, such as Rosemary Leach, Jack Watling and Marius Goring, and, it was hoped, attract larger audiences.

A number of new plays were among the 16 plays put on that season, but each one cost about £400 more than had been budgeted for and the star names did not draw the hoped-for crowds. Marius Goring's revival of Irving's famous play, The Bells, was a very expensive production and unfortunately it proved a financial disaster, both in Birmingham and later in London.

A season of Sadler's Wells opera, on which the theatre would normally hope to recoup some of its losses on repertory, did nothing of the sort. Indeed, the Alec lost about £1,000 on it largely because, in Derek Salberg's opinion, the operas chosen were too unfamiliar — and English audiences have long been suspicious of anything new on stage or in concert hall.

In fact, 1967 was just "one damn thing after another." The 1967 pantomime did not recover its production costs but fortunately these were roughly covered by £4,700 from a repayment of Corporation Tax and both the repertory and the touring seasons were better, but again it was a case of too little and nearly too late.

"A theatre like ours has to budget for a loss on the year," Mr. Salberg said. "If you close, you lose the whole benefit of patronage, as well as paying out £900 a week in overheads including what you still have to spend on advertising to let people know you are still in existence. We budget to lose £700 a fortnight on repertory, during the summer when most theatres close or go over to Bingo, and in 1967 we lost more than that. The days when we could make good our losses from pantomime and touring shows have gone, perhaps for ever.

The problem of rising costs

"In my father's time it probably cost about £9,000 to stage a pantomime before it even opened; today it is nearer £30,000. The top money he ever paid anyone in a week was £175. Now the sort of star who can fill a theatre is hardly ever obtainable under £2,000 a week and the theatre can hold just over £7,000 a week even when playing daily matinees during the pantomime.

"Most touring shows won't come out of London without a big guarantee or won't tour at all. We have been asked as much as £3,000 a week, which would leave us with about £200 after all expenses had been paid.

"By the end of 1967, the bank was allowing us to overdraw up to a limit of £15,000. Last year it started squeezing like mad for us to come down to £10,000 and then in March, told us it must come down to nothing, otherwise our cheques would not be met. At this time we were booking in advance for the D'Oyly Carte company, and we were worried to death.

How the bank was staved off

"In April I went to the bank and asked for more time and begged it not to press us for the £10,000, but it could not agree, though we had bills coming in for drinks for the bars and for advertising, both absolute essentials, which we didn't know how to meet. People with bills were even coming and knocking on the door of this office. It wasn't pleasant.

"The D'Oyly Carte company came to us on May 20. When we

139

had worked it all out we realised we could not pay their share at the end of the run. The bank would not help, so there was only one thing to do. That was when I made the telephone call to Frederick Lloyd.

"Even with the D'Oyly Carte's co-operation our troubles didn't end. Again on June 25, the bank said that the overdraft had to be reduced to nothing. As it was midsummer they knew that it was an extremely bad time for us and that by this time we were negotiating for another loan from the city. I think the bank was very harsh, though of course, it hadn't got any security. But firms with whom we dealt stood by us, specially the small ones. You find out who your real friends are at times like these. and we were very touched by the work of the Playgoers Club which raised a substantial sum towards furnishings.

"I didn't know what I was going to do. In desperation, I called on Leslie Grade in London and told him our position. He lent me £5,000 not repayable until this month and then came another generous gift of £1,000 from A T V, which between them just staved off the bank.

"We were keeping our bar and cafe supplies down to a bare minimum, asking the booking libraries to pay us their commission right on time, and we opened the advanced booking for the Welsh National Opera Company much earlier than usual; in fact, we were scraping from everywhere.

"In May I had made an impassioned appeal to the Arts Council, even though I knew it they were not able to help the commercial theatre. 'Is there nothing you can do?' I asked. They were very sympathetic, but replied that it was not possible. This was a terrible blow, but nevertheless, by arrangement, I went to see the chairman, Lord Goodman, on June 20.

"At last came a letter from him saying that the Council was prepared to make a grant of £9,000, but only to a non-profit distributing company. We had just formed one, anyway, but we still couldn't touch the £9,000 because this money could not be used to pay debts incurred earlier. So there was a cheque for £9,000 in the drawer, but we couldn't touch it.

"I made a further appeal to the Arts Council and then Clifford Woodridge, our secretary and business manager, proposed an arrangement under which the non-profit distributing company took over the presentation of repertory, thus enabling us to draw on the £9,000. The Arts Council agreed and that just kept everyone at bay.

"It was only on June 26 last year that the non-profit distributing company was formed. The immediate benefit of doing this is that you qualify for a subsidy from the Arts Council and the local authority — if they will grant one. You also get relief from S.E.T. — that was another body blow, for £10,000 — and a reduction on the rates.

"So it seemed that our only hope was the corporation. I had first had talks in July, 1967, when it was in the lap of the gods whether we could hang on or not. I asked for an immediate loan of £50,000 and said that we should require a continuing subsidy of £15,000 to £20,000 in future years.

"The talks, which began with the Town Clerk and the City Treasurer, gradually gained impetus and scores of conferences were held. They were told that the theatre would certainly die at the end of the D'Oyly Carte season when its share would have to be paid unless some help was forthcoming.

'Something to show for its money'

"Eventually it was felt that it would be better for the corporation to buy the theatre so that the city would have something to show for its money and it was finally decided that this should be done at a figure not exceeding £85.000.

"Our accountants and theirs are still working out the details, under which we are hoping that future losses will be met equally by the Arts Council and the city. We shall have to pay rent to the corporation — we have never had to pay this before, of course — but it has not been fixed yet. The leasehold is for 77 years.

"But we still haven't had a penny from the city under this agreement and we are having to plan completely blind, but we have kept going on the proceeds of the repertory season—we ran three comedies in successive weeks and made about £600 over the six weeks instead of a budgeted loss of £2,100—an extremely successful touring season and the Arts Council's £9,000.

"The people of Birmingham should understand that by selling the theatre for £85,000, the directors here have given up any profit, but under the new regime our salaries can only improve, we hope."

When I asked Mr. Salberg how much he himself had sacrificed to keep the theatre going all he would say was that he had been offered a job in the theatre, not the Alec, which would have brought him in one year what he has been earning in three. He added that other members of the staff, out of loyalty, had also turned down jobs worth three times as much as the Alec could pay them.

One of the ironies of the situation is that all the time the management was wondering where to turn, private developers were going ahead with providing the new bridge entrance at no cost to the theatre. It must have seemed the only thing which wasn't costing anything.

I asked Derek Salberg if, looking back, he thought there was anything he could have done which he did not do, or anything he did which he now regretted and would do differently if he had to face the same situation again. He thought for a long time and then shook his head.

His main regret he said, was the time the negotiations with the city had taken and what seemed the "red herring" of the merger with Birmingham Repertory Theatre which held up everything for a long time.

'I always believed it would be saved'

"On the other hand, in my father's day, it would not have been possible for the city council to do what it did to save the theatre.

"Deep down in my heart," he said finally, "I always believed it would be saved." There spoke his faith in the theatre in general, but especially in his beloved Alec.

The article might give the impression that we were trading very nearly illegally. This, of course, was emphatically not the case as neither Edmund King, whose firm were at that time our accountants, myself, nor any member of the Board would have countenanced such a thing. In fact, we had assets, including the building, in excess of any liabilities we had accumulated, but these could not have been maintained for much longer.

I must pay tribute to all the shareholders, almost entirely members of my family, who knew that selling the theatre, if only for the ground it stood upon, would bring them in a substantial sum, but nevertheless put the Alex and Birmingham before financial gain, for they derived no benefit, whereas I remained in the theatre I loved.

One shareholder, however, who was not a member of the family, was David Wiseman who, although knowing he would almost certainly never see his money again, had earlier infused some much needed capital into the theatre. David, who is best known for his football activities both as a past vice-chairman of Birmingham FC and a former member of the Football League Governing Committee (and could be seen each year on cup final day accompanying a member of the Royal family on to the field at Wembley), only did this as a gesture to me and to Joan, of whom he was very fond. He was recently awarded the OBE but, as far as I am concerned, for all he has done for football, for innumerable people who needed a helping hand and, of course, not least for the gesture he made to the Alex, a Knighthood would have been more fitting. He later became a member of our Board where his advice and experience was of enormous value, and on the formation of the Council of Management he resigned and Alan, one of his two sons, became, and still is, a member. Although there is no longer a Salberg connected with the Alex, which I fervently hope will not always be the case (though at the moment I cannot quite see how this will be avoided), I trust that there will always be a Wiseman.

Soon after the article appeared the financial details were settled, and apart from purchasing the theatre, we now receive an annual grant of £55,000 a year. Of this, the City receives £9,000 in rent and £4,100 in rates, there is thus little burden on the taxpayer. The City have also given supplementary grants on one or two occasions and have always been most sympathetic towards our problems.

The hope expressed that salaries would improve was justified. At an inital meeting Nancy Burman said that she could not remain a member of the Council of Management if this did not happen, a view I know shared by the other members. Most of the staff, of course, were receiving Union rates (usually above), in themselves in no way excessive, and they were mostly (and still are) working for less than they could obtain outside the theatre, but were content to take a chance and 'sink or swim' with the theatre, not only in the hope of a better financial future, but because of their deep affection for it. Certainly our secretary, Cliff Wooldridge, could have earned considerably more money in industry and it was very sad that with his brilliant brain and having done so much for the theatre he did not entirely gain the confidence of either the Council of Management or the local authority. This was due chiefly, I think, to a manner which could be very difficult to understand at times, and was not helped by his tendency to show his (often justified) impatience at Board meetings. I greatly admired him but he had one failing, however hard we tried (and I had done so for many years), we could not get him to produce figures with any regularity, thus making budgeting very difficult (to put it mildly), and possibly the reason some members of the Council of Management assumed I was not good at producing estimates. In fact, I always considered this to be one of my stronger points, just as it was my father's and is my brother Reggie's.

The purchase naturally eased the strain for me although I continued to work a very long day, starting normally about 9 a.m. until early or late evening (although I would, in the summer especially, get many free afternoons). I was responsible for an average of four to five pantomimes each year; read plays continuously and, with the producer, cast them; ran the theatre with a first class staff to help me; visited London regularly; almost weekly addressed one or even two societies; served on many committees, both local and national, to which I have referred elsewhere. I sat as a magistrate and captained (in a senior capacity) the Warwickshire Colts Cricket Team, so magnificently coached and run by Derief Taylor.

I cannot now recall my exact salary before the 'take-over' but it was minimal, though it was all the theatre could afford. Fortunately, it was augmented by a small private income of Joan's and her very small design fee from the theatre. My daughters' school fees (we opted for private education) were eventually almost entirely met by a covenant on the part of one of my cousins until they went to technical college (where they widened the range of their acquaintances).

There was very little effect on the day to day running of the

143

theatre. The Council of Mangement, formed earlier, had replaced the previous rather 'cosy' board, with Edmund King, the only remaining member of that board, as chairman (as he has remained ever since), and a very hardworking Finance and General Purposes Sub-Committee was formed. Everyone has given yeoman service and I know all of them are devoted to the cause of the Alex. I have, of course, sometimes disagreed with them, usually the Sub-Committee, as must be the case over such a long period and have, naturally, sometimes been criticised, no doubt often rightly, but sometimes unfairly — and indeed just occasionally have been rather hurt. But compared with the average relationship between theatre manager and Board, mine has been almost idyllic and it would not be possible to find a more pleasant group of people.

My chief criticism would be that, although people serve on a Board for the special qualities they bring to it, and I realise that some are very busy or live far away, too few of them come to the performances often enough. Unless they do, it is impossible for them to get the 'feel' of the theatre or to know the staff, to whom they remain faceless. In this respect, somewhat belatedly, I find that the board of the Birmingham Rep. are more aware of the importance of communication with staff, but it is probably more necessary at that theatre.

Nevertheless, they have done many good things for the Alex, not least when, on the departure of Cliff Wooldridge, they appointed Michael Bullock, at that time our Production Manager, as Administrator. Mike, whose somewhat austere face, when in repose, hides a great sense of humour (possibly it is by the law of compensation that his attractive wife, Laurie, is rarely seen not wearing a smile), was appointed with such wide powers that life could have been made both difficult and embarrassing for me. But, being the person he is, our relationship was always of the happiest and he never at any time even remotely 'went over my head'. Mike has now taken over my position at the theatre and realises, as well as I do, that he has inherited a wonderful staff and a great tradition, which everyone agrees he is carrying on splendidly.

144

CHAPTER 25

THE ALEX BECOMES ENTIRELY A TOURING THEATRE

With repertory discontinued at the end of 1973, we were now only producing our own pantomimes, which we were not to do for much longer as we engaged another management to provide the 1976-77 pantomime. This policy is much less exciting but has been dictated by economics.

As stated earlier, I was very doubtful whether I would find sufficient tours of reasonable quality to keep the theatre open throughout the year. In the event, they were forthcoming and 1974, the first full touring season, opened with Robert Morley in "Ghost on Tiptoe", which was afterwards to enjoy a long London run. This was soon followed by an unusual event, a twice-nightly variety bill headed by Ken Dodd. We arranged with him that he would pay the orchestra's overtime money with the result that we all got home before midnight — no mean feat with Ken on the bill. The performance was, of course, largely a virtuoso one as was, entirely, Spike Milligan's brilliant one-man show which later in the year practically filled the theatre. I found him a most unpredictable person, most affable one night, but quite remote the next. We gave him a bottle of gin on the first and last nights, and he wrote me a most charming letter of thanks afterwards, in which he paid tribute to me, our staff and audiences. I read, some time later, that he so disliked Birmingham's new architecture that he would never play in the city again! Obviously more important to him than the audience.

Roy Dotrice, and later Ron Moody, also presented their superb one-man shows. Roy, like Spike Milligan, packed the theatre, but Ron Moody played to very poor houses, proving yet again that it is difficult to know exactly what determines the public's decision whether or not to patronise a particular production. Here, for example, were two well known actors, both giving first rate performances, yet with totally opposite box office results. If only we knew!

"Time and Time Again", a comedy by Alan Ayckbourn, with James Bolam of "Whatever Happened to the Likely Lads" and John Junkin, played to excellent houses, whereas two weeks later "My Fat Friend", a play of similar calibre and with, on this occasion, two stars from the same series, Rodney Bewes and Brigit Forsyth, received very little support.

D'Oyly Carte, Royal Ballet and John Hanson in "Lilac Time" all played to near capacity, as did Barbara Mullen in "Murder at the Vicarage", Peter Wyngarde in "Present Laughter", "The Jolson Revue" and "I'll Sleep in the Spare Room" (with the cast of "The Brothers"). Brian Rix did rather less well than usual (which still meant near capacity audiences) with "A Bit Between the Teeth", and the National Theatre's production of Anthony Hopkin's "Next of Kin", directed by Harold Pinter, an absorbing play but not a 'comfortable' one, did only moderate business. The season was rounded off by "The Deja Revue", a pun title which I thought was 'off putting' but Bill Kenwright, the presenter, once of "Coronation Street" and now in management and doing his best to help keep the touring provincial theatre alive, did not agree. We could not prove who was right as it had no chance anyway coming, as it did, just after the terrible IRA bombing in Birmingham — about which it is still hard to write without feeling physically sick.

The season had been a tremendous success and in an interview in the *Birmingham Mail* with Fred Norris (that good friend of the Alex and theatres generally), Mike Bullock, not noted for his ebullience, said "Last year was a howling success — so much so that it tended to frighten us. It's the old, old show biz problem of — follow that!"

Happily, the following year did, and opened where the previous one had left off. John Hanson in "The Dancing Years" packed the theatre, as did "Glamorous Night" and Richard O'Sullivan in "Boeing-Boeing". On the other hand, a special one-night engagement of Humphrey Lyttleton and his band proved again that, for some reason, the Alex is not a good venue for Sunday shows — the exception being "Gilbert and Sullivan for All" which always filled the theatre.

146

The least said about an entertainment called "The New Minstrel Show", the better. But for the close relationship which existed between our house manager, Norman Wood, himself (among many things) an ex-musician, and the local MU representative, owing to salary queries from the orchestra, the curtain would never have gone up on the Friday. It only did so by the skin of its teeth on about two other occasions, perhaps it would have been a mercy if it had not! Happily this sort of occurrence is very rare, in fact virtually a non-existent one nowadays.

Peter Wyngarde, who only a year earlier, at the height of his 'Jason King' fame, had packed the theatre, proved again the transient nature of TV success when "Dracula" drew very poor houses. "Joseph and His Amazing Technicolour Dreamcoat" paid the first of its visits, staying for a fortnight and, after a quiet opening, played to nearly full houses. "Ipi Tombi", which filled the theatre, was followed by "A far Better Husband" which was enlivened by a hilariously funny performance by Ronnie Corbett.

The New London Ballet, with little-known ballets, including a dull world premiere of "Simorgh", played to empty houses reflecting, once again, that a ballet public's taste is conservative, but given what they want, they will flock in. In September the Wombles, playing at an assortment of times varying from 11 a.m. to 6.30 p.m., delighted over 12,000 children. That month the theatre closed for a week for the installation of a counter-weight system which replaced the hemp lines previously being used to haul scenery up and down. This brought us into line with most theatres and has effected an enormous technical improvement.

The Arts Council and the Birmingham Metropolitan District Council helped to meet this outlay. Unhappily for us though, the cost of steel rose between the years it was ordered and its delivery and installation from £19,000 to £31,000 which was a big financial blow, especially as the Council felt unable to help us by meeting any part of the additional cost.

Except for the week before pantomime opens, when the stage is being used for rehearsals, this was our only closure (apart from one week in the sixties for re-decoration* and the
*See footnote * on following page.

period immediately following the outbreak of World War II when all places of entertainment were closed by government order). I firmly believe that the function of a theatre, particularly if it receives subsidy, is to remain open if humanly possible.

In almost successive weeks we played to the highest and lowest attendance figures of the season. The lowest was with a double bill which Bill Kenwrigth, hearing that I had no attraction, organised for me at short notice. It consisted of a one-act play of Agatha Christie's, which even the kind Maurice Patching of the *Birmingham Post* compassionately described as "not the best of Christie", and "Zoo Story" by Edward Albee. Strange bedfellows indeed, and the mere 1,519(!) people who came during the week could make little of them. Nevertheless, Bill and I are still the best of friends! The highest was with "Big Bad Mouse" which contained side-splitting performances by Jimmy Edwards and Eric Sykes.

The success of this week was somewhat marred for me on the Tuesday when the theatre was almost entirely occupied by a branch of the Conservative Party. During the interval a Councillor who, I thought, intended merely to draw the audience's attention to a collection which would take place on the way out and to which, of course, no one who did not wish to do so was expected to contribute, unhappily chose the occasion to make a long political speech — to which, not unnaturally, a number of the audience volubly objected. Jimmy, himself a failed Conservative candidate, was incensed and verbally attacked the speaker in the wings after he finished his speech. When I apologised to him on the Bridge Bar after the show, he (by then in a somewhat exuberant state) accused me of having engineered the whole thing and loudly (with such a voice it had to be 'loudly') attacked me in front of staff and patrons. However, we soon became friendly again and later in the week I discovered, to my surprise, that this epitome of an English gentleman hates cricket and all sports, except his ruling passion — hunting. A great, if somewhat volatile character, and frankly I think the theatre could do with more like him.

*Carried out by F.S. Sharman Ltd. who, father and son, have done much excellent work for the Alex and have occasionally helped us out of grave crises. Sam is now my regular companion to the rugger internationals at Twickenham.

The penultimate production was "Charley's Aunt", and so blows the wind of change that this famous farce, once guaranteed to fill a theatre, no longer seemed funny, except in patches, and received no public support. Now that ladies *do* smoke cigars and men and women look much alike, I suppose a great deal of the point has been lost.

The season ended with near capacity houses for The Little Angels of Korea who, as was customary on their visits, were received at the Council House by the Lord Mayor. He had met them the previous evening after the performance when he received a kiss from each one of them. They were delightful youngsters, who were ordered by their Government to eat one Korean meal a day which they cooked in the theatre with resultant unfamiliar odours.

The 1976 season opened quite well with "John, Paul, George, Ringo and Bert" followed by John Thaw and Richard Coleman in Alan Ayckbourn's "Absurd Person Singular", a big success, repeated recently at the Birmingham Rep. A disastrous revival of "Miranda" followed which, frankly, was not worth reviving. Unfortunately a number of managements have dug up modest comedies which may have been good enough in their day, but had dated with the years. So, many revivals caused a great deal of dissatisfaction among our regular theatregoers.

Fortunately the season immediately recovered with — again — "Joseph and the Amazing Technicolour Dreamcoat", Honor Blackman in a thriller, "Motive", and Sidney James, who packed the theatre, with "The Mating Season". Tragically, the Saturday night performance was to be his last full one anywhere as this delightful man and brilliant comedian died on the following Monday during the performance at the Empire Theatre, Sunderland. I recall almost his last words to me on the Saturday night which were that, as he had a matinee there on the Saturday of the Cup Final, he would be unable to see it on TV. How sadly prophetic those words turned out to be.

Some excellent productions, notably "Godspell", "Equus" and "The Three Sisters", followed — all doing splendidly unlike, I must admit to my secret pleasure, "Pyjama Tops" which I regretted having booked, under some persuasion, and which, unlike "Equus", was an exploitation of nudity for nudity's sake, and unfunny into the bargain. This play marked a downward trend, and with "There's a Girl in my Soup" unexpectedly flopping, our next success was not until several weeks later when "Magic of Vienna" did excellent business but was so costly that it resulted in a financial loss. Although "Arms and the Man" (the best production I have ever seen of it) and "The Seagull" both provided artistic statisfaction, they achieved poor box office returns.

The season continued to flag for several weeks until "Out on a Limb" with Ian Carmichael, disguised with a beard (which I and most people thought detracted from his own very special personality and added nothing to the part), did outstandingly well, as did D'Oyly Carte who, on this occasion, were only able to play for one week. The other big box office successes in a season which, after opening so well, had been rather patchy were "Dear Daddy" (misleadingly titled, as mentioned elsewhere) with Nigel Patrick and Phyllis Calvert, a play not to the liking of most of our audience; "The Student Prince"; "An Ideal Husband" with Wilfred Hyde-White, Sylvia Sims and Simon Williams (once a member of our repertory company); and Margaret Lockwood, Peter Byrne and John Stone in a clever thriller, "Double Edge".

Only occasionally were we able to offer productions solely for youngsters, a function which is, of course, fulfilled by the Midlands Art Centre for young people, but when we did (such as "Basil Brush", "The Wombles", "Sooty", etc.), they always made a big appeal. But this season "Animal Kwackers", trading on its TV name, drew — and disappointed — thousands of children. I was thoroughly upset and when I received complaints (and I received many) took the unusual, and somewhat dangerous, step of returning money or offering tickets for a performance of a production which parents might consider suitable, such as pantomime.

The Little Angels of Korea were due to end the season and the theatre was heavily booked, but at the last moment the Korean Government refused to grant an exit visa which resulted in disappointment both to us and to patrons, who had to receive their money back. One way and another we were involved in a heavy financial loss, especially as the last minute replacement could not be properly publicised* at such short notice, and we had absolutely no redress.

So ended, on a disappointing note, a season which was to be my last full one at the theatre in which I had spent the major part of my life. But a lot was to happen before I finally retired, which I will relate in the final chapter.

*I have so far hardly referred to the very important matter of publicity for which a theatre can only spare a pitifully small amount of its budget. We were almost the first theatre to engage two girls, Penny Mortimer and Lynne Mills, solely to make contact with firms, Women's Guilds, etc. and to accompany organised parties round the theatre and generally promote and market the theatre. Under the expert guidance of Gordon Price, who advocated and masterminded the scheme, they did a splendid job. When Penny left she was replaced by Sue Richards. With the spade work successfully achieved, only Sue remains in the publicity department, where she is doing excellent work.

CHAPTER 26

PANTOMIME

So far I have only obliquely referred to our pantomimes which, in many ways, have been the Alex's mainstay and are renowned well beyond the confines of the Midlands. Their tradition was commenced by Lester Collingwood, then built up further by my father and continued by myself. I have even been referred to as a 'pantomime king' — (horrible expression!) and was very flattered when J.C. Trewin, one of our foremost drama critics and a man for whom I have the highest respect, wrote in his notice for one of our pantomimes, headed "Mr. Salberg's genius for pantomime", "Mr. Salberg, I suggest, knows the secrets of the craft as well as anybody in the land.... his work in its chosen field is superb English pantomime." Praise indeed from such a connoisseur.

As a theatre goer my tastes lean more towards, say, Chekhov's "Uncle Vanya" or an Alan Ayckbourn play at the other end of the scale — in fact the straight theatre in general. But as a producer and entrepreneur of pantomime I find something magical in an entertainment which can bring together people of all ages and all types with its combination of fun, music, tinsel, acrobats, colourful scenes and costumes together with special effects, such as my favourite water and U.V. spectacles. Neither did the excitement ever lessen for me of watching a pantomime gradually evolve from merely a title on a piece of blank paper in, say, March to its emergence as a full-scale production when the curtain rose on that frightening, but magical moment on Christmas Eve (or thereabouts).

When, in 1976-77, the pantomime was presented by an outside management, a critic referred to it as "the usual Alex hotchpotch". Let me assure him that to create a pantomime from scratch, as we did at the Alex annually, can be no 'hotch-

152

potch'. Innumerable conferences will take place with each artiste to discuss material which must fit into the pattern of the pantomime if it is to be used; then, and not until then, the book starts to take shape (and will be continually altered).

Costume and scene designs are submitted and almost as frequently rejected, as are suggestions for dance routines, musical numbers, special scenes and indeed every facet of the production, for the entire construction and balance is planned with almost the same care a general would exercise when preparing a battle. In fact, so meticulous is the planning, and this may sound boastful (but any artiste who has worked for me in pantomime will confirm it), that I used to write down, when rehersals commenced, the time we would ring down at the first performance and was rarely more than a few minutes out. All this is very hard work, but I have loved every.......well, nearly every......minute of it.

Pantomime has gradually evolved from the Italian comedies of the 16th century and its roots in medieval morality plays until its emergence in 1717 when, under the aegis of John Rich, the description 'pantomime' was first used. The formula then remained much the same until around 1806 when the clown became pre-eminent with the rise of the greatest one of all, Grimaldi, whose comic genius elevated the Harlequinade, which almost disappeared with his death.

It was not until the early seventies that music hall artistes were imported into the casts, introducing, as they do to-day, their own business. The greatest of these was Dan Leno who brought the pantomime dame to the fore.

Fascinating though it would be to investigate the complete history of pantomime, the temptation must be resisted for it would take a separate book to cover it, in any way, adequately.

Suffice it to say that pantomime is one of the few remaining British traditions, although it has been consistently written off. As early as 1859 *Chambers Journal* stated ".....the spell of pantomime is broken", in 1885 the *Sporting and Dramatic* announced categorically ".....pantomime is dead", Max Beerbohm in 1904 wrote in his collected essays ".....pantomime will never again be what it was". Like Punch it probably never was and the same was being said in the twenties and now in the seventies. I cannot help feeling, though, that there cannot be much wrong with a tradition whose sole purpose is to spread

153

fun and jollity in a world not over-endowed with these qualities and which very rarely indeed, in spite of accusations to the contrary, introduces 'smut'. I must admit, however, that a former secretary, mishearing me, wrote to a comic for his 'suggestive' material, whereas I had dictated 'suggested'!

To attempt to trace the full story of pantomimes at the Alex would also require a separate book so I must, from necessity, confine myself to some rather disjointed recollections dating from my own personal involvement in 1938, first as director, then as director and producer (or should it be the other way round? I never know.) However, I have included an appendix which contains the titles and names of leading members of each pantomime since the days of Lester Collingwood, whose pantomimes were, as already indicated, a little rough and ready but suited to the taste of his audiences.

When my father took over and presented his first pantomime, "Mother Goose", in 1911 it followed a similar pattern, but his pantomimes became gradually more artistic without losing the Alex's reputation for comedy which is, to me, still the most important ingredient. He possessed Lester Collingwood's talent for discovering people *before* they became stars, for in those days people did not 'shop' for star names as they do today and the good reputation of the pantomime itself would usually suffice to fill the theatre. As a result many famous names appeared in Alex pantomime before they became stars.

Certainly, by the time my father died, Alex pantomimes had greatly increased their fame and were nationally acclaimed. He was keenly looking forward to maintaining and, if possible, to further increasing it with "Aladdin", for which he had re-engaged Barry Lupino, one of the great dames of all time. Barry was not the easiest person to handle, and he soon faced me with a challenge in this, my first pantomime (I was only twenty-five then and he a seasoned campaigner). The BBC had arranged to broadcast an excerpt of the pantomime but would not allow some commercial references used by Barry who announced firmly that he would rather be left out of the broadcast than omit them. In those days radio had as much, if not even more, impact than TV does today, so he posed me with a grave dilemma. I took my courage in both hands and told him he either appeared in the broadcast or withdrew from the pantomime. Heaven knows what I would have done if he had stuck to his decision; mercifully, he gave way, but my heart was in my boots.

The next pantomime, "Robinson Crusoe", was the first to come fully under my management and I must pay tribute to the tremendous help I received from David Cochran, for years my father's producer. A man of many accomplishments, he not only produced the pantomimes but designed the dresses and conducted the orchestra. He died soon after a war time dress rehearsal, having spent twenty five years all told with our management. I was also much indebted to Roy Cooke, the brilliant painter and designer of whose death in South Africa I was sad to learn recently; to Sidney Jones who made the sets so magnificently, and equally, of course, to Madam Lehmiski who for so many years supplied the dancers and arranged the choreography.

It was very important to me that the pantomime should be a success and I booked George Robey, the biggest name thus far to appear at the Alex, in his day in fact there was no bigger, although I soon realised he was not quite the George Robey of his heyday. The pantomime opened comparatively well but the balance was not quite right, so I asked George if he would move until later, a scene which he finished holding a Greta Garbo mask in front of his face as he walked off stage. Obviously he forgot he was now in a front cloth and had much less space, with disastrous results, which I watched helplessly from the back of the stalls. This is how M.F.K. Fraser described the event in his book:

"On about the fourth afternoon of the run, George Robey fell from the stage onto the floor of the stalls in trying a new exit into the wings, his sight obscured by a comedy mask. He was back on the stage without delay — trust the spirit of a confirmed trouper — but, though he actually finished the show, it was his last for nearly two months. Apart from the shock, he had broken three ribs, injured his spine and bruised his face most painfully. For the young manager, the accident was a potential disaster of the most alarming magnitude, threatening the continuance of his first solo pantomime and the prosperity of his newly undertaken enterprise. Of course, the show went on. All the cast did trouperly especially Chic Elliott* (until then playing the part of the Dusky Queen) who cleaned off the black, thickened her eyebrows, reddened her comely nose, and became Mrs. Crusoe for the duration of the emrgency. No more fuss about it than that. The show went on."

'Crusoe' ran for seventeen weeks and gave the box office an extremely busy time and me a formidable baptism! George, with amazing fortitude, returned in mid-February — marvellous, bearing in mind that he was sixty nine and that when he fell, so great was the impact that he broke the arm of a front row seat. In a comparatively recent book on George Robey, it was said that he had over-imbibed, which is absolutely untrue. On the occasion of the pantomime dinner (then an annual event) George said "I've enjoyed all my Birmingham pantomimes, but this one has been my happiest — apart from one little slip."

My next pantomime was "Jack and the Beanstalk" with Dorothy Ward, Shaun Glenville and Georgie Wood, then, shall we say, mature artistes, referred to by some wag as 'Derek Salberg's discoveries'! It was played under wartime conditions and this fact, added to the opposition at the Prince of Wales of that most delightful and brilliant little man Arthur Askey who was then the biggest draw in England, resulted in very moderate takings. But I still cherish the recollection of Shaun Glenville, who liked a 'drop', making a solemn promise of abstinence to Dorothy Ward, his wife, on Rocket Night, when she knew he would meet many old friends prior to the performance. Temptation proved too strong however and, for possibly the only time in pantomime history, the cow had to prompt the dame with the words of his opening song!

The pantomime which followed, and my last before I joined the army, was "Dick Whittington". To beat the blackout, performances were daily at 2.30 p.m. with three mornings at 10.30 a.m. causing the leading comic to say that he couldn't be expected to be funny at that hour in the morning. I didn't like to tell him, but in my opinion he was not particularly funny at 2.30 either! Later in the run, with lighter nights, some early evenings were introduced and in March two performances a week were twice nightly. Although still in England for the next

*She shortly fell ill and I had hurriedly to get a replacement, George Hirste. Summoned by telephone, he arrived on the train at noon and played the matinee at 2.30.

pantomime, I was obviously only able to take a limited part in the planning, and none for the next four pantomimes as I was overseas. A large gap then ensued until 1946 when I returned in time to see "Simple Simon" which, as mentioned earlier, I did not feel was a true Alex pantomime. But from all reports the pantomimes produced during those years were extremely good, especially "Dick Whittington" with Noele Gordon in the name part making a big success, as she had done (as Prince Charming) in the previous year's "Cinderella".

I soon started to prepare for my first pantomime since demob. — "Babes in the Wood", which I naturally wished to be top-class but, unfortunately, turned out to be rather disappointing. Since then I have presented about thirty Alex pantomimes, and over a hundred away from Birmingham, and have gained much experience which I lacked at that time after an enforced absence of so many years. It was extremely important, therefore, that after a moderate start my next pantomime "Robinson Crusoe" should be a winner. I engaged a seasoned performer, Eddie Leslie, as dame and a number of other artistes who I felt would make a strong comibination, but I had not found an adequate 'second' comedian to support Eddie.

But luck was with me and the solution found after visiting a matinee at my brother's repertory company at Preston. I bought a local newspaper and read that a young comedian, about whom I had heard excellent reports, was playing at the nearby Opera House, Blackpool. I told Joan I thought we should go and see him, and drive back after the show. She was not anxious to do so as she knew I was very tired, but reluctantly agreed. We arrived just as the curtain went up at the vast Opera House to only a handful of people as it was out of season. The variety bill was 'dying' when on came this comic who set the sparse audience alight. I, usually hesitant to take quick decisions, went round to see him immediately his act finished. His name was Norman Wisdom, and he treated my interest in him with the utmost suspicion!

Next day I telephoned his agent, Keith Devon, who, in his usual effervescent manner, said "this boy will be one of the greatest of all time".* He pushed his salary up to what I thought

*See footnote * on following page.

157

was an exorbitant figure, but I gave him a 3-year contract with the salary rising each year, as I felt confident he would be a big success. He was — and so was the pantomime.

Norman eventually played four successive years for me, alternating between Birmingham and Wolverhampton, but it was not until his fourth appearance (at Wolverhampton) that he had achieved national (and indeed international) stardom. That year it was impossible to get into the Grand Theatre and I believe we could have run until the summer!

"Queen of Hearts"**, an unusual subject, occupied the stage in 1949/50. It was predictably robust, featuring as it did, two members of the Lupino family, Lauri Lupino Lane and his uncle, Wally, two good old fashioned slapstick artistes. Dumarte and Denzar's skeleton act, as in future pantomimes, caused a furore, especially with the youngsters. Eddie Kelland Espinosa added a lighter touch, but my chief recollection was, and I hope he will forgive me for saying so, of John Le Mesurier playing the Wizard and transparently hating every moment of it!

The next year Norman returned to play Buttons in "Cinderella", a part in which he was first-class and in a pantomime which was deservedly a big box office success. The cast also included, for the first of many occasions, The Monarchs who were a riot as always. The bearded one, Les Henry, is, for me, one of the funniest men, both on and off the stage. He has a wonderful range of Jewish stories which he will tell to anyone who cares to listen. Although of distinctly Semitic appearance, and with parents who were very orthodox Jews, he is married to a delightful, tall, blonde lady, Anne, who usually wears a large crucifix around her neck. When walking down the road together no couple could appear more incongruous, but they are ideally suited in every way. He and his partner, Eric Yorke, brought me luck in every pantomime they played for me.

At this time, all seemed to be serene in our pantomime

*Down the years he told me this about at least twenty artistes. I would assess his ratio of successful predictions, in my case, was an adverse one of about 18½ : 1½!

**A happy outcome of this pantomime was the pantomime association it commenced with that wonderful designer and painter, Rex Spencer, whom I brought in as I was not satisfied with the scenery. He became head of design for Midlands ATV until, at his own request, he returned to designing only.

world and I was very hopeful of the next, "Sleeping Beauty", for which I had engaged Freddie Forbes, who specialised in the part of 'Queen' in that subject. The first rehearsal arrived but he did not. Soon after I had greeted the rest of the company and was waiting to give the signal for the opening of the champagne, which always accompanied our first rehearsals and was drunk after my speech of welcome, I was called to the telephone. He had been taken seriously ill and would have to withdraw from the pantomime (sadly, he died very shortly afterwards). I informed the cast, quickly engaged a replacement, which was extremely difficult at that time of the year, and along with Oliver Gordon, the producer, reshaped the book as we were forced to scrap most of Freddie's scenes and to substitute others to suit the new dame. But time was too short, the replacement not strong enough, and as a result the pantomime never really 'got off the ground' as far as the comedy side was concerned, although Wilson, Keppell and Betty certainly provided a superb comedy interlude. Scenically it was first class, particularly the Highland waterfall and glade scene which commenced my long association with Jimmie Currie, who specialised in these scenes.

The following year (1953/54) was to be "Dick Whittington", and for the part of Idle Jack I booked Jimmy Wheeler, an error of judgement, for although a great 'stand-up' comic, he was too static for pantomime. He had appeared in the George Robey pantomime with his father when they were known as Wheeler and Wilson, and I paid them, then, the princely sum of £30 a week. Soon after they signed the contract they made a big success in a radio series, and old man Wilson, a delightful man but an inveterate moaner, was 'not too happy'. I recalled this in my last night speech saying, "Then they only got £30 in 1939 and Jimmy's father never stopped grumbling." A member of the cast standing behind me called out "What are you paying Jimmy this year?" I replied, "A lot more and I've never stopped grumbling!" To my astonishment, Jimmy came up to me after the curtain fell and said (and meant it) how delighted his father would have been to hear my comment. Probably he would, as unfortunately he had, by then, long retired to his eternal rest.

Faced with two successive 'below standard' pantomimes (by our yard-stick at any rate) I was becoming worried and for my

159

next one, "Aladdin", I engaged Harry Bright as producer. He was a very clever man of whom I was very fond outside the theatre and who my children adored. In the theatre I found his methods too bullying and I never felt really happy when dealing with him.

The pantomime, which included Clarkson Rose and the Monarchs, although not the best, was up to standard and contained some splendid production touches from Harry. The subject for the following year was "Robinson Crusoe" for which Harry Bright was very anxious to have a male principal boy which, although very much accepted nowadays, was a great novelty then. As a result the newspapers, both local and national, gave us great coverage. (I will not enter here into the pros. and cons. of male v. female principal boys, except to say that, on balance, I prefer the latter.) In deference to his wishes, especially as he was writing the 'book', I left the major part of the casting to him, something I had never done with a producer before. The pantomime had some splendid features, but I disagreed with a lot of it and it was a financial disaster. Partly because the star of that year, although famous and talented, was a female comedienne and the public prefer pantomime dames to be male.

So bad were the figures towards the end of the run that the Board and I began seriously to wonder whether pantomime had lost its hold, especially as attendances had now dropped for three years running. Again we seemed to be at the crossroads, and not because of any ego on my part, I decided to take over the whole production myself which entailed not only the casting and planning, as formerly, but also responsibility for virtually every detail including partly writing the 'book'.* I directed it from the 'producer's chair' for I had been finding it increasingly frustrating to possess ideas and to see faults in the finished article which I had to discuss with the producer, rather than making the necessary alterations myself. I think that with all the mistakes one inevitably has made, this decision proved to be correct.

So, in 1955, I 'produced' my first pantomime, "Cinderella".

*During Oliver Gordon's years as producer, and sometimes afterwards, the book and music was by Henry Marshall. From the late fifties Joan Benyon wrote most of the lyrics and provided the book which I would then rewrite to fit in with my requirements.

The cast included Adele Dixon, a most lovely principal boy, Teddy Johnson and Pearl Carr who were delightful, a splendid double act Connor and Drake, Tommy Rose (who played so often for me) and Terry O'Neill, a top class Buttons. Everyone co-operated and backed me up to the hilt. It was a very good pantomime and business boomed, in spite of the fact that the advance booking had not been good.

This was very encouraging and my next pantomime, "Babes in the Wood", was equally successful with a cast including, once again, The Monarchs, Terry Hall (a delightful and talented man) whose Lenny the Lion shot him to fame just after he was booked, Fay Lenore, one of the best principal boys, and not least, Jack Stanford (married to my sister-in-law, but now deceased), to whom Max Wall referred, in a recent television interview, as "One of the great eccentric dancers of all time", as indeed he was.

From an entertainment standpoint the 1957/58 "Dick Whittington", which starred Sonnie Hale, was less successful. He was extremely ill both before and during the run but somehow managed to finish it (he died not so very long aftewards). Sharing the comedy was Arthur Haynes who had become a big star after signing his contract, and Baker and Douglas who have now gone their own separate ways, both achieving individual success. Next year's "Puss in Boots" was an extremely good pantomime with Norman Vaughan, Terry Hall again, and that great dame, George Lacy, making his first of many superb appearances for me. Dennis Lotis sang charmingly, but was rather lost in the hurly burly of pantomime, and Daphne de Wit was brilliant as the human cat.

1959/60, "Cinderella" included Bartlett and Ross, Mike and Bernie Winters, who regularly over-ran their time* and, as Buttons, George Martin, a charming man and excellent performer who now writes the scripts for the Basil Brush show. Dandini was played by Terry Fearis, a beautiful redhead, who started at the Alex as a dancer and who I always considered possessed star potential. The four male singers included a delightful man called Val Doonican who later married Lynette Rae, principal boy for me the next year. I did not feel it was

*I eventually threatened them that if they continued to do so, I would personally write anti-semitic slogans on their dressing room door!

one of our best pantomimes, but the public seemed to like it.

Strangely enough, "Cinderella", the best story of all, has never appealed to me as a producer, probably because it does not offer as much latitude for imagination as many other subjects. "Sinbad the Sailor" which followed, included a brilliant double act who had only recently completed a ghastly television series. They said to me during the run "If we don't make it soon, we never will!" They did, their names? Morecambe and Wise — and they even managed to compete with Geroge Lacy. Next came "Aladdin" which I have always considered to be one of our best pantomimes, in the true sense of that word. Edmund Hockridge, who played Abanazar, a bad character, was a piece of casting against type, but was quite outstanding. I count him and his lovely wife, Jackie, as two of my best friends to this day although, alas, we rarely meet. Terry Fearis played the part of Aladdin excellently in a cast which included that talented couple, Miki and Griff, Joe Church, a tower of strength as Wishee, Tommy Rose as Widow Twankey and the Patton Brothers, great troupers, appearing in their first of many pantomimes for me, always with great success. Others who further strengthened the pantomime included that wonderful fantasy act, Emerson and Jayne, and Martin Dell, a powerful Emperor of China.

"Mother Goose" which followed, was surely the best Alex pantomime ever and the nearest I ever came to feeling entirely satisfied with one. The cast included Beryl Reid playing a specially written part (not dame). She is, of course, a most brilliant artiste and much more than a comedienne as she has proved since 1965 when she appeared in "Sister George", then in films and with the National Theatre Company. She made a huge success, as did Ted Rogers, then unknown, the Dallas Boys and Jack Tripp, playing dame for me for the first time. He has since appeared for me somewhere, virtually every year since. He ranks with Barry Lupino of pre-war years and George Lacy, as the best dame ever to play the Alex.* In fact he became part of the Alex pantomime tradition. He is a complete perfectionist who, I was warned, might be a little tempera-

*I would also include Terry Scott, the dame in this year's "Aladdin" which, as I write, is playing to packed houses. Arthur Askey, one of the greatest, played for me at Bournemouth, but never at Birmingham.

mental — if he is, it is only because he wants everything in the show (not just his part of it) to be absolutely right. The relationship between Jack, Allen Christie (his partner) and I has always been much more than that of a manager and artiste; we have been great personal friends, as indeed I am proud to say, have so many artistes.

The pantomime included yet another fine artiste, for before it was fully cast, I had heard from my friend, Albert Knight, one of the great gentlemen of the theatre who has, amongst many activities, for many years produced the Palladium pantomimes, that a very good young singer who had not long moved from Australia was worth looking at. I did so, liked him and booked him at a very small salary. His name was Frank Ifield, and soon his song, "I Remember You", swept the country. Before the pantomime even opened I was offered a huge sum to release him, but resisted the temptation. He is now a superb artiste, but was then rather raw and only one cog in a wonderful machine. On the scenic side, it included superb sets by Rex Spencer and special effects, such as the Highland scene, and one in which the girls dived below the stage before Mother Goose (actually a 'double') entered the pool in search of beauty. Yes, I am sure it was our best ever pantomime and will be very hard to surpass — anywhere. Never at any time during the run, matinee or evening, was it possible to obtain a seat, and we had such a long waiting list that it was a pleasure to receive cancellations!*

Strangely enough, this pantomime was one of the few which have not been entirely happy backstage. I think it was based on the fact that Beryl Reid, when engaged, was clearly the star with, of course, top billing. But by the time the pantomime opened Frank had become virtually the biggest name in England and whatever the billing stated, to the public he was the star name. Although Frank never, in any way, took advantage of this fact, it created a situation which could easily cause unrest.

*"Mother Goose" created a record by playing to 150,000 people; it was closely followed by "Jack and the Beanstalk" in 1964 with 147,000; "Puss in Boots" in 1966 with 136,000; and "Crusoe" the year before with 135,000. All these played ten weeks, but in one week less "Jack and the Beanstalk" played, in 1973-74, to 122,000 people. The lowest attendance was 92,000 in 1969-70.

The following year at Wolverhampton, it was very pleasing that, with almost the same cast, except for Frank, Beryl's name and the excellence of the pantomime resulted in many weeks of capacity business.

This extremely high standard was not maintained in 1963/64 with "Babes in the Wood". Ronnie Carroll was not at his best in pantomime, but there were splendid performances from Arthur Worsley (a supreme ventriloquist), Billy Burden*, the rustic comic, and from those tremendous workers, Gordon and Bunny Jay, the delightful vocalists, Overton and Stock and, as always, George Lacy. The girl babe was played by Sally Thomsett, since of "Man About the House" fame. On paper it should have been a great show, but almost every experiment I made just failed and if it was not one of our better pantomimes, it was entirely my fault.

Fortunately we came right back to form with "Jack and the Beanstalk", nearly up to the standard of "Mother Goose". The Bachelors, who I had booked before their record "I Wouldn't Trade You for the World" made them amongst the biggest draws in the country, combined with Jack Tripp who made his usual success, and a strong supporting cast, achieved a splendid and happy pantomime. However, it did give me one nasty moment when a comedian, now famous but then little known, was missing when 'called' at about 9 p.m. He eventually emerged from the pub next door saying he did not intend to rehearse as it was so late. Although the pantomime was due to open in three days' time, I wished him "Goodnight" but, as he neared the exit, added — "By the way, don't bother to come back tomorrow." Luckily, this shook him and he returned to rehearse.

I was again lucky as I had engaged The Barron Knights to appear in "Robinson Crusoe" before their "Call Up the Groups" went to the top of the charts. They were a great success, as was Denny Willis, especially with his hilarious "Post Horn Gallop". The Cox and Miles Twins were, as always a great asset but Kathleen West, a late replacement for a dame who had died suddenly, and in her own sphere a wonderful artiste, proved

*Apart from being a delightful fellow and first rate comedian, he had, and I expect still has, the ability, when cycling, to reverse within a space of three inches if a pretty girl happens to pass by!

again that dames should be male not female.

The 1966/67 "Puss in Boots" with Des O'Connor, who had come right to the fore by that Christmas and has, of course, subsequently achieved even greater fame, packed the theatre. It had a very strong supporting cast including Rikki Fulton, a hilarious dame who fully justified the gamble of bringing him so far from Scotland, where he is a household name. Jean Barrington with her lovely voice, and yet again The Monarchs, helped greatly towards its success. "Goody Two Shoes" followed with the New Vaudeville Band who had enjoyed brief fame with such numbers as "Winchester Cathedral". Unfortunately they were a totally undisciplined group and did not do themselves justice, which could not be said about Jack Tripp and Fay Lenore. The Scottish Highland Pipers, whose only entrance was in the highland glade scene just before the interval, remained for the next 1½ hours for the 'walk-down', between times creating a dramatic upsurge in our Leon Bar takings! Robert Marlowe was responsible, for the first time, for the choreography which he did brilliantly, and Paul and Peta Page commenced a long, happy and very artistic relationship with me.

The following year Ted Rogers starred in "Dick Whittington" and was excellent in a not particularly outstanding pantomime, in which Pat Lancaster, one of my favourite principal boys, Cy Grant and The Dallas Boys did fine work. The Dallas Boys are one of the best acts of their kind, but because they are not a pop group, but a great deal more, have never achieved the recognition they deserve. Gordon Peters, who has done splendidly for me elsewhere, somehow never quite realised his full potential except in a duet with Cy.

Next year's "Aladdin" was a comparative disaster. It starred Michael Bentine, a brilliant man and one of the world's charmers, who loved pantomime but was almost impossible to 'tie down' at script conferences (as Dave Allen had warned me might be the case). He teemed with brilliant ideas, many of which would have entailed re-building the stage (if not the entire theatre). I settled for some of the more possible ones, although even they called for props of the utmost intricacy, but became progressively worried as these conferences continued. To make matters worse, after an anti-flu injection, Michael (in spite of being an old Etonian!) turned out to be allergic to the vaccine and did not appear at the first rehearsals, neither did his props! These arrived three days before the dress rehearsal in an apparently unfinished state. Anyway they completely baffled Michael, and scenes which had once sounded so hilarious had to be cut out. During the last few weeks of the run he suffered a leg injury and did not finish the pantomime. In some ways he never started it! Donald Peers, who co-starred, and an equally delightful man, gave a splendid if somewhat light-weight performance, but lost his voice during the course of the run. There were, however, many compensations, notably from Jasmine Dee as Aladdin, Billy Burden and Ravel. Two items choreographed by Robert Marlowe — a butterfly/dragon routine and a novel version of the Willow Pattern Plate — were outstanding. A long association began with Jane Harrod who played the genii, and each future year choreographed 'outside' pantomimes for me with great success.

The 1970/71 "Cinderella" pantomime which followed played to near capacity. It starred that brilliant artiste Ronnie Corbett as Buttons when he was on the edge of his now tremendous fame. Strangely enough, although I have naturally had the occasional differences of opinion with artistes, Ronnie is the only one who has made me unhappy at rehearsals. He seemed to assume from the very first rehearsal (possibly quite rightly) that I knew absolutely nothing, and after only two hours, rather a short time in which to form a judgment, he announced in front of all the cast that he didn't like my methods of rehearsing. From then onwards, apart from telling me that the pantomime was very under-rehearsed, we had little communication, although he did once ask me, towards the end of rehearsals, how long I thought the pantomime would run and when I told him (correctly as it turned out), said he didn't see how I could know! We were never unfriendly, and once the pantomime was launched got on extremely well together and I am very fond of him. I bow to no one in my admiration for his work ("The Two Ronnies" must be just about TV's best ever entertainment programme) and although, in a recent interview with Derek Nimmo (of whom I am a great fan), Terry Scott said he was the best Buttons he had co-starred with, I did not feel his particular qualities made him an ideal for the part. Cinders was played by Jean Bayless who had starred in "The Sound of Music" and in several pantomimes, including two at the Palladium. She has a really exquisite voice and (like Terry Fearis) is a beautiful redhead and a lovely person. Lynn Kennington was a dominating Prince Charming and Noelle Finch a lively Dandini, a part she loved. (She once told me that even if she was not playing pantomime, she still put on her Dandini wig at Christmas!)

"Robinson Crusoe" was the next subject, with Les Dawson and Jack Tripp (partnered, of course, by Allen Christie). Les, surely one of our very funniest men, was then very inexperienced in pantomime and at several conferences with him during the year, I emphasised that having established him in the opening scene, I would delay his next entrance, but it was essential that he then came back with something really strong. Had he any ideas? He described to me a routine for about half an hour and had me helpless with laughter. I could not wait to see it at rehearsal, but when I did it lasted exactly 1½ minutes, which included the time it took for a table to be brought on by the Miles Twins (who, like their husbands the Cox Twins, would do anything to help a show). It never got a laugh even from the assembled company and had to be scrapped. Receiving large billing was the group 'New World' who had just made a big hit with "Tom, Tom, Turn Around", and were excellent whilst singing seriously, but unfortunately John ('Fuzzy') Lee was under the misguided impression that he was a comedian. I think his biggest comedy contribution to the pantomime was made when he threw a bucket of water from his dressing room window over a traffic warden he saw booking him outside the stage door. He gave her a bunch of flowers later, as they left the court!

The 1972/73 pantomime, "Puss in Boots", was sound but unexciting. Jack Douglas assisted by George Truzzi had many funny routines, but that talented artiste, Millicent Martin, was not really at her best in pantomime which is a very specialised medium, a fact not always appreciated. Great work was done by Reg ('Confidentially') Dixon and Ken Roberts. Both these fine performers worked for me many times, always with success and absolute expertise, for they are true artistes. Jacqueline Toye, one of the many artistes who started their career as a dancer at the Alex, was endearing as the human cat.

Next year's "Jack and the Beanstalk" had a very strong

cast including Jimmy Tarbuck, George Lacy and The Grumble-weeds, a riotous success, who were to become 'the talk of the town' and were as nice a group to have in the theatre as the Barron Knights. Jimmy, on the other hand, drove me mad. A most delightful chap and a very funny comic, he would not take seriously any of the straight scenes which he had to play as 'Jack', a part in which he had insisted on being cast, thus losing their effectiveness and, therefore, to some extent failing to obtain the best contrast from his comedy scenes. I never felt he really believed in pantomime, and without this belief one should not appear in one. In any case he would certainly much rather have been playing golf, at which he is an expert. When I told him he must make at least one extra entrance in the second half and that the scene with the princess, after he had rescued her from the giant's clutches, must be extended, his reply was that he was not 'stage struck'! At the money we were paying him he should have been! George Lacy, as always, was superb. Unfortunately Nicholas Brent, a tower of strength for me in several pantomimes and again doubling the parts of the old woman and giant, had an accident on the opening night during his fight with Jimmy and had to withdraw from that part. As a result, and at only a few hours notice, we engaged an actor, on a temporary basis, who could claim to be either the world's smallest giant or biggest dwarf!

It was an excellent pantomime, as was "Babes in the Wood" which followed in 1974, with Leslie Crowther as the star. Leslie scored a great personal triumph and was, with Edmund Hockridge, the greatest leader of a company I have known. No pantomime with him in it could fail to be anything but extremely happy. We share the same sense of humour and love of cricket.

It is repetitious to say that once again Jack Tripp was stupendous, especially in his scenes with Leslie. Jimmy and Brian Patton were excellent, and Johnny Vyvyan who, with only two lines to speak, of which 50% were inaudible, was a riot. Linda Williams, the principal girl, had only limited oppor-tunities and it was not easy to predict the enormous success she was soon to make in "A Chorus Line". The Three Squires, who were making their first appearance for me at Birmingham, were a tower of strength, as they had always been elsewhere.

Michael Redgrave and Joan Plowright
in The National Theatre production of "Uncle Vanya", 1964

The author has selected Laurence Olivier, Marlene Dietrich, Eric Morecambe and Ernie Wise as the greatest artistes, in their respective spheres, to have appeared at the Alex.

Marlene Dietrich

Morecambe and Wise

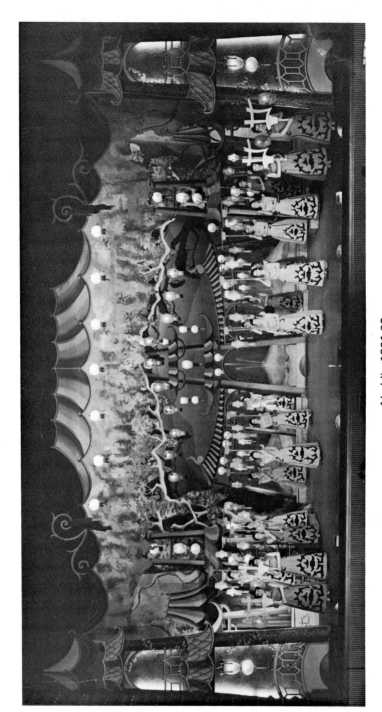

Aladdin 1961-62
(Designed by Norman Smith)

Repertory season 1969: A Man and his Wife
Sheila Brownrigg and Emrys Jones as Lady and Sir Winston Churchill

Arthur Lowe and Harry H. Corbett in "Laburnum Grove"
Presented by Triumph Productions.
(Arthur was at one time a member of our Hereford company)

DEREK, BEST WISHES ALWAYS

Dear Derek,
    When we first met in Blackpool to discuss
the pantomime, "Robinson Crusoe" I had several
misgivings: I thought to myself, "This chap is
a born worrier" and in that assumption I was
quite correct... You were a worrier. You worried
about the theatre, you worried about the business,
but above all you worried about the artists who
worked for you, and their welfare. You see Derek,
you are most unusual in theatre management, you
actually care about people, and now that you are
about to retire, I find myself realising that
there is nobody who can take your place. The word
"Gentleman" is applied to all sorts of odd bods,
but in your case, it really does apply, you are
one, and you are stuck with it. With all my heart
I wish you well in your retirement from active
participation in show business, but not from your
friends in it, and Derek, I count myself as one
of them. Good luck to you, and God Bless.

Les Dawson

The first of two hundred letters in an album
presented at the author's gala performance.

Michael Bullock — the author's successor at the Alex

Leslie Crowther making presentations to the author at
the Gala performance

The line up at the author's final curtain call
(Not included are John Alderton, Arthur Askey, Jack Tripp and Georgie Wood)

"Cinderella", in 1975/76, was to be the last completely Alexandra pantomime as a decision was soon to be taken by the Council of Management that, in the interests of economy, our production department, sadly, must close. I would like to feel, therefore, that it was an outstanding one, but unfortunately this was not quite the case. It was dogged by bad luck. Peter Goodwright, to my way of thinking a 'Buttons' in the very best mould, was taken ill and could not appear during a large part of the run. This, naturally, in spite of a noble effort by the under study, Raymond Savage, had a very detrimental effect on the pantomime which was, in any case, rather patchy. However, it contained many attributes, notably, Terry Hall and Lenny the Lion, the ugly sisters' costumes designed by John Inman who I released for his TV series but was booked to play sister alongside Barry Howard, and a lovely flying ballet beautifully arranged by Virginia Courtney. Jane Terry, another local girl who started at the Alex as a dancer, continued the long line of excellent Dandinis.

Dai Francis, though, was not entirely happy casting and his black face spot, which is so very strong, could not, much as I tried, be fitted successfully into "Cinderella". The fault was entirely mine.

At Christmas 1976 we broke with a long tradition, and instead of presenting our own home-produced pantomime, entrusted it to an outside management, Triumph Theatre Productions which, under the leadership of Duncan Weldon and Louis Michaels, is undoubtedly the most progressive theatrical management in the country.

The pantomime was "Dick Whittington", but as the final decision was not taken until August, by which time our intended production was virtually completed, only minimal savings could be effected. So, in the event, the pantomime was a compromise between the two managements. The cast included Frank Ifield who was superb, Patrick Cargill whose dame developed greatly as the pantomime progressed, Jim (Nick Nick) Davidson who I feel sure will become a star name, the Cox Twins, together with the Miles Twins, stalwarts for me of so many pantomimes at the Alex and elsewhere, and Terry Doogan, a superb pantomime cat. It was expertly produced by Alan Curtis who, as 'Ratman', confirmed his reputation as the best 'baddie' in the business.

169

This delightful company, I know, sensed my feelings at having an 'outside' management produce an Alex pantomime and made it so very much happier for me than it might have been. I was very proud of the fact that at the end of the run, in spite of not being 'our' company, they gave a party for me at which the whole company, which included the stage management and orchestra, presented me with a beautiful illuminated address (which now hangs in the Leon Bar alongside those presented to my father in earlier years). The opening words were "To Derek Salberg, a great gentleman of the theatre". I was very touched and only hope those words were merited.

This chapter has, I realise, mostly referred to the stars, but they are, of course, but part of the story and I fervently wish I had room to mention the names of the many hundreds of outstanding supporting artistes who have appeared in them; such as Arthur ('Not Now') Tolcher whose father before him worked loyally for mine for very many years. Arthur has appeared in countless pantomimes for me and given 100% at every performance, he has understudied virtually every male performer in each one of them and gone on for many, with the result that the pantomime would run for at least an extra ten minutes. Jimmy Tarbuck may not be stage struck, but Arthur certainly is! Each year I awaited a letter from his famous Mum* telling me in which of our pantomimes she wished him to appear! He was just one of the huge number of artistes who, although not receiving top billing, made a large contribution to our pantomimes. Particularly do I wish I had space to mention by name the backbone of any pantomime — the dancers and singers.

But pantomime is indebted not only to its artistes, but to a host of other people without whom the curtain could not rise. Foremost in this category I would place the Musical Director and his orchestra who can make or mar a show. We have been lucky down the years and have maintained a consistently high musical standard under such musical directors as Larry Macklin, Harry Hudson**, Arthur Roberts, Tony Davidson, Peter Day and Tony Stenson.

*I heard with profound sorrow of Beatrice's passing just as I completed this book. She was part of theatre lore.
**See footnote * on opposite page.

170

Equally important is the choreographer who is also the producer's right-hand man, and I have already mentioned the wonderful work, over so very many years, of Madame Lehmiski, Carol Hinsley, Robert Marlowe and most recently of Virginia Courtney. (I was also most grateful to Denise Shaune who stepped into the breach for the Ronnie Corbett "Cinderella".) In fact we have been blessed in every department, not least in the Wardrobe where a first class staff was for so many years headed by Mrs. Mitchell ('Mitch') under a succession of wardrobe heads, most recently Yvonne Cooper and Eric Laight who took over the construction and designing of the head-dresses after Joan died. Their immediate predecessor was Terry St. Dennis (once one of the famous St. Dennis Sisters).

Not a whit less important are stage managers whose work is rarely appreciated by the public. Our longest serving were Brian Hayle (13 times), Roy Astley, now one of London's top stage managers (7 times), Michael Bullock (six times), and Bill Morton (3 times) — all superb at their job.

The public, naturally, more easily acclaim the work of property masters and carpenters, such as Sydney Jones (whose father was at the Alex almost from the time it opened). He loved every grain of wood and every piece of timber used in building his marvellous sets. We were very fortunate to have such worthy successors to him as Fred Reeves and the almost legendary "Big Dick" Turner.** Our electricians down the years, Jimmy Neale, Billy Warwick, Alan Chester, Roy Bastiman, Bill Graham and now Eric Otto, have all been devoted to their work which, with changing techniques and more sophisticated equipment, becomes yearly more intricate and important. A major contribution is, of course, made by designers and painters. Here again we have been fortunate and have been blessed with brilliant designers such as Roy Cooke, Len Hudson, Elizabeth Dorrity, Rex Spencer, Norman Smith*** and, most

*Knowing my partiality for kippers, Harry who each summer season conducted at Yarmouth, arranged to send me some from his favourite shop. However, a note came saying, "I can't send the kippers yet as they are on holiday for a week."

**He now receives great assistance from his right hand man, Peter Howes.

***Norman designed the superb settings for the 1977 Royal Variety Performance.

recently, Kenneth Turner (who also created the costumes after Joan died). Ken, who originally worked for us at Wolverhampton, is a great character who rarely eats, never seems to go to bed, imbibes vast quantities of beer, but always appears fresh as a daisy next day! He usually arrives late for appointments (which drives me mad) — not just by ten minutes but sometimes by a day — with such plausible excuses that I usually ended up apologising to him! During the latter years he also became our production manager, a position held by Michael Bullock before his appointment as administrator.

Mike had followed Bill Avenell who left us to play the part of 'Mr. Lovejoy' in "Crossroads". A wonderful character, he joined us as an actor having previously appeared at (amongst others) the Birmingham Repertory and Royal Shakespeare Theatres. He was not noted for remembering his lines and at one rehearsal, having staggered painfully through his scenes as Alderman Fitzwarren, he reached the last front cloth of which he barely knew a word. But never entirely at a loss, he invented some sort of drivel until a sentence completely defeated him. After a long pause he recalled the opening words and grasping them as a drowning man would a lifebelt, uttered to the principal boy, "What can I do to help you?", then stopped dead. By this time I was fed up to the teeth and shouted from the stalls, "I'll tell you what you can do to help her Bill, you can learn your bloody lines!" Bill was quite unabashed and, indeed, seemed to accept my remark as a compliment!

In another pantomime, whilst declaiming his lines with his usual gesticulations, he had to light a piece of flash paper from which a spark caught on his voluminous costume, with the result that the staff off-stage kept calling out "Bill, you're on fire!" Quite oblivious, he went on happily with the scene until finally, looking down, he realised the awful truth, and never has anyone left the stage so rapidly! At one rehearsal, apropos of nothing, he walked on to the stage, called together the artistes, who had been entirely co-operative throughout the rehearsal period and, to my astonishment, announced in very stern tones that "Mr. Salberg wants no trouble from you. You are to take the rehearsal with all seriousness and to keep on your toes." With which (he was responsible for lighting the pantomime) he went to the lighting desk, lifted his hand for

172

a minion to alter its position, clapped his hands for another to change the mike, summoned a member of the stage management staff to sit by him for lighting notes and when, five minutes later, I called out for him he was fast asleep, and indeed snoring. There was a famous rehearsal when, after he had lunched(!) well but not too wisely, we were taking a scene in which he and Terry Fearis were standing surrounded by water on a narrow bridge. In the space of five minutes Terry only just prevented him from falling in the water on three separate occasions. I threatened her with instant dismissal if she did so again! Stories about dear old Bill abound; he was a great, but sometimes complex, character and one could not help but love him, even if he was exasperating at times.

Characters such as Bill, and incidents such as these, will remain in my memory as part of the joy of presenting pantomime. But uppermost is the recollection of walking into a packed auditorium composed sometimes of deprived children, sometimes of senior citizens, sometimes of Rotarians or a works party, or maybe a matinee full of parents with their children. Always though, of an audience alive with an expectancy which it was one's duty to fulfil to the best of one's ability. Then afterwards to feel enormous pleasure on those occasions when one had succeeded. For what greater thrill is there than hearing children's laughter, or indeed that of grown-ups?

*   *   *   *   *   *   *   *

The economics of pantomime demand that, having spent a large capital sum on its construction, it is necessary to spread the cost over a number of years. Each pantomime was, therefore, presented under our own management for two or three years, then hired out to other managements and eventually either sold or broken up for part use in one of our future productions.

This, of course, greatly widened our field of activities and we have presented pantomimes, under our direct management, in very many venues including Wolverhampton, Nottingham, Bournemouth, Belfast, Bradford, Hull, Torquay and (when they existed) some London suburban theatres. We hired out productions to such diverse cities as Cardiff, Chester, Swansea, Sunderland and Dublin. Before the war, as already mentioned, our pantomimes were also seen in South Africa.

173

When under our management, the pantomime was very similar to the original production at Birmingham with usually some (or occasionally many) changes of cast. These changes might call for additional scenery and nearly always, costumes. Therefore, the workshops and wardrobe who, in any case, had to maintain the various pantomimes in good condition, were kept busy all the year round.

To hire out pantomimes, as we did, entailed a tremendous amount of prior organisation for the number of things which can go wrong are legion. Invariably we would receive frantic telephone calls near opening night to say various items (often discovered a few hours later) were missing. We naturally did not relish these calls as they came at a time when we were all 'up to our eyes' with the Alex pantomime.

One year, my father (heaven knows how) was responsible for 12 pantomimes, including one at the Garrick Theatre in London (which 'flopped' badly). Our longest 'outside' association was with the Grand Theatre, Wolverhampton where we presented pantomime with only a year's break from the late thirties until 1971 when Humphrey Stanbury and his Chairman, Tony Southall, made the wise move to present their own pantomimes. I was very sorry when the relationship ended for it had been not only financially rewarding, but extremely happy. However, I did have one very tricky visit there when Teddy Johnson, Pearl Carr, Jack Tripp, Bert Weedon and Janet Brown were starring. Teddy, the most reasonable of people, had telephoned me to say that he and Pearl had agreed to cut some numbers as the pantomime was too long, but other artistes were not doing likewise. They were upset and asked me to come over as soon as I could. As, in any case, I visited each of my pantomimes within three or four days, I went immediately.

After hearing Teddy and Pearl's grievance, I went to see Bert who explained that all his numbers were going so well he could not decide which to cut. He intended to eliminate at least two and, therefore, resented the complaint being made so quickly. I then called on Jack Tripp and Allen Christie, just for a chat, but foolishly said I thought the Fairy they had recommended to me was pretty bad (or words to that effect). Soon after I left the dressing room I ran into her and she told me she

174

had heard I had said that "she was the worst Fairy in the business". I replied that I could not possibly have said that, because the girl playing Fairy for me at Birmingham entirely fitted the description! The principal girl then cornered me to say she was very unhappy at having one chorus cut from her only number. I next met Arthur Tolcher, a great trouper, who broke down and cried his eyes out because, having almost lost his voice, he could not give his usual robust performance. The wardrobe mistress then saw me and said the dancers were dissatisfied with many of their costumes and she was having problems with some of them. Very depressed by this time, I knocked with trembling hand on the dressing room door of my friends the Cox and Miles Twins. I need not have worried though, for as soon as I entered all embraced me saying "Lovely to see you, Guvnor, and you know we are such a happy family." Every subsequent year, whenever they were working for me (and that was virtually every year), Jack Tripp and Allen Christie sent me a telegram containing the words "Guvnor, we're such a happy family!" As I was leaving I was given a consolation kiss from the principal boy, Janet Brown, so my visit was not without its compensations!

Wolverhampton also provided one of my saddest and most worrying moments when I received a telephone call just before the pantomime was due to open. It was from Terry Bartlett to say his partner, Colin, had collapsed and would never work again (he died soon after). Somehow a replacement was found and, as always, 'the curtain went up', but for Terry it meant the end of the act of Bartlett and Ross, the outstanding ugly sisters of their time, perhaps of any time. (John Inman and Barry Howard ran them very close.)

Just as our pantomimes were invariably successful at Wolverhampton, so (with few exceptions) were those at Bournemouth, always produced expertly by Frank Adey and stage-managed by his wife Betty. With great help from Sam Bell*, the Corporation's entertainments officer, we built up the run from four weeks to nine. At Nottingham, one of the best pantomime dates in the country, we played to attendance figures beaten only by Ken Dodd. Hedley Claxton, one of the theatre's great characters,

*When Sam retired we received the same co-operation from Leslie Beresford and all his staff.

175

who was our conscientious company manager there, never ceased announcing this, for he has never lost his enthusiasm, in spite of advancing years. Our two other most successful strongholds were Belfast (for many years) and Bradford (for a shorter period), where our relationship ceased a little unfairly, I felt, when a new manager took over. But whether our pantomimes were successful or not, and they usually were, we always received splendid co-operation from the managements of the various theatres, all of whom made my companies and myself extremely welcome.

****   ****   ****

I include, with his permission, an hilarious letter sent me by Peter Powell when he was producing a pantomime for another management. I doubt whether I ever had to face quite such a combination of circumstances!

PETER POWELL'S LETTER

"My dear Derek,

How's your's going? Thought you'd be amused to hear that we have had the usual mess-up over rehearsal rooms, misunderstandings over pianists, delay over arrangements for props — we also have a blind comic who gets over not being able to read his present script by reciting from past successes (playing his own feed) — the other comics take turns with........he started off on a long gag from a kitchen routine (Aladdin, Blackpool 1936) which got unfunnier as the minutes ticked by — in the end Cardew Robinson stopped him very seriously by saying 'just a minute Dave, I must write all that in my script!' The fairy of course has been sitting in a corner for two days waiting for her scene to be called, talking to a man who's on nobody's list but swears he's been engaged for King Rat. The Ballet mistress, who has to go back to London tomorrow says the choreographer should be ashamed sending such inexperienced girls etc. etc. The Babes are still at school and haven't broken up yet....and then I suppose they'll have their Christmas shopping to do before they can rehearse.

176

The scenery won't fit, there aren't enough lines, a rostrum's missing, there are only two limes and one won't work if the other does. There are only three singers instead of four and one of those is willing to fill in anywhere with a spot. The company manager is very old, very experienced, and a sweetie, but you daren't say good morning unless you've an hour to listen to his reply. The Stage Director is very young, very inexperienced, and is already gibbering incoherently. We have a dwarf, and in the chorus an unbaptised Jehovah's Witness who wants, during the second house on Boxing Day, to be totally immersed in the local swimming bath. One of the singers (not the singing one) has told me he wants to get in Rep and Ken Keeling* has told him he can get him into the Alex next season — he seemed very pleased about this.

We have no wardrobe mistress, but there aren't any digs left even if they send one. Taken all round I imagine we are much the same as any panto up and down the country, probably a bit better off than most.

Funny how I love it, but I'd rather be going through it all for you.

As ever,

      Peter"

*A great stalwart of many Salberg companies and once manager of the Grand Theatre Wolverhampton, he is now manager of the Dundee Repertory Theatre. His wife, Doreen Andrew, has given many brilliant performances for me, Reggie, and many theatre and TV directors.

CHAPTER 27

FUTURE OF THE ALEX AND OTHER
TOURING THEATRES

The past has been difficult, the present in many ways even more so, and the future will obviously present serious problems for, self-evidently, the provincial theatre is no longer commercially viable.

As I write these words there is a question mark over the future of the Birmingham Theatres, and I fervently pray that by the time they are in print a decision will have been reached which ensures the continuance of all three.

This situation is in no way peculiar to Birmingham though. The Coventry Theatre has just been given at least a temporary reprieve, and the Palace, Manchester saved by a property and building firm who intend to run it as a theatre, but the nearby Opera House appears almost certain to close. In Liverpool an agreement has been reached between the County Council and Moss Empires which will rescue the vast Empire Theatre, but it seems unlikely that the Liverpool Royal Court Theatre, which has been closed for some time, will be re-opened. The Bristol Hippodrome, the only touring theatre there, is in danger of closure as is the New Theatre, Oxford.

The National Theatre, although playing to capacity in all three of its auditoria, has put out a plea for help to the tune of £400,000 otherwise, they say, they will be faced with closing entirely the small Cottesloe Theatre where most of their experimental work is done, and the largest auditorium, The Olivier, for six months a year and ending provincial touring.

The D'Oyly Carte Company*, who have given so much

---

*It has just been announced that they are, at last, to receive Arts Council subsidy.

pleasure to millions, has stated through its administrator, Freddie Lloyd, (who, as related in an earlier chapter, helped the Alex to surmount a severe financial crisis) "Declining audiences is not our trouble, but even operating on modest budgets the company walks on a financial tightrope, being unable to afford even one bad season let alone major new or ambitious productions." They have already been forced to scrap their centenary production of Gilbert and Sullivan's first full-length opera, "The Sorcerer",

Should the National have to curtail its activities and D'Oyly Carte cease to operate, it would be a major tragedy which would further reduce the amount of product available to the provinces.

It has largely been the lack of attractions (coupled with ever escalating costs) which has caused the demise and threat of closure to so many theatres. As Bernard Delfont said, when reprieving the Coventry Theatre which was due to become a Bingo Hall, "I've got a shop in Coventry, but nothing to put in it."

Whereas, when I entered the theatre, *The Stage* newspaper listed in its 'On Tour' column over two hundred shows (a figure admittedly inflated by revues and No. 2 theatres, both now non-existent), the most recent issue contains a mere nine. These include those of Triumph Theatre Productions, without whom many more provincial theatres would probably have closed during the past few years. They, together with D.A.L.T.A. (Dramatic and Lyric Touring Association), who are responsible for administering the tours of the major ballet and opera companies as well as those of drama companies such as the National Theatre and Prospect, have been the main source of supply.

But a debt of gratitude is also owed to managements such as Cameron Mackintosh (whose splendid production of 'Oliver' occupied the Alex stage for four weeks last year and is currently playing to capaicty in London), David Kirk, Llewellyn Rees and Lionel Harris, Charles Vance, Bill Kenwright, John Newman, Malcolm Knight, Walter Jokel and Mark Furness — all of whom are, fortunately, stage-struck and prepared to face the hazards of touring with only the prospect of small, if any, reward*.
*See footnote * on following page.

179

(I have omitted such excellent managements as Peter Saunders, John Gale, Ray Cooney, etc. whose work is mainly in the West End.)

There is, nevertheless, a great shortage accentuated by the fact that, unfortunately, there are now less prior-to-London tours. Many managements faced with the heavy cost of touring, and the reluctance of the stars to do so, prefer, if they have fixed a London theatre, to run a series of previews in it before the actual opening night.

Many towns have no theatre, some have one or possibly two, but Birmingham, as befits a city of its size, possesses three, the Alex, the Hippodrome and Repertory Theatre. They each have a different although linked role to play, but to some extent the available productions are split between them. The operas (excluding D'Oyly Carte, who come to the Alex) and big ballet companies go to the Hippodrome which has a bigger seating capacity, excellent orchestra pit and slightly larger stage than the Alex**. It can stage big musicals (although some of them play the Alex in preference), but is totally unsuited to straight plays.*** The Birmingham Rep., who have always been extremely co-operative (and continue to be under Clive Perry, the director, and John Greenwood, the administrator), now receive some of the National Theatre's tours. One, which included Albert Finney, entailed the resident company being paid but 'laid off', but so great was the demand that their 901 seats proved totally inadequate. At the Alex 1562 seats would have been available and there was no company to pay off; madness personified and DALTA knew my view.

*These are managements presenting 'straight plays'. There are many others, too numerous to mention, doing splendid work in other fields such as summer shows, old time variety, music, etc.

**Nevertheless, I refute the suggestion that these Companies would be unable to visit Birmingham in the unhappy and, I think, unlikely event of the demise of the Hippodrome. In a letter to the *Birmingham Post*, whilst not denying that the Hippodrome is the better venue, I pointed out that the big Opera and Ballet Companies had most successfully appeared at the Alex from the mid-40's until 1974, since when a counter-weight system has been installed and a considerable number of back-stage and front of house improvements made.

***So much so, that a leading actor, due to play Birmingham this year, stipulated the Alex.

180

But, although its objective must be primarily to uphold its position as one of England's leading repertory theatres, it cannot be blamed for entering into the touring field, within certain clearly defined limits. For, in common with everyone, they are faced with very severe financial problems and must do their utmost to make their theatre viable.

Once again the inevitable word finance crops up so, as it is largely at the root of all evil, let us consider that mundane subject. It is possibly best understood by examining the way in which a theatre such as the Alex operates.

The theatre's weekly overheads, now greatly lessened by the closure of the production departments, are approximately £4,500 (naturally they vary somewhat with each production, and by several thousand during the pantomime season). After allowing average profits on all ancillaries such as Bars, Cafe, Programmes, etc. (but excluding grants), they are reduced to around £3,500. Touring managements usually demand a guarantee for straight plays of anything from £3,500—£5,500 against a percentage which varies between 62½% and 70%. For musicals the guarantee may well be in excess of £10,000 against an even higher percentage. The financial implications become obvious when, to take just two examples, last year's splendid production by the National Theatre of Alan Ayckbourn's "Bedroom Farce" attracted near capacity audiences at every peformance and yet the theatre's share was only £3,300. D'Oyly Carte played two weeks to full houses as always but required, quite understandably, a guarantee that their share of takings would be a minimum of £10,000*. I heaved a huge sigh of relief when this figure was reached and we were left with a small margin. But it's not good for the nerves!

It must be borne in mind too that these were our 'bankers'. So was a package show which I booked knowing that for six performances we were certain to fill the theatre — which we did. But I was unable to obtain it (and then after much negotiation) for less than 87½% of our takings. Even though we were able to show a small surplus, these terms give the theatre no opportunity of compensating its inevitable bad weeks by its good ones. At the same time they put the theatre at tremendous risk should the show not turn out to be a draw or some

*It is now considerably more.

181

calamity, such as the Irish bombing, extreme weather conditions or bus strikes etc., occur.

The high percentage was based mostly on the salaries paid to the stars which I firmly believe, with sur-tax as it is, are founded largely on prestige. For stars, quite understandably, must maintain a salary bracket as high as that of equivalent artistes. But if only (and I know this is a pipe dream) a system could be evolved which gave a substantial but ceiling salary, I am convinced artistes would be barely less happy and, indeed, only slightly less well off. It will never happen, but it would be lovely! So many more productions would become viable, especially pantomimes which, faced also with huge production costs (an entirely new one would require nearly a quarter of a million pounds to assemble), are being gradually squeezed out.

High salaries are, of course, only part of the problem and many people may be surprised to learn that they are nothing new. Pavlova in the twenties received £1,200 a week when she appeared at the Palace Theatre and Little Tich and Vesta Tilley £500 each. As early as 1795, Master Betty, an infant prodigy, who in his day achieved fame equal to that of the Beatles later, earned £100 a performance and was able to quit the stage entirely when still in his teens having amassed a huge fortune.

It must be realised too that these high salaries apply only to a very small percentage of artistes (usually current TV idols or pop stars, whose career at the top may only last for a limited time).

The average actor is not overpaid and in any case will almost certainly not work fifty-two weeks a year, or have a pension (other than the state one) to which to look forward. Furthermore, he is very vulnerable, for as he grows older he may become unsuitable for the roles he has been playing, a hazard not shared by those in most other occupations.

Nevertheless, I see danger signals being hoisted by the actors' union — Equity, who are in danger of being taken over by their activist-leftist members. This is partly because of the apathy of the average moderate who is either unable, or does not wish, to attend meetings, for a majority of actors do not want to concern themselves with union matters.

Negotiations with Equity are conducted by highly qualified

people, such as my brother Reggie, who (unlike me) is a brilliant negotiator. I do not feel entitled, therefore, to comment at length on some of the projected claims or on one or two of those already agreed, but will restrict myself to saying that the theatre is not, in my book, and never can be regarded in the same light as a factory. I oppose the structured week with its demand for further limitation on the number of performances and daily hours, hint of time clocks, and an increasing move towards claiming unsocial hours. These are already in operation to some extent, for artistes travelling from one town to another on Sundays, now receive a third of a day's pay for doing so, which sounds fair enough, but when people entered the theatre they knew they must expect to travel on Sunday and would work when other people were relaxing. I am certain the majority of artistes would agree that, although this is one of the disadvantages, their work offers a number of compensations.

I consider that the regulated entry rule, necessary when introduced, has played its part and should now be very greatly relaxed. It is heartbreaking for promising young actors to complete their drama school training and then to be virtually barred from entering the profession.

I also see danger in the demand for £60 basic minimum*, even for beginners in the non-subsidised areas of the theatre. It may well have the effect of reducing the salaries of the middle range, older and experienced actor, as budgets may be pruned accordingly. If demands become too great it will reduce the amount of employment available, which has already occurred in some sections of the theatre. Whereas, once, we employed thrity-two dancers in our pantomimes, the average is now between eight and twelve; orchestras which once filled the pit now have wide gaps between musicians, or have even disappeared. Already smaller cast plays are increasingly presented on tour and included in the programme of many repertory theatres. I quite understand the argument that it is better to pay less people a higher salary than to employ more people at a lower one, but this argument can be carried too far.

It might be imagined from these comments that I do not

*A lower, two tier minimum has now been agreed. I have been invited to act as arbitrator in any case where Equity and the managers are unable to agree when the lower figure should apply.

appreciate what Equity has done for actors, but this is far from being the case. Furthermore, I have always had the most cordial and co-operative relationship with them. I was absolutely delighted when they took space in my Gala programme, and especially that their President, Birmingham-born Hugh Manning, who I admire both as an actor and a man, should have included in it the words:

> "It was at this theatre that I had my first experience of theatre-going . . . . much enhanced by the happy atmosphere created by the Salberg family. It has been my good fortune since, to share that joy backstage with many hundreds of actors, dancers, variety performers, singers, stage management and staff who have worked with Derek who has been the 'Guvnor', Management and always the friend to us all, audience and performer alike . . . . . . To be under the Salberg banner with Derek, his brother Reggie or their cousin, Basil Thomas, was to have a plum job with a marvellous family management . . . . . generosity prevailed when it came to salaries . . . . . there was always the happy occasion of Derek's end of the week parties."*

Just as my relations with Equity have been of the happiest, so have those with the Musicians' Union and NATTKE (the National Association of Theatre, Television and Kinematograph Employees) who represent the staff, many of whom I know are not well paid. But until more money is available it is difficult to see how theatre wages can be made to equate with those in a factory, or many other forms of employment. Admittedly, people working in a theatre do so in a more congenial atmosphere, but this should not in itself be a sufficient reason for a lower wage structure.

NATTKE naturally feels this but I believe there is a realisation of the theatres problems on their part for they have always been reasonable, although hard negotiators. I certainly cannot see them adopting the attitude of their American equivalent related in *The Curtain Falls*, a fascinating book lent me by that delightful and talented couple, Brian Oulton and Peggy Thorpe-Bates:

> "....Everyone connected with our venture was eager to keep the play running, the actors all consented to take a cut in

*This referred to the Alex's famous 'offices' mentioned elsewhere in the book.

salary, so all of us now agreed that it would be only fair if the union men would also help. The stage-hands, when approached on the subject, said that they would have to refer the case to their Union for consideration. Several days later a Union representative attended one of our matinees to judge the show. He told us that it would be impossible for his men to take a cut, but that perhaps he could help us by removing some of the backstage workers whom his Union had forced upon us. After the play this Union delegate called upon Kenneth and me. 'Gentlemen,' he said, shaking his head, 'I'm afraid I can't do a thing. In fact, I'm going to have to ask you to put on an extra man. You've got a clock in the second act and—'

'Of course there's a clock,' said Kenneth, 'it's vital to the action of the play. It strikes the hour and—' 'That's just it,' replied the Union arbitrator. 'it strikes the hour. I suppose the stage manager works it?' 'He does. He steps behind the clock for a minute and strikes out eleven o'clock.' 'Well, you'll have to have a Union man to do that from now on. Our rules call for one of our men, not your stage manager, to work all effects.'

'But there's nothing for the man to do but just that one thing......' Despite all further remonstrance on our part, thereafter an additional Union stage-hand turned up for each performance. He sat idle in the wings until the hour appointed for him to step up to the clock. And every time he rang out eleven strokes on the silver bell, he was paid the sum of 6.75 dollars."

No, I'm sure it will never happen here, but at the same time NATTKE must do its best for its members. How then are managements to satisfy the unions, meet inflation and yet stay in business?

One short answer would appear to be an increase in admission prices, which, of course, carries with it the possibility of audience resistance, especially as the increase would need to be a sharp one in order to make any significant contribution. For let us examine what happens to each £1 charged by a touring theatre. 8% goes in VAT, of the balance between 62½% - 72½% (or even more, as we have seen) goes to the touring company. The theatre is thus risking the loss of a patron for the gain of just a few shillings.

Prices have, of course, risen quite considerably over the past few years, but not at the same rate as most commodities. I was interested when reading a programme for the leading Manchester theatre in 1901 to find that the top price was, even then, 10/6d at a time when the advertisements in it proclaimed: "Whisky, 3/6d a bottle", "Coal, 1/- a cwt" and "Tobacco, 3½d an ounce"* (as quoted at the beginning of the book).

They will, of course, continue to rise, but the real answer to the problem lies, I fear, in greatly increased subsidy at local and national level, for although the country is slowly moving to the realisation that the Arts are an important part of the community life, we still lag behind most countries. Germany, for example, spent £30,000,000 on three opera houses in 1976, whilst we spent but three and a half million pounds on the Royal Opera House, Covent Garden.

As Mr. Norman St-John Stevas, the opposition spokesman on Education and the Arts, said recently when speaking in a private capacity, "It is impossible to go on running the Arts on a shoe-string." I absolutely agree, but at the same time I would make four points.

First, I see no excuse for subsidising a theatre where the public have clearly indicated that they do not want one.

Secondly, civic and national patronage is not a 'carte blanche' to unnecessary spending — quite the reverse.

Thirdly, some opponents of subsidy for the theatre claim that it is only used by a minority. But then so are museums, art galleries, parks, libraries and, probably, public lavatories. In fact, what is not?

But *is* the theatre really supported by such a minority? This 'minority' attracted 320,000 to the Alex alone last year; a big musical not long ago played to full houses for twenty eight weeks at the Hippodrome, where Tommy Steele in "Hans Christian Andersen" played to capacity for four weeks, and opera has just filled nearly every seat for three weeks. The Birmingham Rep has rarely had an empty seat for three months, which included the period when the Alex and Hippodrome pantomimes and the nearby Coventry Theatre (with "Emu in Pantoland") were all drawing vast audiences. The Grand Theatre, Wolverhampton anticipate that by the time their pantomime finishes it will have been seen by 100,000 people. As Fred Norris once wrote in the *Birmingham Mail*, "Give 'em the shows and they will flock in." But, as we have seen, it is not

*At that time it was possible to get a meal at Miles, by the old Birmingham market hall, for 3d (just over 1p in present coinage).

186

always easy to find the shows to give 'em. However, there are very hopeful signs, both in quantity and quality for, in conjunction with the Arts Council, Triumph Productions have just formed a touring grid of eighteen theatres, which prominently features the Alex. It is a most important development.

As further proof that theatre-going is not just for the few, it is worth noting that more people are attracted annually to the Birmingham theatres than to the three local football teams. Their average combined attendance (if all three were playing at home) would be approximately 100,000 composed largely of the *same* regular fans at each match, whereas theatres draw from a much wider and ever-changing (according to the type of attraction) field.*

My fourth point, an obvious one, is that theatres must not accept subsidy as their right, but must help themselves. They must go out to fetch the public, not just sit back waiting for them to arrive, in other words they must market themselves**. They must keep a careful eye on changing trends as, for example (and this is only one of many), the reluctance of patrons to come into town to book, preferring to do so by telephone, only to find, owing to insufficient lines and undermanning, that it is continually engaged.*** In this connection the opening of the Birmingham Arts shop, financially supported by West Midlands Arts, was a very definite step in the right direction.

It provides regional and local information and sells craftwork, but its main function is that of acting as a booking venue

*In a survey on theatre attendances in Great Britain, it was shown that the attendance figure for League football in 1976 was 25 million and for the theatre 37 million. And, of course, it must be borne in mind that many attend both the theatre and soccer matches.

**Shining examples of what can be achieved are the success of Peter Tod at the Civic Theatre, Darlington, at one time a complete white elephant, of Richard Condon at the Theatre Royal, Norwich where, although he has admittedly everything in his favour, his enterprise has been the major factor, as it has been with John Counsell at Windsor.

***In fairness, I must point out that there are very many problems to overcome in order to give even an adequate service. Patrons often imagine that when they continually hear the ringing tone that the two telephonists are not answering. It is more than likely, however, that they are dealing with calls from other patrons. These may well take a long time and meanwhile the other lines go on ringing.

for regional theatres*. It is excellently managed by Jill Grayson, but I very much doubt whether it can ever achieve the highly optimistic forecast contained in the original survey (which included many excellent suggestions, alongside some absurd ones such as the closing of all theatre box offices until the evening). But it is playing its part in helping to make a theatre efficient and its facilities more easily accessible to its patrons

But help from an outside source, although invaluable, can only achieve limited results. For in the final analysis a theatre will stand or fall by its own efforts. It must create a feeling of trust among its patrons on whom it has imposed a positive image of itself. Above all it must provide a happy and 'anxious to please' atmosphere in which theatre-goers can enjoy their evening out.

Whilst I would certainly not claim that the Alex is perfect in every respect, it is held in deep affection, and most assuredly deserves to receive not only continued, but increased financial support and greater realisation in certain quarters, not only of it's importance to the life of Birmingham and its environs, but of the almost unique position it holds nationally. Given this support, I am confident that the Alex will outlive not only "The Archers" and "Crossroads" but . . even "The Mousetrap"!

*Last year they sold over 37,000 tickets for Birmingham theatres alone.

188

CHAPTER 28

MY CURTAIN CALL

And so I come to the final chapter which, because I retired on the 31st July, 1977, the day after I became 65, must contain probably the two saddest words in the English language — "Good Bye".

But before it became time to write them very much was to happen, and even now, as I look back on my last six months at the theatre, I am filled with emotion at the amount of affection and kindness shown to me, not only by the staff, patrons and actors, but by people in so many walks of life. This took me completely by surprise for, although I realised that after 46 years there would be some reaction, possibly a few kind letters and maybe a farewell lunch, I had done no more than my job during the course of which I had been rewarded by making so many friends and by the emergence of the Alex to its present status.

The first event, before the announcement that I was to retire, occurred when I re-visited my Bournemouth pantomime in February. They knew, of course, that with the change in policy this would be my last pantomime there, or indeed elsewhere, and several of the artistes sensed that perhaps the year might see my retirement.

Nevertheless, although most of that company, led by Leslie Crowther and Jack Tripp, had worked for me in the same subject for the two previous years, it came as a complete, but very pleasant, surprise when, after a speech by my old friend and great pantomime producer, Frank Adey, I was presented with a lovely wine cooler on which were inscribed the words — "You should have been in last night."

These were the ones which many of them knew I said would be inscribed on my tomb, for whenever I was "in front" things invariably went wrong, or the show 'died', and as soon as I went backstage this was the phrase used by each member of the cast.

Soon afterwards, following speeches by Frank Ifield and Patrick Cargill, I received from the Birmingham cast and orchestra the illuminated address to which I have already referred.

In May my retirement was announced and both the *Birmingham Mail* and *Post* tell me they received, as I did, a very large number of letters, some of which they were good enough to publish. One of my first enclosed a pair of cuff-links engraved with the masks of comedy and tragedy which, said the donor, were "in appreciation of many happy hours spent at the Alex"— a sentiment re-iterated many times over. Many papers in the area gave complimentary coverage with an especially kind one from Fred Norris in the *Birmingham Mail*, and the *Post* honoured me with a leader.*

Many kind remarks were made to me. I enjoyed the one made by a patron who told me that a friend of hers had retired three months ago and then, putting her hand on my shoulder, added, "He's dead and buried!" Another blamed the government! They have been blamed for many things but this, I felt, was unfair.

From then onwards life was punctuated by a series of parties. The first was given by Lorna and her husband, Gordon, at their week end caravan site. Lorna, our second in command in the Box Office,** is an irrepressible person who could so organise a funeral that everyone, including, in all probability, the corpse, would enjoy themselves! It was a great party and consisted, apart from Lorna, of Joan Vaughton, her delightful parents and her sister, Ira; Elsa, very circumspect when carrying out her box office duties but equally uninhibited on these occasions; Sal, the only member of the box office staff with whom I can discuss cricket; Selema, the best telephonist (and that includes a multitude of duties) in the business. Her exact nationality has never been entirely resolved. Basically Arabic,

*On reading these words again I must repeat that no one was more surprised than I at the goodwill and kindness I received, so I hope I do not sound too self satisfied or indeed conceited.

**They refer to themselves as 'the ticket factory'.

190

she is, nevertheless, entitled to wear a Jewish 'Shield of David', a French beret and a kilt. Jackie, my secretary, remembers arriving at the party and knows she got home safely but recollects little in between. The volatile Peggy Ashby added greatly to the occasion. A versatile artiste, she often appeared in our repertory productions and started her career as a dancer with us. To round off a happy day, they made me the gift of some most attractive shirts (later in the year they presented me with most of the clothes I stood up in — dress suit and underpants excepted — to make my farewell speech).

Another happy recollection of that day was of the beautifully inscribed cake made by Pam, the accomplished wife of Norman Wood, our House Manager. He is a worthy successor to Charles Kraus, Brook Sinclair, Colin Burley, Norman Florence, Stephen Sandford, Michael McGrath and Martin Williams (who, tragically, recently died so very young whilst the administrator of the New Theatre, Cardiff, when on the threshold of an outstanding career). Norman has a delightful manner, is a wizard at figures, possesses a tremendous fund of knowledge and, although only young, "you mention it ..... and he's done it". Mike Bullock and I once decided to discuss a subject of which even he could know nothing — the obscure one of 'sewers'. This mention immediately reminded Norman of the occasion when an agent offered him a band engagement which he could not accept as he was, at that time, working down the sewers! He went on to recall a party he had once attended down a sewer and, never lost for words (to put it mildly), held forth at great length on the subject. I did score off him once though, when he told a long story, the gist of which was that he once got locked up in a railway carriage for a long period with a goat. After the story had proceeded for what seemed like hours, in desperation I asked, "Did the goat mind?" This stilled even Norman's tongue! His memory is not infallible, and not long before I left I asked him to let me retire a happy man by buying himself a notebook. He did, and I believe in due course he may even use it! In case these remarks might convey a contrary impression, I hasten to add that I am extremely fond of Norman.

Soon after Lorna's outing I had a lovely day with them at the Vaughtons' family cottage in Wales, only marred for me by Lorna's insistence that we all hired double bicycles to ride down

Barmouth front. I shared one with Selema who never put her foot on the pedals, and as a result my retirement date was almost advanced by several weeks! It was a very happy day and I realised, once again, how fortunate I was to have so many friends.

As July 30 drew near I was interviewed on the Jack de Manio programme, on Radio Birmingham, and on Nationwide by Tom Coyne who expertly combined talking to me with flashing over to the theatre to speak to some of the artistes who were appearing that day in my Gala Performance. Just after I retired Ed Doolan, of BRMB, who has done so much to help the theatre in general and the Alex in particular, gave me an equally expert interview, mostly about matters non-theatrical, which made a very pleasant change.

On the day following my retirement Anthony Everitt, of the *Birmingham Post*, gave a cocktail party for me attended largely by people connected with the theatre, TV or associated activities, which was a most enjoyable occasion. That evening the Playgoers' Club put on a wine and coffee evening at which they presented me with a most attractive and useful wallet inside which was a substantial cheque. Several members, old friends of mine, gave me personal presents. I was, needless to say, extremely touched and gratified.

Later in the year the Civic Society honoured me with a scroll to add to the gold medal they awarded me in 1968. One of the happiest events was a complimentary supper given me by the Midlands Arts Centre for Young People. The Sutton Coldfield Photographic Society, who had taken photographs of our pantomime dress rehearsals for many years, made me a presentation of one of their silver spoons, and to end a year, which had been nothing if not eventful, and in which I had already received the Queen's Jubilee Medal, I was honoured by being elevated from the Order of the British Empire to that of Companion of the Order.

But these were preceded by a tremendous event, a Gala Performance, given with the backing of the Council of Management. A special brochure programme containing 58 pages, which entailed weeks of hard work, was produced by Michael Bullock and Jackie in conjunction with Alan Davies (a fellow cricket enthusiast) of the printers, John Goodman & Sons Ltd.

It contained, on the first inside page, a very kind message from Laurence Olivier, which is reproduced at the beginning of this book, and one from Anna Neagle. On the last, in their own inimitable style, was one from Morecambe and Wise. It also included a short history of the theatre, a biography of myself, a list of all the repertory and pantomime artistes who had played for me, interspersed with advertisements, which mostly included kind remarks about myself.

The ontire organieation of tho porformanco, a most formid able task, was in the more than capable hands of Alan Curtis who assembled a wonderful cast whose names, along with many who helped, were included in the two middle pages of the programme which I append at the end of the book. All of them, including the orchestra, superbly led by Peter Day, who had to conduct the show with only one rehearsal, gave their services, as did virtually the entire staff. A wonderful and in fact quite unique show resulted and was played to a capacity audience which included the Lord Mayor, Councillor Freda Cocks and many local and theatre notabilities.

It began at 7.30 p.m. and when Leslie Crowther, who had also compered much of the show, appeared last, it was 12.15 a.m. Even so, he achieved the remarkable feat of getting the audience 'rolling in the aisles'. It is a great tribute to Alan and all con- cerned that only a few people (with transport problems) left before the end, and a large number stayed on to attend a buffet supper. A happy thought was the appearance of all the members of the staff, not otherwise engaged* at the curtain call.

I then came on to give the speech which I had been dreading for weeks, and indeed had wondered whether I would be emotionally capable of making. For some weeks I had been recalling the words spoken by David Garrick at his last perform-

---

*Joyce Pegg only just found time to appear in the photograph of the Final Curtain in this book. She is a wonderful and invaluable person who came originally to help with the books on the understanding that she did not work on Saturday mornings. Not only has she done so ever since, but has taken over a multitude of duties. They include the voluntary ones of visiting sick members of the staff or sending them flowers and organising cards on staff birthdays. I was delighted to know, from a letter she wrote me just before I retired (for neither of us is very good at speaking our deep feelings), that she reciprocated at least some of the deep admiration I feel for her.

ance which were, "This is to me a very awful moment; it is no less than parting for ever with those from whom I have received the greatest kindness and favours and on the spot where that kindness and those favours were enjoyed." These words seemed so very apt, but because the evening had been made so happy for me, my task was made much easier and it was unnecessary to use this theme.

Before making my speech Leslie Crowther presented me with a number of gifts which included a tape recorder (one of many staff gifts) on which it had been arranged to tape the performance, and a book containing messages from hundreds of actors which I shall always treasure..

It was an evening I, and I am sure none of those present, will ever forget, and is perhaps best summed up by remarks in just a few of the very many letters I received afterwards.

One from Peter Arculus* ended by saying, "Birmingham audiences seldom stand en masse — in doing so spontaneously for you last night, they unquestionably bestowed on you its own elusive accolade."

Another, from an inveterate and much travelled theatre-goer, Max Berner, said, "I am now in my 82nd year and retired last March after 62 years in business which included three journeys round the world. In a number of countries I visited I attended many 'final functions', 'last appearances', 'farewell parties' and listened to many valedictory talks, but none comparable to the emotional and heart-warming greeting of last night's well deserved tribute to you. To the end of time, July 24th 1977 will be a 'Red Letter Day' in your life of devoted service to the Theatre. The standing ovation and the spontaneous singing of "Auld Lang Syne" demonstrated the affection and esteem of the vast audience."

Richard Leech, the accomplished actor, who graduated with a medical degree from Dublin University and worked for me soon afterwards at Hereford, wrote in an article in *World Medicine*, which I would blush to include in full, "to be a Salbergian was the non-pareil because Derek was part of a family

*At the time I had never met Peter Arculus, who is senior science master at Solihull School. I have since seen him playing, quite brilliantly, Widow Twankey in their staff production of "Aladdin.". Produced by the headmaster, Giles Slaughter, who was excellent as Wishee, it was one of the best amateur productions I have seen.

business and he saw to it that his companies became happy families............his farewell performance was notable for the waves of affection which inspired the evening and were totally eclipsed by Derek's own restrained and dignified performance at the end."

This gave me great pleasure as did all the letters, but I think the one from which I derived the most came from a dear friend who wrote, "In your farewell speech you said friendship was more important than money   then you must be one of the richest men in the world."

In many ways I think I am for I can say, as did Agatha Christie at the end of her recently published "An Autobiography", "I thank God for my good life and for all the love that has been given to me."

After all, it is not vouchsafed to many men to have possessed a wonderful wife and family, a host of friends and a job which, in spite of some trials and tribulations, has enabled me to enjoy a prolonged love affair.

APPENDIX "A"

The original members of the Council of Management, with brief biographies of them as they appeared in our house magazine at the time, are appended below. Since then many of them have either changed or extended their activities. Edmund King, for example, has retired from the firm of Agar, Bates, Ledsam & Co (now Deloittes) and from the chairmanship of Warwickshire County Cricket Club, but has increased his activities with the MCC in which he now holds one of the most important administrative offices. Robert Oulsnam, who has been the honorary secretary to the Council since its inception, has since formed his own very flourishing estate business, Robert Oulsnam & Co. John Owen has left the Warwickshire cricket staff.

Jack Carney Smith, sadly, died before he was able to attend a meeting and his place has never been filled but the other members are still serving.

EDMUND H. KING, F.C.A.

(Chairman). The senior partner of Agar, Bates, Ledsam & Co., Chartered Accountants: for many years a director of the Alexandra Theatre; elected Chairman of the present Council of Management of the new company; serves on the board of two public companies and is a director of a further twenty companies.

A keen sportsman, he played cricket for Warwickshire in the 1920's and also as a hockey player, played in the final trial for England also in the 1920's; he is now the chairman of the Warwickshire County Cricket Club and a very important member of MCC Committees. *(He had, of course, been a member of the previous board.)*

MISS H. NANCY BURMAN, M.A.

Miss Burman was born in Edgbaston and educated at Malvern Girls' College. Stage Director of the Basil C. Langton Company 1941/46; Production Manager Shakespeare Memorial Theatre, as it was then called, in 1946/49; Assistant Director of Birmingham Repertory Theatre 1949/61; Administrator 1961/64; member of Drama Panel, Arts Council of Great Britain from 1966; Life Governor, Birmingham University; member of

National Theatre Board, member of Executive on Council of Cannon Hill Arts Centre; member of Victoria Theatre (Theatre in the Round), Stoke on Trent.

J. CARNEY-SMITH

Born in Birmingham. Prior to R.A.F. service, a director of a printing firm. After the war, Chairman and Managing Director of Elliott Advertising—now merged to form Cogent-Elliott Limited; Vice-Chairman of The Birmingham Federation of Boys' Clubs; Chairman of the Committee responsible for Midnight Matinees presented at the Alexandra Theatre for fifteen years, during which time the sum of £35,000 was raised for the Federation; Past President of Birmingham Publicity Association and Council Member of Marjory Fry Trust (discharged prisoners).

EDWIN H. HEAPE

Born in Burton on Trent and resident in Birmingham since 1948; civil servant; member of the Alexandra Playgoers Club (now the Birmingham (Alexandra) Theatre Club) since 1950; Chairman of The Playgoers Club from 1954 to present day; founder member of federation of Playgoers Society of Great Britain in 1957—still actively interested as conference delegate; has particular affection for the Alex, and is also actively concerned with the welfare of ex-servicemen.

ROBERT M. OULSNAM, F.A.L.P.A., A.I.A.S.

(Secretary). Born in Barnt Green, where he now resides, educated at Chipping Camden Grammar School. A well-known Birmingham estate agent; partner in the firm of H. Donald Dixon, Barnard & Dobson, Auctioneers, Estate Agents, Surveyors and Valuers. Chairman of Bromford Housing Association—at present building £3,000,000 worth of houses and flats; director of a number of property companies; was ENSA Advanced Agent for Southern India during the war; apart from theatrical business interests, was a professional musician and has broadcast on numerous occasions. He instigated and negotiated with the City and Developers for the present extension being built at the front of the theatre, this to ensure adequate theatre frontage on Suffolk Street. A member of the Association of 41 Club (Ex-Tablers).

JOHN M.B. OWEN
The youngest member of the Council of Management. Born in Knowle where he is now residing, educated at Yarlet Hall, Stafford. Up to National Service trained to be an auctioneer; after National Service, a member of the TA during which time he completed the now famous Nijmegen March in Holland (one hundred miles in four days); joined the County Ground Administrative Staff (Warwickshire Football Pool) 1961; Social Secretary of Warwickshire County Cricket Supporters' Association for many years; Secretary of the Warwickshire Supporters' Social Club since its conception; a keen tennis player.

ALAN DAVID WISEMAN, A.M.I.P.
Born in Birmingham and educated at Solihull School. Joint Managing Director of David S. Wiseman & Son Limited— founded by his father, David S.F. Wiseman, OBE, a well-known city figure and for many years a director of the Alexandra Theatre, during which time he gave it invaluable support. Alan Wiseman is President of Alvechurch Football Club (although he no longer plays); farms extensive land at Weatheroak; enjoys hunting with the West Warwick Farmers' Foxhounds.

The original city representatives were:

Alderman Stanley BLEYER   )
Alderman Ernest HORTON   ) all of whom are still members
Alderman V.G. SIMPSON   )
Alderman A.M. BEAUMONT DARK
Alderman J.S. MEADOWS
Alderman Harold TYLER

in addition to the first three, present city representatives are:

Councillor G.A. GOPSILL
Councillor John SEVER   (now an MP having recently won
                             the by-election at Ladywood)
Councillor E.J. FRANKLIN

198

APPENDIX "B"

REPERTORY PLAYERS FROM 1927

1927

Producer: SIDNEY PEASE

Players:

Henry Hallatt	Cameron Hall	Victor Fairley
Prudence Vanbrugh	Sheila MacEvoy	(stage manager)
Karen Stanley-Alder	Maisie Crowley	Muriel Henshaw
Max Avieson	Arthur Rigby,	Harry Brayne
Norman Leyland	the younger	Janet Jordan
Janet Hodson	Harry Tresham	Edward G. Wood
Nancy Tetley	Harry Scott	Frank Moore
Arthur Bawtrey	Morval Carr	

1928

Producers: GERALD SAFFREY and F.V. MAXWELL-STEWART

Players:

Henry Hallatt	Maisie Crowley	Victor Fairley
Karen Stanley-Alder	Rita John	(stage manager)
Vernon Fortescue	Nancy Tetley	James C. Prodger
Arthur Rigby,	Edward Morton	Daphne Wellings
the younger	Daisie Mitchell	Stella Camberian
John Drew-Carran	Milton Vaughan	Edward J. Wood
Cameron Hall	Percy Braithwaite	Fred Essex
Sheila MacEvoy		

1929

Producer: GERALD SAFFERY

Players:

Bruce Belfrage	Everley Russell-Gregg	Lionel Scott
Faith Liddle	Daisie Mitchell	(stage manager)
Cherry Hardy	Jocelyn Huband	Bushill Matthews
Stella Florance	Kathleen O'Dell	Henry Lewis
Ruth Robinson	Sheila Raynor	Cyril L. Musto
Nesta Lloyd	Phyllis Shand	Douglas Vigors
Horace Wentworth	Eileen Beldon	Mickey Brantford
David Mackane	John Blake	Members of the
Robert Wallace	Joan Preston	Birmingham Amateur

199

| Claude Saunders | Madge Lackland | Dramatic Federation |
| John Lauriston | | |

1930

Producers: GERALD SAFFERY and J.G. MAINE

Players:

Rupert Harvey	H.M. Vanderfelt	Joel Harris
Karen Stanley-Alder	Nancy Tetley	Peggy Hughes
Frank Pettingell	(stage manager)	Henry Lewis
Terence Maxwell	Cyril Musto	Gwen Carlier
Anita Carol	Arthur Freeman	Gladys Beston
Efga Myers	Wendy Lessar	Mary Richards
Peter Coleman	Edwin Turner	Rosalind Copley
Basil Bowen	Rita Cave	Sheila Crocker
Julia Hart	Godfrey Baseley	Edward J. Wood
Aletha Orr		

1931

Producer: GERALD SAFFERY

Players:

Raymond Huntley	Mary Gauntlett	H. Celestine Print
Doreen Moss	Joan Preston	Dorothy Neville
Claude Bailey	H.M. Vanderfelt	Muriel Henshaw
Frederick Rivenhall	Frank S. Henry	Mary Cutting
Laurence Rushworth	Hazel Carnegie	Arthur Freeman
Christian Milne-Thomson	Nita Valerie	Adrienne Andrews
Florence Tressillian	Alfred Richards	Sidney Renneff
Joan Denton	(stage manager)	Phyllis Bailey
Aletha Orr	Gerald Lennan	Vera Ashe
Will H. Glaze	(stage manager)	

1932

Producer: GERALD SAFFERY

Players:

Henry Hallatt	Hilary Fisher-White	Gerald Lennan
Ennis Lawson	Harold Mortlake	F.V. Maxwell-Stewart,
Helene Simon	June Wenner	(stage manager)
Laurence Rushworth	H.M. Vanderfelt	Joan Pat Smith
Christian Milne-Thomson	Mary Gauntlett	Diana Marks
Ernest Holloway		

200

1933

Producers: SIDNEY PEASE, CLIVE WOODS, GEORGE OWEN

Players:

Betty Bowden	Paddy Chalmers	Phil Marco
Clive Woods	Kathleen St. John	Muriel Henshaw
Alice Darch	Valerie Larg	Marjorie Lyon
Thelma Fenwick	Gerald Lennan,	Duncan Blyth
John Morley	(stage manager)	Arthur Freeman
Phil Ray	F.V. Maxwell-Stewart,	Diana Marks
Eric Howard	(stage manager)	Joan Pat Smith
George Roche	Suzanne Hudson	Mary Tinley
Myrtle Richardson		

1934

Prodcer: GEORGE OWEN

Players:

Phil Ray	George S. Wray	Diana Marks
John Morley	Gerald Lennan	Molly Randle
Eric Howard	Kathleen St. John	Lucy Griffiths
Reginald Newson	Hal Henshaw	Joel Harris
Anthony Viccars	Brian Hayle,	Gwen Muspratt
Betty Bowden	(stage manager)	Sidney Renneff
Thelma Fenwick	Mary Tinley	Joan Pat Smith
Valerie Larg	Robert Leighton	Duncan Blyth
Paddy Chalmers		

1935

Theatre being re-built

1936

Producer: GEORGE OWEN

Players:

Barbara Spicer	Aletha Orr	Lucy Griffiths
Kathleen St. John	Lee Fox	Sheila Crocker
Wilfred Babbage	John Arnold	Trude Peake
Brefni O'Rorke	Penelope Shaw	Philip Frost
Campbell Singer	Gerald Lennan	Douglas Kerr
Moira Cusack	Bruce Walker	Robert Anderson
Linden Travers	Gerald Cuff	Peggy Sergeant
Anthony Viccars	Joan Preston	Cecil Mumford

201

Betty Bowden
H.M. Vanderfelt
Stanley Illsley
Lorraine Clewes
James Viccars

Nora Parsons
Michael Peake
Duncan Blyth
William Munton

Anthony Barrie
Brian Shelley
Frank Pettitt
Sidney Renneff

1937

Producer: GEORGE OWEN

Players:

Brefni O'Rorke
Dorothy Galbraith
Kathleen St. John
Marjorie Battiss
James Viccars
Moira Cusack
Mary Graham
Sidney Renneff
Gwen Muspratt
Viola Glover
Elsie Goulding
Anthony Viccars
Arthur Rees
H.M. Vanderfelt

Sheila Millar
Ethel Hope Johnstone
Pamela Sharpe
Brian Hayle,
(stage manager)
Philip Garston-Jones
Frances Macklin
Robert Anderson
Anne Pichon
William Roderick
Eric Howard
Kathleen Holdernesse
Thomas Reynor
Michael Eden

Peggy Ditcham
Bryan Shelley
Robin Graham
Gladys Payne
Doris Pallett
Stanley Illsley
F.V. Maxwell-Stewart
Gerald Lennan
Yvonne le Dain
Lorraine Clewes
Lucy Griffiths
Cecil Mumford
Mary Tinley
John Taylor

1938

Producer: GEORGE OWEN

Players:

Winifred Griffiths
Diana Caird
Norman Melrose
James Viccars
John Young
Stanley Illsley
Sheila Millar
Brian Shelley
Eric Howard
Anthony Viccars
Moira Cusack

Bruce Humphries
F.V. Maxwell-Stewart
Anne Pichon
Kenneth More
Robert Anderson
Brefni O'Rorke
Kathleen St. John
Vivien Grenville
Gerald Lennan
Thomas Reynor
Mary Graham

Brian Hayle,
(stage manager)
Sidney Renneff
Lorraine Clewes
Peter Rosser
Phillipa Grayling
Lee Fox
Bruce Walker
Gerald Cuff
Cecil Mumford
Michael Peake

202

1939

Producer: GEORGE OWEN   Associate Producer: PHILIP STAINTON

Players:

Betty Bowden
James Viccars
Florence Hunt
Kathleen Holdernesse
Beryl Johnstone
Peggy Emmerton
Kenneth More
Brian Hayle,
(stage director)
Joan Pat Smith
Norman Melrose
Kathleen St. John
John Farries-Moss

Nancy Roberts
Kay Delius
Sheila Millar
Lee Fox
Antony Rutter,
(stage manager)
Gwen Muspratt
Anne Pichon
Anthony Viccars
Robert Ginns
Gerald Cuff
Elizabeth Sumner

Douglas Quayle
Vernon Fortescue
Cecil Mumford
Noel Johnstone
Peter Rosser
Ninka Dolega
Gerald Lennan
Sheila Brownrigg
Mollie Cooper
Aletha Orr
Phil Ray
Robert Anderson

1940

Producer: GEORGE OWEN

Players:

Betty Bowden
Anthony Viccars
Antony Rutter
Penelope Shaw
Malcolm Russell
Gerald Cuff
Robert del Kyrke
Elisabeth Crowfoot,
(stage manager)
Gwen Muspratt
Cecil Mumford
Thelma Hughes
Felicity Devereux
Brenda Bruce
Robert Ginns
Kathleen St. John

Thomas Raynor
Lee Fox
Mary Graham
Lorraine Clewes
Robert Long
Barbara Holtham
Gwen Barryman
Marjorie Lyon
Eileen Draycott
Philip Howard
Philip Stainton
Pamela Edmunds
Alan Haines
Marjorie Matthews
Russell Waters
Robert Anderson

Lucy Griffiths
Barry Ferguson
Philip Thornley
Vernon Fortescue
Phil Ray
James Viccars
Beryl Johnstone
Jess Sweet
Audry Hesketh
Brian Hayle,
(stage director)
Joan Carter
Jayne Grey
Axel Moller
Gordon Dane

1941

Producer: GEORGE OWEN

Players:

Betty Bowden   Lee Fox   Robert Anderson

Gerald Lennan
Kathleen St. John
Jayne Grey
Pamela Blake
Guy Verney
Barbara Holtham
Vernon Fortescue
Marjorie Matthews
Hazel Tucker
Robert Ginns
Barrie Cameron
Pamela Gibson

Gwen Berryman
Sandford Gorton
Ruth Robinson
Vittorio Rietti
Brian Hayle,
   (stage director)
Denis Goacher
Eileen Draycott
Aletha Orr
Lucy Griffiths
Bernard Sarron
Pamela Edmunds

Joan Duan
Alan Haines
Elisabeth Crowfoot,
   (stage manager)
Philip Stainton
Nora Parsons
Robert Victor
Malcolm Russell
William Lloyd
David Read
Betty Mallett

1942

Producer: GEORGE OWEN

Players:

Betty Bowden
Gwen Berryman
Audrey Hesketh
Gerald Lennan
Wilfred Boyle
Robert Anderson
Vernon Fortescue
David Langley
Penelope Shaw
Richard Lancaster
Elisabeth Crowfoot,
   (stage director)
Duncan Ross

Kathleen St. John
William Senior
Emerton Court
Joan Haythorne
David Read
Jayne Grey
Hazel Tucker
Eileen Draycott
Dennis Goacher,
   (stage manager)
Richard Hannan
Andrews Buck
Francis Drake

Lionel Dunn
Hubert Langley
Philip Stainton
Maxine Audley
Michael Bird
Marjorie Matthews
Richard Tregea,
   (stage manager)
Aletha Orr
Joan Salberg
Robert Ginns
Alec Mason
Barbara Holtham

1943

Producer: GEORGE OWEN

Players:

Leon Darrell
Eileen Draycott
David Ashe
Robert Ginns
Philip Stainton
Geoffrey Miller
Barrie Cameron
Betty Bowden
Kathleen St. John
Hazel Court

Dennis Goacher
Joan Miller
Bettina Forest
Vernon Fortescue
Richard Lancaster,
   (stage manager)
Hubert Langley
Vanda Godsell
Iris Darbyshire
Jayne Grey

Eric Rutherford
William Senior
Robert Anderson
Sylvia Williams
Andrews Buck
Jeanne Butler
Angela Wyndham-Lewis
Gerald Lennan
Douglas Vigors
Lisa Brunelle

204

1944

Producer: GEORGE OWEN

Players:

Sylvia Williams	Denis Goacher	Beryl Johnstone
Philip Stainton	Vanda Godsell	Frank Pettitt
Iris Russell	Maud Gill	Betty Bissett
Jayne Grey	Robin Bailey	Eileen Draycott
Jimmy Viccars	Anthony Davies	Pauline Loring
Marianna Harvey	Hugh Kelly	Andrews Buck
Joan Miller	Richard Lancaster,	Lionel Dunn
William Senior	(stage manager)	Vernon Fortescue
Janet Joye		

1945

Producer: GEOFFREY STAINES
Associate Producer: PHILIP STAINTON

Players:

Vernon Fortescue	Eileen Draycott	Richard Littledale
Pauline Loring	Patrick Alleyn	Cecil Mumford
Trevor Denis	Leslie Parker	Hugh Kelly
Vanda Godsell	Larry Noble	Iris Russell
Gladys Tudor	Nellie Sheffield	Doris Pallett
William Senior	Jayne Grey	Kenneth Thornett
Charles Mardel	Beryl Johnstone	Robin Bailey
Tom Gray	Patricia Bailey	Gwen Muspratt
Marianna Harvey	Betty Bissett,	Ena King
Margaret Ward	(stage manager)	Bertram Dench

1946

Producer: GEOFFREY STAINES   *Associate Producer:* JOHN GABRIEL

Players:

Andrew Osborn	Margaret Ward	Geoffrey Quaife
Gennie Graham	Bruce Baker	Margaret St. Barbe-West
Hamilton Dyce	Vera Gould	Philip Lennard
Monica Verney	Ann Titheradge	Ann Lancaster
Peter Norris	Eileen Draycott	Cyril Wentzel
Elizabeth Kentish	Ronald Lane,	Cecil Mumford
Brian Hayle,	(stage manager)	Alec McCowen
(stage director)		

1947

Producer: JOHN GABRIEL

Players:

Geoffrey Quaife	Leslie Yeo	Pauline Williams
Eileen Draycott	Ethel Ramsay	Jennifer Edmonds,
Brian Hayle,	Ronald Lane,	(asst. stage manager)
(stage director)	(stage manager)	Meg Maxwell
Bertram Dench	Raymond Francis	A.J. Brown
Larry Noble	Noel Owen	Stephen Ward
Cecil Mumford	Barrie Cameron	Roy Hannah
Laurence Rushworth	H.M. Vanderfelt	Joan Painter

1948

Producer: JOHN GABRIEL

Players:

Neil Firkins	Betty Grant,	Anthony Niner
Raymond Francis	(asst. stage manager)	Roy Hannah
Stephen Ward	Gwen Berryman	Frank Royde
Ronald Lane,	Jean Harvey	Robert Blow
(stage manager)	Herbert Vanderfelt	Alec McCowen
Jennifer Edmonds	Ted Butterfield	Brian Hayle,
Lister Skelton	Colin Laurence	(stage director)
William Avenell	Pauline Williams	Hilary Vernon
Dick Turner	Geoffrey Chater	Jack Pulman
William Warwick	Larry Noble	Laurence Rushworth
Val Vaux	Gwen Harris	Nan Marriorr-Watson
Elspeth Duxbury	Mysie Monte	Victor Heath
John Derrick	Fred Beck	Avril Conquest
Eileen Draycott	John Gabriel	Maud Gill
Philip Lennard		

1949

Producer: PETER POWELL   *Associate Producer:* FRANK DERMODY

Players:

Sydney Arnold	Michael Harris	John Hanby
Geoffrey Mason	John Le Mesurier	Jean Owen
Con Kenna	David Aylmer	John Blake
Geoffrey Chater	Roy Hannah	Ray Langford
Eileen Draycott	Peter Vaughan	Derek Reade
Peter Greenwell	Betty Nelson	Susan Wade,
Elspeth Duxbury	Theo Bryan	(stage manager)

Pauline Jackson	Mary Anderton	Kay Drummond
Ida Shepley	Elizabeth Kentish	Jenny Trafford
Richard Turner	Alice Hannam	John Evans
Alex McDonald	Pamela Abbott	Colin Laurence
Michael Maddox	Leslie Allen,	Stella Hamilton
Robert Ginns	(stage manager)	Dorothy Rolston
George Holding	Peter Wilde	Lawrence Ayris
Michael Spokes	Michael Martin	John Crocker
Campbell Grey	Anthony Niner	Leslie Sands
Pauline Williams	Gillian Stanton	Jimmy Holland
Brian Hayle,	Patricia Driscoll	Joanne Davies,
(stage director)	Dennis Egan	(stage manager)
John Blake	Earl Cameron	Geoffrey Mason
Arthur Lane	John Clifford	Rosa Picken
Philip Howard	Dorothy Lamond	

1950

Producer: PETER POWELL *Associate Producer:* MICHAEL FINLAYSON

Players:

Pauline Williams	Nicholas Meredith	Peter Rosser
Stella Hamilton	Susan Wade,	Cynthia Cruxton
Elspeth Duxbury	(stage manager)	Paul Morgan
Eileen Draycott	Peter Vaughan	Ian Middleton
Leslie Allen,	James Kenney	Gerald Saffery
(stage manager)	John Moffatt	Leslie Sands
Harold Lang	Alan Wilson	Colin Laurence
Keith Faulkner	John Franklyn	Edward Waddy
Zena Walker	Beryl Cruxton	Herbert Vanderfelt
Julia Lang	Brian Stuart	William Moore
Gregory Scott	Betty Nelson	Tony Davies
Vernon Fortescue	Ingrid Burke	Stewart Ruttledge
Kenneth Crow	Jean Harvey	Winifred Bradfield
John Le Mesurier	John Franklyn	Peter Zander
Brian Hayle,	Theo Bryan	Marie Church
(stage director)	Michael Redington	Hugh O'Neill
Tony Steedman	Terence Alexander	

1951

Producer: PETER POWELL
Associate Producer: VERNON FORTESCUE & MICHAEL FINLAYSON

Players:

David Dodimead	John Taylor	Martin Quinn

207

Nigel Fitzgerald
Hugh Kelly
Patricia Kerry
Herbert Vanderfelt
Brian Stuart
Derek Prentice
John Hobday
Janet Latimer
Alec Roebuck
Shirley Hall
Patricia Grey
Cecil Mumford
Leslie Parker
Griffiths Moss
Stella Hamilton
Eileen Draycott
Brian Hayle,
   (stage director)
Edgar Wreford
Kenneth Crow

Pamela Abbott
Alexander Archdale
Nevill Whiting
Sutton Jones
Rita Cashmore
Victor Heath
Diana Wilding
Alec McCowen
George Skillan
Betty Nelson
Fenella Scott
Stewart Ruttledge,
   (stage manager)
Bertram Shuttleworth
James Hudson
Russell Wood
Eddie Sutch
June Rodney
Clem Coulson

Jeannie Starbuck
Betty Bowden
Ursula Granville
Olwen Griffiths
Antony Cullen
Tony Steedman
Colin Laurence
Patricia Mahoney
Eve Gardiner
John Probert
David Oake
Elspeth Duxbury
Harry Brunning
Kenneth Sterne
Grahame Clifford
June Martin
Arthur Lane
Eleanore Bryan
William Moore

1952

Producer: PETER POWELL   *Associate Producer:* COLIN LAURENCE

Players:

Robert Ginns
Tilsa Page
Tony Steedman
Brian Hayle,
   (stage director)
Pauline Williams
Fred Fisher
John Gooding
Edward Mulhare
Eileen Draycott

Leslie Dunn
Stewart Ruttledge,
   (stage manager)
Carol Hinsley
Harry Crossman
Shirley Hills
Colin Laurence
Anthony Sagar
Patricia Gould
   (asst. stage manager)

Joan Blake
Robert Moreton
John Hobday
Jimmy Holland
Ronald Radd
Leslie Sands
Fenella Scott
Elspeth Duxbury
Philip Dudley
Hugh O'Neill

1953

Producer: PETER POWELL   *Associate Producer:* C.B. PULMAN

Players:

Pauline Williams
Anthony Sagar
Leslie Sands
Brian Hayle,
   (stage director)

Stewart Ruttledge,
   (stage manager)
Peter Vaughan
Malcolm Johnson
Brian Rider

Michael Myatt
John Miller
Ruth Porcher
Pamela Eaves
Rosemary Towler

208

Edward Ballard	William Patrick	Tilsa Page
David Harries	Patricia Kerry	Joan Blake
Donald Lightwood	Emerton Court	Leslie Dunn
Jill Hipkiss	Eileen Draycott	Lawrence Davidson
Muriel Rowan	Jeannette Hutchinson	Frank Veasy
Billie Whitelaw	Ronald Radd	Alec Audley
C.B. Pulman	Roy Astley,	Dawn Belas
Nicholas Meredith	(asst. stage manager)	Edward Mulhare
Pearl Catlin	Jennifer White	Janet Latimer

1954

Producer: PETER POWELL   *Associate Producer:* GERALD CUFF

Players:

Anthony Sagar	Leslie Dunn	Emerton Court
Margaret Stallard	Eileen Draycott	Shirley Cooklin
Pauline Williams	Elspeth Duxbury	John Baddeley
Stewart Ruttledge,	W. Thorpe Devereux	Jeannette Hutchinson
(stage manager)	Deering Wells	Leslie Sands
William Avenell	Edward Ballard	Rex Garner
Ken Freeman	Joan Blake	Peter Rosser
Richard Turner	Roy Astley,	Mary Tennant
Brian Hayle,	(asst. stage manager)	William Warwick
(stage director)		

1955

Producer: PETER POWELL   *Associate Producer:* WILLIAM AVENELL

Players:

Michael Barrington	John Baddeley	Kenneth Thornett
William Avennell,	Ward Williams	John Brown
(stage director)	Ursula O'Leary	Elspeth Duxbury
Julia Somers	Patricia Corfield	Pauline Williams
Leslie Sands	Eileen Draycott	Brenda Jones
Rex Garner	Stewart Ruttledge,	Rosemary Towler
Janet Hollander	(stage manager)	Philip Lennard
John Ormand	Jeanette Hutchinson	Donald Leaver
Robert Chetwyn	Leslie French	Roy Astley,
Erica York	Julia Lang	(asst. stage manager)
Aimee Delamain		

1956

Producer: PETER POWELL   *Associate Producer:* JOHN BARRON

Players:

James Grout
Eileen Draycott
Pauline Williams
Janet Hollander,
   (asst. stage manager)
John Brown
David Crane
Delena Kidd
Joan Berringer
Eunice Blacks
Stewart Weller
Rex Garner
Ward Williams

Eve Michelson
Terry Farrel
Vernon Fortescue
Phyllis Partridge
Patricia Brewer
Michael Barrington
Ursula O'Leary
William Avenell,
   (stage director)
Anne Luce
   (asst. stage manager)
Rosemary Evans

Leslie Dunn
Enid Freeman
Anthony Sagar
Maureen Beck
Leslie Sands
Roy Astley,
   (stage manager)
Annette Hunt
John Lanzer
Norman Johns
Elise Bernard
Judith Whittaker

1957

Producer: PETER POWELL
Associate Producers: ALLAN DAVIS, PETER ALDERSLEY,
WILLIAM AVENELL

Players:

Eileen Draycott
Kathryn Greenaway
Hilary Scotfield
Pauline Bentley
David Ryder
Roy Astley,
   (stage manager)
Anne Godley
Bryan Pringle
John Lanzer
Bernard Hepton
David Baron
Hazel Hughes
Rex Garner
Jean Innes
Anne Coombes
Linda Hayne

Andrew Vale
Ursula Smith,
   (asst. stage manager)
Laurence Bourne
Martin Friend
Laurence Turner
Vivien Merchant
Frank Veasey
Nan Munro
John Brown
Patricia Rogers
Jonathan Matthews
Terence Lodge
Edmond Bennett
Pauline Glenar,
   (asst. stage manager)
Alan Browning

Basil Gill
Geoffrey Lumsden
Hugh Kelly
Barbara Atkinson
Anne Jameson
Tony Steedman
Graham Harper
Stephen Rich
William Avenell,
   (stage director)
Pauline Thompson
Emerton Court
James Lloyd
Georgine Anderson
Michael Robbins
Norma Kaye

210

1958

Producer: PETER POWELL   *Associate Producer:* JORDAN LAWRENCE

Players:

Eileen Draycott	Nancie Jackson	Pauline Thompson,
William Avenell,	Susan Short,	(asst. stage manager)
(stage director)	(dep. stage manager)	John Scott
John Standing	Jeremy Hyams	Carol Hinsley
Roy Astley,	Alison Morris	Georgine Anderson
(stage manager)	Brian Tipping	Donald Carter
Ann Zane	Maureen Tracey	Nicholas Selby
Reginald Gillam	Patricia Rogers	Brian Rawlinson
Judy Black	Brian Kent	Meurig Wyn Jones
John Lanzer	Derek Royle	Clive Vale
Tony Steedman	Arthur McFarlane	Philip Garston Jones
Margaret Denyer		

1959

Producer: PETER POWELL   *Associate Producer:* ALLAN DAVIS

Players:

Meg Wynn Owen	William Avenell,	Trevor Davis
John Standling	(production manager)	Margery Field
Terry Scully	Peter Boretski	Harry Lockart
Alison Morris,	Edward Clayton	Ursula O'Leary
(asst. stage manager)	Allan Izzard	Derek Royle
Penelope Lee	Judy Black	Alan White
Ewan Maclean	Ronald Magill	David Crosse
Roger Redfarn	Tony Steedman	John Boden
Joan Peart	Roy Astley,	Brian Miller
Kathleen St. John	(stage manager)	Rex Garner
Brian Kent	Ross Hutchinson	David Kirk
John Rudling	Richard Turner	

1960

Producers: JOHN RUDLING, GUY VAESEN, OLIVER GORDON,
ANTHONY SHARP, FRANK DUNLOP, RONALD MAGILL,
WILLIAM AVENELL, NANCY POULTNEY, NICHOLAS GARLAND

Players:

Tony Steedman	Alan White,	Bernard Smith
Ian Gane	(asst. stage manager)	Catherine Woodville
Ronald Magill	Alison Morris	Robert O'Leary
Roy Astley	Kate Cameron	David Macmillan

Elspeth Duxbury
Margery Field
Ronald Cunliffe
Anne Cunningham
Richard Hicks
Eileen Draycott
Ursula O'Leary
Helen Dorward
Derek Royle
Terence McSparrow

Judy Parfitt
Paul Dane
Jennifer MacArthur,
  (asst. stage manager)
Pauline Williams
Brian Kent
Heather Canning
Grace Newcombe
Cicely Paget-Bowman

Philip Elsmore
William Avenell,
  (production manager)
Millard Williams
Judy Black
Mary Watson
Peter Farrell
Richard Fox
Tina Matthews

1961

Producers: BASIL DEAN, EDGAR METCALFE, PETER POWELL,
IAN MULLINS, BRIAN BELL, DENNIS RAMSDEN,
ANTHONY SHARP, WILLIAM AVENELL, IAN CURTIES

Players:

Michael Ingham
Philip Garston-Jones
David Macmillan
Frank Woodfield
Judy Parfitt
Eileen Draycott
Beryl Johnstone
Michael Graham
Ross Hutchinson
Philip Elsmore
Heather Canning
Tony Steedman

William Avenell,
  (production manager)
Roy Astley,
  (stage manager)
Anne Aubrey
Pamela Marwood
Derek Royle
Rex Robinson
Brian Kent
Desmond Stokes
Alan White,
  (asst. stage manager)

Eileen Helsby
Richard Hicks
Vanda Godsell
Vincent Ellis
Ian Gane
Arthur Cox
Martin Carroll
Jennifer MacArthur,
  (asst. stage manager)
Gay Cameron
Elspeth Duxbury
Ross Hutchinson

1962

Producers: DAVID PAUL, BERNARD HEPTON, WILLIAM AVENELL,
ANTHONY HOLLAND, MICHAEL INGHAM, WILLIAM GAUNT,
ANNE STUTFIELD, HUGH GOLDIE, OLIVER GORDON

Players:

William Avenell,
  (production manager)
Beryl Johnstone
Allen Green
Michael Hawkins
Roy Astley,
  (stage director)
John Gill
Roslyn Langdon

Michael Julian
Nadine Hanwell
Walter Gennie
Frank Shelley
Ross Hutchinson
Jeffrey Alexander
Pamela Charles
Henry Millin
Eileen Draycott

John Ringrose
John Lennard
Gordon Clyde
Adrienne Finch
Eileen Helsby
Frank Woodfield
Peter Price
Alan White,
  (stage manager)

212

Arthur Cox	Derek Royle	David Daker
Alan Edwards	Roderick Griffiths	John Carlisle
Patricia Prior	Elizabeth Stern,	Patrick Carter
Paul Mead	(asst. stage manager)	Conrad Monk
Heather Canning	Michael Ingham	Frank Millman
Brian Kent	Janet Butlin	Doreen Andrew
Adrian Ropes	Charles Workman	

1963

Producers: JAMES GILLHOULEY, WILLIAM AVENELL,
ANTHONY SHARPE, GEOFFREY EDWARDS,
MICHAEL FINLAYSON, DEREK ROYLE, BERNARD HEPTON,
ANNE STUTFIELD

Players:

Brian Kent	Diana Barrington	Claire Davenport
Alan Partington	Lyn Bartlett,	Henry Manning
Derek Royle	(asst. stage manager)	John Jefferson-Hayes
Janet Whiteside	Olivia Hamnett	John Murray-Scott
Ronald Hooper	William Lyon-Brown	Michael Hawkins
Michael Ingham	David Glover	Eileen Draycott
Anne Angel	Roger Clissold	Timothy Carlton
Ronald Magill	Pamela Greenall	Don Maclean
Peter Cook	Frank Woodfield	Susan Short,
Brian Coburn	William Avenell,	(asst. stage manager)
Terence Ratcliffe	(production manager)	Jane Bond
Arthur Cox	Eileen Helsby	Fred Ferris
Beryl Johnstone	John Leonardt,	Duncan Livingstone
Rosemary Leach	(stage manager)	Doreen Godwin
Conrad Monk	Linda Morgan	Peter Price
Alan White,	Philip Garston-Jones	Michael Julian
(stage director)		

1964

Producers: ALLAN DAVIS, WILLIAM AVENELL, ALAN EDWARDS,
MICHAEL INGHAM, GUY VAESEN, JOHN BARRON,
WILLIAM DAVIS, GEOFFREY OST, DAVID BELLAMY

Players:

Brian Kent	William Morton,	Carolyn Lister,
Janet Whiteside	(stage director)	(asst. stage manager)
Jan Carey	Valerie Van Ost	Elizabeth Paget
Graham Williams,	Leroy Lingwood	Susan Tebbs
(asst. stage manager)	Martin Williams	Frank Woodfield
Michael Behr	Michael Ingham	Anthony Howard

213

Margery Field
Michael Cooke
Malcolm Young
Beryl Johnstone
Pamela Greenall
Paul Marklew
John Alderton

William Avenell,
  (production manager)
Victor Lucas
Jenny Rushton,
  (asst. stage manager)
Ray Mort

Carol Evans,
  (stage manager)
Caroline Monkhouse
Diana Irvine
Patsy Trench
William Ingram

1965

Producers: GEOFFREY EDWARDS, MICHAEL INGHAM,
GEOFFREY OST, OLIVER GORDON, ALLAN DAVIS,
DAVID BELLAMY, ROY PATRICK, PETER ZANDER,
WILLIAM AVENELL, LIONEL HAMILTON, ROBERT CARTLAND

Players:

David Daker
Paul Marklew
Brian Kent
William Morton,
  (stage director)
Roy Patrick
Helen Dorward
Marian Forster
Robert McBain
Patricia Brake
Christopher Dunham
Mary Chirgwin
Geoffrey Denton
Roger Dwyer
Christopher Maudsley
Paulet Tu
Paula Claddo
John Citroen
Geoffrey Edwards
William Avenell,
  (production manager)
Janet Whiteside
Carole Walker
Carol Evans,
  (stage manager)
David Raynor
Allan Weston

Sonja Crosbee,
  (asst. stage manager)
Alvis Cooke,
  (asst. stage manager)
Anthony Mathews
Derek Carpenter
Dennis Spencer
Doreen Keogh
Jennifer Whitworth
Peter Keen
Alan Brown
Victor Woolf
Lee Fox
Jan Carey
Michael Ingham
Frank Woodfield
Paul Carson
Richard Astbury,
  (asst. stage manager)
Peggy Mount
Harold Brookstone,
  (stage manager)
Audrey Noble,
  (stage manager)
Gladys Taylor
George Waring
Elspeth Duxbury

Reginald Long
Marina Martin
Gail Ensor
Gordon Wiseman
Patricia Cooke
Dennis Edwards
Anthony Howard
Ian Beavis
Beryl Johnstone
Patricia Leach
John Pickles
John Roberts
John Bradburn,
  (asst. stage manager)
John Gray
Claire Davenport
Ronald Russell
Malcolm Young
Eric Longworth
Jennifer Wood
Michael Bullock
Varinder Verma
Peter Benson
Paul Smith
Nicholas Brent
Raymond Somerville
Eric Longworth

1966

Producer: MALCOLM FARQUHAR
Associate Producers: WILLIAM AVENELL, ALLAN DAVIS,
MICHAEL INGHAM, DENNIS SPENCER

Players:

Janet Whiteside
Jenny McNae
Ursula O'Leary
William Morton,
(stage director)
Frank Woodfield
Raymond Holden
Clint Morris
Laurence Rew
Michael Behr
Peter Daley,
(asst. stage manger)
Dorothy Bear
Martin Norton
Edward Chapelle
Peggy Mount
Vivien Sherrard
Anthony Healey
Clare Owen
John Maxim

Ronald Russell
David Daker
Richard Hicks
Yvonne Quenet
Reginald Long
Barbara Atkinson
Alan Wassall
Hazel Hughes
Catherine Johnston
John Maxim
William Avenell,
(production manager)
Margery Field
Jennifer Whitworth,
(stage manager)
Nicholas Walker
Richard Turner
Paul Mills
Josephine Tewson
Jennifer Hill

Michael Bullock,
(stage director)
Daphne Heard
Elna Pearl
Jennifer Foster
Anthony Donovan,
(stage manager)
Elizabeth Choice
Desmond Gill
Elaine Page
Melanie Walker
Graham Williams
John Rowe
Rosamund Burne
Katherine Harvey,
(asst. stage manager)
Dorothy Primrose
Peggy Ann Wood
Beverley Collins
Peggy Aitchison

1967

Producer: MALCOLM FARQUHAR
Associate Producers: HUGH GOLDIE, LIONEL HAMILTON,
DENNIS SPENCER

Players:

James Copeland
David Simeon
Anne Rutter
Douglas Wilmer
Walter Gitzgerald
Jenny McNae
Jo Richardson,
(asst. stage manager)
Douglas Wilmer
Christopher Robbie
Michael Behr
George Waring
Raymond Graham

Michael Bullock,
(stage director)
Joan Huet,
(stage manager)
Nicholas Smith
John Nathan Turner,
(stage manager)
Sharon Gurney
David Lloyd Meredith
Joseph Greig
Gillian Francis
Marion Forster
William Avenell

Kathleen Michael
Vivien Sherrard
Michael Reeves
Sarah Golding
Antony Linford
Anthony Ainley
Frank Woodfield
Raymond Bowers
Rosemary Leach
Richard Greene
Anthony Howard
Peggy Aitchison
Christopher Dunham

215

Rosamund Burne
Ursula O'Leary
Madelaine Christie
Dermot Walsh
Michael Napier Brown
Elizabeth Choice
Simon Williams
Michael Gwynne
Marius Goring
Dennis Spencer

Janet Hargreaves
Jack Watling
Naunton Wayne
Desmond Gill
Janet Whiteside
John Figg,
  (stage manager)
John Gale
Kathleen St. John

Jacqueline Maude
Trevor Smith
Howard Lang
Joanne Hayden,
  (asst. stage manager)
Gerald Tarrant
Brian Kent
Annabel Littledale
Jack Allen

1968

Producers: DENNIS SPENCER, JENNY McNAE, TERENCE LODGE, NANCY POULTNEY, EDGAR METCALFE

Players:

Mark Heath
Michael Reeves
Paul Marklew
James Hazeldine
Peter Bissell
Peter Wright,
  (asst. stage manager)
Gillian Francis
Victor Woolf
David Lloyd Meredith
Dennis Spencer

Bernard Shine
John Guest
Peter Biddle
Frank Woodfield
Peter Templar,
  (asst. stage manager)
Barry Lineham
Margery Field
Jenny McNae
Noelle Finch
Terence Lodge

Michael Bullock,
  (production manager)
Margaret Robertson
Patrick Parnell
Olivia Farjeon
Raymond Bowers
James Leonard
Joanne Hayden,
  (stage manager)
Jacqueline Firth
Valantine Dyall

1969

Producers: JENNY McNAE, GEOFFREY EDWARDS, JOHN GORDON ASH, KEITH BEATTIE, DENNIS SPENCER, ANTHONY CORNISH

Players:

Adam Faith
Daphne Riggs
Derek Seaton
Sylvia Howard,
  (stage manager)
Brian Hewlett
Bernard Shine
Jenny McNae
Adele Strong
Nadine Hanwell
Henry Moxon

Anna Cooke,
  (stage manager)
Isobel Stuart
Helen Dorward
Rosemary MacVie
Lynette Erving
Jill Meers
Robert Lankeshear
David Downer
George Cooper
Rosemary Davis

John Quartermaine
Amelia Baynton
Adrian Pearson
Douglas Malcolm
Frank Woodfield
Margery Field
Madelaine Mills
Michael Bullock,
  (production manager)
Clement McCallin
Dennis Spencer

Peter Gregory,   Penelope Shaw   David Bedard
(asst. stage manager)   Mary Laine   James Tomlinson
George Woolley   Richard Quick   Rosamund Burne
Emerys Jones   Alan Buckman,   Sally Templar
Derek Anders   (dep. stage manager) Peter Macknel
Kathleen Worth   Norman Comer   Philip Garston-Jones
Tina Roach   Carolyn Lister   Sheila Brownrigg
Ursula O'Leary   Jennifer Hill   Ronald Bain
Simon Browne   Raymond Bowers   Noelle Finch
Carmen Blank   Lionel Hamilton

1970

Producers: KEITH BEATTIE, ROGER CLISSOLD, DEREK SEATON,
GEOFFREY EDWARDS, DENNIS SPENCER, RONALD MAGILL,
DOUGLAS NEILL, NANCY POULTNEY

Players:

Amelia Bayntun   Mary Laine   John Griffiths,
Helen Dorward   Aileen Raymond   (asst. stage manager)
Judith Fellows   Hilda Schroder   Janice Younger,
Nicholas Brent   Jeanette Tomsett   (asst. stage manager)
Geoffrey Davion   Christopher Tranchell Nick Frost,
Allan Haley   Susan Maddock,   (dep. stage manager)
Brian Kent   (asst. stage manager) Heather McConachie,
Michael Lomax   Sue Derrick   (dep. stage manager)
Adrian Reynolds   Pamela Rooason,   Susan Hanson
Kay Wilson   (dep. stage manager) Jennifer Hill
Amanda Saunders,   Raymond Bowers   Ursula O'Leary
(asst. stage manager)   Michael Cotterill   Jo Richardson
Jeanette Rae   Philip Garston-Jones   Marlene Sidaway
Gillain Evans   Paul Henry   Dennis Spencer
Kathleen Worth   Tony Leary   Michael Bullock,
Ken Marples,   Adrian Pearson   (production manager)
(stage manager)   Joan Turner   Tony Craven,
Noelle Finch   Frank Woodfield   (stage manager)
Yvonne Guest   Gillian Francis   Derek Seaton
Janet Hargreaves

1971

Producers: KEITH BEATTIE, DENNIS SPENCER, CHRIS DUNHAM

Players:

William Avenell   Sue Nicholls   Roger Stephenson
Veida Draisey   Kathleen Worth   Alan Weston
Frank Woodfield   Hilary Graham   Liz Charles

217

Adrian Pearson
Richard Scott
Paul Spinetti
Michael Bullock,
(production manager)
Andrew Betts
John More
Geoffrey Davion
John Marquand
David Rayner
Lynette Erving
Gillian Francis
Yvonne Guest
Charmian May

Amanda Saunders,
(dep. stage manager)
Ann Bradley
Raymond Savage
Lorraine Baxter
Brian Kent
Michael Cotterill
John Bromley
Lewis Michael
Norman Comer
Dennis Spencer
Philip Trewinnard
Leslie Lawton
Noelle Finch

Pauline Garner
Moira Hughes
Patricia Michael
Jeannette Rae
Tony Craven,
(stage manager)
Ken Marples,
(stage manager)
Heather McConachie,
(stage manager)
Peter Tyrrell,
(stage manager)
David Sparks

1972

Producer: CHRIS DUNHAM   *Associate Producer:* DENNIS SPENCER

Players:

Peggy Aitchison
Christine Edmonds
Margaret Hayden-Davies
Mary Laine
Ursula O'Leary
Raymond Savage
Roderick Horn
Philip Garston-Jones
Emma Shaw
Peter Robert Scott
Frank Woodfield
Dennis Spencer
Angus Lennie

Heather McConachie,
(stage manager)
Peter Roper,
(dep. stage manager)
Paul Imbuch
Nicholas Brent
Liz Charles
Lynette Erving
Patricia Kerry
Audrey Murray
Eileen Page
Richard Frost
Paul Spinetti

Paul Haley
Vanessa Davies
Robin Wentworth
Michael Bullock,
(production manager)
Adrian Pearson
Raymond Bowers
Kathleen St. John
Graham Parkes,
(asst. stage manager)
Hilary Graham,
(dep. stage manager)
George Woolley

1973

Producer: CHRIS DUNHAM
Associate Producers: LIONEL HAMILTON, BERNARD KRICHEFSKI

Players:

Peggy Ashby
Carole Boyd
Jill Graham
Louise Nelson
Ursula O'Leary
Jill Stanford

David Blake Kelly
George Woolley
Frank Woodfield
Susan Shaw
Joy Andrews
Ruth Jastrzabek

Eric Stark
Gerald Wallace,
(asst. stage manager)
Raymond Savage
Michael Sanderson
Adrian Pearson

218

Gladys Taylor
Brian Moorehead
Phidius Kouttis
Richard Shurey
Glyn Worsnip
Anthony Smee
Alan Bennion
David Aldridge
Richard Frost
Jack Niles
Al Garcia
Heather McConachie,
 (stage manager)

Dafydd Harvard
Carl Andrews
Lorraine Baxter
Lynette Erving
Susan Mansell
Liz Norman
Penelope Shaw
Adele Strong
Kathleen Worth
Arnold Locke
Chris Cooksey
Frank Marlborough
Brian Honeyball

Bob Garson,
 (dep. stage manager)
Helen Neil,
 (dep. stage manager)
Derek Bergmann,
 (dep. stage manager)
John Marquand
Chris Lethbridge-Baker
Michael Balding
Michael Poole
Paul Spinetti
Norman Pitt
Lionel Hamilton

From 1974 Repertory discontinued

219

APPENDIX "C"

PANTOMIME CASTS
(from Lester Collingwood's first in 1903)

1903-04 — ALADDIN
Minnie Jeffs, Trixie Toole, Bert Atherton, Burley and Crilley, Oliver J. Round.

1904-05 — DICK WHITTINGTON
Florence Bruns, Nellie Valentine, Albert Darnley, Will Letters, Barrett and Knowles.

1905-06 — BLUEBEARD
Minnie Jeffs, Lilian Stanley, The Bogamys, Bert Atherton, Dorothy Ward.

1906-07 — CINDERELLA
Minnie D'Aubyn, Bessie Butt, the Brothers Obo, Fred Barnes.

1907-08 — THE BABES IN THE WOOD
Susie Beaven, Yvonne Lamor, Fred Arthur, Barrett and Knowles.

1908-09 — LITTLE RED RIDING HOOD
Ellaline Thorne, Dolly Denton, Maudie Olmar.

1909-10 — ALADDIN
Ethel Beech, Molly Wynne, Ray Ford, Nellie Taylor.

1910-11 — DICK WHITTINGTON
Marie Reeve, Lily Eyton, Maudie Olmar, Madge White, Harry Cooke.

1911-12 — MOTHER GOOSE
Madge Clifton, Gertie Gavagan, the Brothers Rich, Elsie Roby.

1912-13 — ROBINSON CRUSOE
Myra Hammon, Ray Ford, Monica Ellstree, Mona Magnet, Bert Harrow, Joyce Barbour.

1913-14 — CINDERELLA
Myra Hammon, Nelly le Breton, Teddy Lewis, Leo Bliss.

1914-15 — ALADDIN
Mona Magnet, Ennis Lawson, Sid Dean, George Franklin.

1915-16 — JACK AND THE BEANSTALK
Josie Delaine, Betty Green, Tom Nelson, Leo Trainor.

1916-17 — THE BABES IN THE WOOD
Myra Hammon, Sybil Coulthurst, Willy Cave, Gus Elton, Freddie Foss, the Brothers Brookes.

1917-18 — THE FORTY THIEVES
Victoria Carmen, Aimee Stewart, Fred Hutchings, Sam Hilton.

1918-19 — CINDERELLA
Victoria Carmen, May Ralph, Barrett and Knowles.

1919-20 — LITTLE RED RIDING HOOD
Emmie King, Doris May, Bert Harrow, Fred Hutchings, Edna Randall.

1920-21 — DICK WHITTINGTON
Victoria Carmen, Blance Mayne, Harry Brayne, Willy Cave, Charles Falla, Harry Gilmore.

1921-22 — ALADDIN
Clarice Chesney, Mildred Telford, Harry Barrett, Arthur Carlton.

1922-23 — BO-PEEP
Mabel and Hester Reeve, Teddy Stream, Jack Shires, Will Gardner.

1923-24 — ROBINSON CRUSOE
Victoria Carmen, Kitty Franklin, Leo Bliss, Jack Shires, Billy Matchett, Mamie Soutter, Claude Lester.

1924-25 — CINDERELLA
Nellie Wigley, Rona Ray, the Brothers Obo, Sandy Powell.

1925-26 — THE FORTY THIEVES
Beatrice Allen, Rona Ray, George Hirste, the Brothers Egbert.

1926-27 — THE BABES IN THE WOOD
Nellie Wigley, Ilene Evelyn, Harry Brayne, Pat Nash, Fred Fields, Ernie Mayne.

1927-28 — JACK AND THE BEANSTALK
Violet Field, Evelyn Ray, the Brothers Egbert, Billy Danvers.

1928-29 — DICK WHITTINGTON
Kitty Franklin, Lennie Deane, Billy Matchett, Lily Long, Rich and Galvin, Sandy Powell.

1929-30 — ALADDIN
Maudie Olmar, Violette Deane, Nadia and Vadim, Albert le Fre, Billy Danvers.

221

1930-31 — CINDERELLA
Nora Bancroft, Maisie Weldon, Melford and Dodd, Gladys Watson, Nor Kiddie.

1931-32 — ROBINSON CRUSOE
Nita Croft, Betty Eley, Billy Matchett, Dick Evans, Sandy Powell.

1932-33 — LITTLE RED RIDING HOOD
Jennie Hartley, Lilian Denton, Barbara Wood, George Hirste, Hal Bryan, Georgie Wood.

1933-34 — THE BABES IN THE WOOD
Dorothy Langley, Babs Valerie, Eddie Henderson, Hannah Watt, Fred Kitchen, Joan and Marjorie Volonoff, Billy Merson.

1934-35 — DICK WHITTINGTON
Lily Lapidus, Irene North, Hannah Watt, Harry Gilmore, the Mariajanos, Jack Williams, Hal Bryan, Clarkson Rose.

1935-36 — CINDERELLA
Muriel Cronshaw, Avril Angers, Kittie Prince, Joan and Marjorie Volonoff, George Betton, Eddie Henderson, Clarkson Rose, Georgie Wood.

1936-37 — MOTHER GOOSE
Hannah Watt, Rita Cooper, Presco and Campo, Eric le Fre, Charles Penrose, Barry Lupino.

1937-38 — ALADDIN
Elizabeth French, Doris Bransgrove, Joan and Marjorie Volonoff, Laurence and Latasha, Jack Morrison, Walter Niblo, Barry Lupino.

1938-39 — ROBINSON CRUSOE
Elsa Stenning, Patricia Stainer, Chic Elliott, Wheeler and Wilson, Bob Lloyd, Norman Griffin, George Robey.

1939-40 — JACK AND THE BEANSTALK
Dorothy Ward, Edna Wood, Nellie Caine, Norman Carrol, Shaun Glenville, Georgie Wood.

1940-41 — DICK WHITTINGTON
Sally Stewart, Joan Brett, Phil Ray, Robert Ginns, Walter Niblo, Dicky Hassett.

1941-42 — ROBINSON CRUSOE
Rosalind Melville, Audrey Eskell, Toni Raglan, the Fayre Four, Chic Elliott, Billy Matchett, Robert, Ginns, George Doonan.

1942-43 — LITTLE MISS MUFFET
Ruby Moule, Edna Thompson, George Bolton, Dennis Lawes, Dave and Joe O'Gorman.

1943-44 — THE BABES IN THE WOOD
Marjorie Clayton, Peggy Sergeant, Herbert Cave, Robert Ginns, the Fayre Four, Dennis Lawes, Eddie Leslie, Sid and Max Harrison.

1944-45 — CINDERELLA
Noele Gordon, Billy Baker, Haver and Lee, Jenny Hayes, Claire Ruane, Percy Manchester, George Doonan.

1945-46 — DICK WHITTINGTON
Noele Gordon, Hermene French, Evelyn Dove, Gerry Lee, Tommy Fields, Michael Cole, Connor and Drake.

1946-47 — SIMPLE SIMON
Paula Grey, Wendy Toye, Jean Telfer, Tarzan, Michael Cole, N'Gai, Jack Farr, Naughton and Gold.

1947-48 — BABES IN THE WOOD
Lisa Lee, Hermene French, Jack Elmont, Tommy Jover, Eddie Connor.

1948-49 — ROBINSON CRUSOE
Norman Wisdom, Eddie Leslie, Betty Huntley Wright, George and Jimmy Page, Pauline Williams, Slim Ryder, Toscaneli, Lehmiski Ladies.

1949-50 — QUEEN OF HEARTS
Lauri Lupino Lane, Elsie Percival, Cyril Wells, Eddie Kelland-Espinosa, Wallace Lupino, Valerie Carton, The Skating Dexters, Pop White and Stagger, Cooper Twins, Maple Leaf Four, Percy Le Fre, John Le Mesurier, Brian Blades, Lehmiski Dancers, Don Cooke, Jean Harvey, Dumarke and Denzer, Brian Hayle (SM), Leslie Allen (ASM).

1950-51 — CINDERELLA
Norman Wisdom, Terry Kendall, Betty Leslie Smith, Ruthene Leclerc, Nick Nissen, Three Aberdonians, Three Monarchs, Betty Nelson, Gotham Singers, Lehmiski Ladies, Alexandra Babes, Michael Moore, Helene Cooney.

1951-52 — SLEEPING BEAUTY
Frank O'Brian, Wilson Keppel and Betty, Tommy Godfrey, Patricia Grey, Slim Rhyder, Phyllis Adrian, Wyndham Milligan, Cliff Weir, Barbara Tyler, Gotham Singers, John and Betty Royle, Thomas Williamson, Lehmiski Ladies, Audrey Penney, Hilda Keenan, Clem Coulson, Walter Myerson, Ricardo Davies, Brian Hayle (SD), Stewart Ruttledge (SM).

1952-53 — DICK WHITTINGTON

Jimmy Wheeler, Jean Inglis, Gordon Craig, Walter Myerson, Anthony Sagar, Sheila Rae, Two Pirates, Julie David, Jimmy Plant, Ida Shepley, Gerry Lee, The Fregolis, Lehmiski Ladies, Gotham Singers, Alexandra Babes, Tilsa Page, Brian Hayle (SD), Stewart Ruttledge (SM).

1953-54 — ALADDIN

Clarkson Rose, Three Monarchs, Tudor Evans, Jean Inglis, Joe Black, George Sylvester, Shirley Brett, The Harvards, Rosemary Banks, Brian Blades, Mayfair Four, Lehmiski Ladies, Brian Hayle (SD), Stewart Ruttledge (SM).

1954-55 — ROBINSON CRUSOE

Tessie O'Shea, John Sangler, Louis Holt, Chris Mann, Phyllis Anderson, Charles Rowley, Arthur Sumner, Evan Williams, Graham Bros., John Cartier, Shirley Williams, Ossie Noble, Melomaniacs, Lehmiski Ladies, Nemecs and Violet, Brian Hayle (SD), Stewart Ruttledge (SM).

1955-56 — CINDERELLA

Teddy Johnson, Pearl Carr, Adele Dixon, Tommy Rose, Terry O'Neill, Ted Gatty, Ursula O'Leary, Rosemarie Hill, Mastersingers, Vernon Drake, Eddie Connor, Shirley Phelps, Gabrielle and Toledo, Lehmiski Ladies, William Avenell (SD), Roy Astley (SM).

1956-57 — BABES IN THE WOOD

Three Monarchs, Terry Hall, Fay Lenore, William Avenell(PM), Charles Harrison, Donovan and Hayes, Julia Sutton, Gillian Taylor, Anthony Spurling, Lynette Mills, Noel Ross, Michael Jordan, Joe McBride, Bernard Albrow, Janet Hollander, Alexandra Babes, Lehmiski Ladies, Roy Astley (SD), Jack Stanford.

1957-58 — DICK WHITTINGTON

Arthur Haynes, Sonnie Hale, Baker and Douglas, Anne Fields, Avril Vane, Pat Somers, Patricia Rogers, Four Jones Boys, Tony Steedman, Tony Vallance, Nobern, William Avenell (PM), Trio Menares, Alexandra Babes, Lehmiski Ladies, Roy Astley (SD).

1958-59 — PUSS IN BOOTS

Dennis Lotis, Terry Hall, Mastersingers, William Avenell (PM), Kathleen Alwood, Joan Ross, Three Graham Brothers, Norman Vaughan, George Lacy, Christine Yates, Derek Royle, Kathleen St. John, Daphne De Wit, Lehmiski Ladies, Roy Astley (SD), Susan Short (SM).

1959-60 — CINDERELLA

Bartlett and Ross, Mike and Bernie Winters, George Martin, Carol Eric, Terry Fearis, Mary Benning, The Four Ramblers, Lehmiski Ladies, Alexandra Babes, William Avenell (PM), Isabel Rennie, Roy Astley (SD).

1960-61 — SINBAD THE SAILOR

George Lacy, Morecambe and Wise, Lynette Rae, Linda Lee, Roselli Singers, Four Playboys, Johnny Stewart, Anton and Janet Morrow, Three Ghezzis, Lehmiski Ladies, Derek Royle, Arthur Tolcher, William Avenell (PM), Roy Astley (SD).

1961-62 — ALADDIN

Edmund Hockridge, Miki and Griff, Terry Fearis, Ann Harriman, Joe Church, Martin Dell, Patton Brothers, Tommy Rose, Emerson and Jayne, William Avenell (PM), Atlas Sahara Troupe, Lehmiski Ladies, Jennifer MacArthur (SM), Roselli Singers.

1962-63 — MOTHER GOOSE

Beryl Reid, Frank Ifield, The Dallas Boys, Jack Tripp, Ted Rogers, Pamela Penfold, William Avenell (PM), Allen Christie, Kay Lyell, Five Olanders, Arthur Tolcher, Judy Whalley, Lehmiski Ladies, Roselli Singers, John Leonardt (ASM), Roy Astley (SM).

1963-64 — BABES IN THE WOOD

Ronnie Carroll, George Lacy, Arthur Worsley, Billy Burden, Gordon and Bunny Jay, Gwen Overton, Clive Stock, Arthur Tolcher, William Avenell (PM), Marrakech Troupe, Jennifer Paul, Clinton Greyn, Julie Mellon, Candy Sisters, Lehmiski Ladies, Sally Thompsett, Ross Clear.

1964-65 — JACK AND THE BEANSTALK

The Bachelors, Jack Tripp, Joy Turpin, Les Oscars, Nicholas Brent, Colin Crompton, Lehmiski Ladies, Pamela Penfold, George Campo (and Lina Marvel), The Renellis, Allen Christie, Ann Shephard, Johnathan Everett, William Avenell (PM), William Morton (SD), Carol Evans (SM).

1965-66 — ROBINSON CRUSOE

The Barron Knights, Denny Willis, Kathleen West, Joy Turpin, Cox and Miles Twins, Johnnie Mack, The Islanders, The Falcons, Alexandra Four, Lehmiski Ladies, Ruth Llewellyn, Stanley Jack, Angela Gulley, Jennifer Whitworth, William Avenell (PM), Peter Norfolk, William Morton (SD), Carol Evans (SM).

1966-67 — PUSS IN BOOTS

Des O'Connor, Rikki Fulton, Three Monarchs, Francis Regan, Dennis Spencer, Alison Griffin, Sue Jones, Clem Ashby, Frank Woodfield, Jean Barrington, Lynn Wynters, Jasmine Dee, Atlas Sahara Troupe, Lehmiski Dancers, William Avenell (PM), Michael Bullock (SD), Peter Daly (SM), Peter Keen (ASM).

1967-68 — GOODY TWOSHOES

New Vaudeville Band, Fay Lenore, Jenny Vance, Jack Tripp, Chris Carlsen, Four Kinsmen, Robert Marlowe, Allen Christie, Valla Bertini, Penny

Harrison, Kay Lyell, Arthur Tolcher, William Avenell (PM), Michael Bullock (SD), Paul and Peta Page's Puppets, Alexandra Dancers, Joanne Haydon (SM).

1968-69 — DICK WHITTINGTON
Ted Rogers, Dallas Boys, Cy Grant, Philip Blaine, Lauverne Richins, Gordon Peters, Raymond Bowers, Claude Zola, Pat Lancaster, Robert Marlowe, Thorey, Brant Brothers, Paul and Peta Page's Puppets, Michael Bullock (PM), Anna Cooke (SM), Alexandra Dancers.

1969-70 — ALADDIN
Michael Bentine, Donald Peers, Billy Burden, Jasmine Dee, Martin Dell, Martin Lawrence, Patricia Garrett, Ronnie Stevens, Sheila Dawson, Deanna Linden, Valerie Wayne, Clare Herbert, Alfred Ravel, Robert Marlowe, Terry Kerr, David Ryan, Raynor Bourton (ASM), Alexandra Dancers, Michael Bullock (PM), Anna Cook (SM).

1970-71 — CINDERELLA
Ronnie Corbett, Lyn Kennington, Tommy Rose, Charlie Stewart, Janet Hargreaves, Sons and Lovers, Noelle Finch, George Raymonde, Jimmy and Brian Patton, Jean Bayless, The Mistins, Paul and Peta Page's Puppets, Alexandra Dancers, Michael Bullock (PM), Ken Marples (SM), Janice Anthony (ASM), Heather McConachie (ASM).

1971-72 — ROBINSON CRUSOE
Les Dawson, Jack Tripp, New World, Pat Lancaster, Allen Christie, Cox and Miles Twins, Helena Garron, Arthur Tolcher, Allister Bain, Emerson and Jayne, Michael Cotterill, Heather McConachie (ASM), Dominic March (SM), Michael Bullock (PM), Alexandra Dancers.

1972-73 — PUSS IN BOOTS
Jack Douglas, Millicent Martin, Reg Dixon, Paul Farla, Jacqui Lewis, Valerie Wayne, Danny O'Dea, Adrian Pearson, William Avenell, Maggie Stride, Ken Roberts, George Truzzi, Michele Summers, Jacquie Toye, Bill Gore, David Frater, Alexandra Dancers, Heather McConachie (SM), Graham Francis Parkes (ASM).

1973-74 — JACK AND THE BEANSTALK
Jimmy Tarbuck, The Grumbleweeds, George Lacy, Wendy Walsh, DuMarte and Denzar, Nicholas Brent, Roger Stevenson Puppets, Paul Farla, Peter Kirby, Helen Neil (ASM), Deanna Linden, Heather McConachie (SM), Douglas Quartermaine, Clio Steele, Alexandra Dancers.

1974-75 — BABES IN THE WOOD
Leslie Crowther, Jack Tripp, Raymond Savage, Philip Anthony, Allen Chrsitie, Three Squires, Arthur Tolcher, Jane Fyffe, Mary Sanchez, Janet Walpole, Linda Williams, Jimmy and Brian Patton, Johnny Vyvyan, Sue

226

Jenkins, Valla Bertini, Paul and Peta Page's Puppets, Alexandra Dancers, Roy Astley (CSM), Pamela Ross (DSM). [The Babes were supplied by Betty Fox who has long been a leading figure in the dance world.]

1975-76 — CINDERELLA
Peter Goodwright, Dai Francis, Terry Hall, Raymond Savage, Neptune Harmony Group, Jane Terry, Gerrie Raymond, Barry Howard, Gerald Moon, David and Tony Webb, Suzanna Beaumont, Jill Stanford, Alexandra Dancers, Anthony Davis (CSM), Jim Capper (DSM).

1976-77 — DICK WHITTINGTON
(in association with Triumph Theatre Productions)
Frank Ifield, Patrick Cargill, Jim Davidson, Alan Curtis, Raymond Savage, Cox and Miles Twins, Terry Doogan, Derek Royle, Olwen Hughes, Madelaine Baker, Paul Shepherd, Judy Allen, Steve Adams, Pamela Beesley, Ray Paul, Alexandra Dancers, John Swain (CSM), Reica Benjamin (DSM), Candyce Brandl (ASM).

A NIGHT WITH THE STARS

A TRIBUTE TO

DEREK SALBERG

Sunday 24th July, 1977

★ ★ ★ ★ ★

Artistes appearing will include:

JOHN ALDERTON	TERRY HALL &
AVRIL ANGERS	LENNY THE LION
ARTHUR ASKEY	FRANK IFIELD
MAXINE AUDLEY	GEORGE LACY
JEAN BAYLESS	PAT LANCASTER
BRENDA BRUCE	LEO MAGUIRE
PATRICK CARGILL	JUDY PARFITT
ALLEN CHRISTIE	SANDY POWELL
LESLIE CROWTHER	DEREK ROYLE
JIM DAVIDSON	TONY STEEDMAN
BETTY FOX	CHARLIE STEWART
MODERN GENERATION	DAVID TOMLINSON
RAYMOND FRANCIS	JACK TRIPP
PHILIP GARSTON-JONES	LESLIE WELCH
PETER GOODWRIGHT	GEORGIE WOOD
NOELE GORDON	HARRY WORTH

also other artistes too late for inclusion in the programme

★ ★ ★ ★ ★

Musical Director: **PETER DAY**

Production under the direction of ALAN CURTIS

Gala devised by **MICHAEL BULLOCK**

Please do not smoke whilst the curtain is up

Two pages from the author's farewell Gala Night programme are reproduced above and on the page opposite.

Frank Ifield, Judy Parfitt and Harry Worth were, due to various circumstances, unable to appear, but Marius Goring and Ray Paul, though not listed above, were welcome additions to the artistes.

We would like to thank the Artistes, Stage Management and Orchestra – without whose generosity and assistance this Gala would not have been possible.

Stage Management – **ROY ASTLEY**
ALAN WHITE
LIZ STERN
HEATHER McCONACHIE

Public Relations – **MALCOLM FARQUHAR**

Orchestra – **TREVOR CHARLTON, TREVOR OERTON, STAN POOLE, ARTHUR ROBERTS, GEOFF SMITH, JIMMY WEDGE**

Resident Stage Manager – **RICHARD TURNER**

Chief Electrician – **ERIC OTTO**

The above was correct at the time of going to press

The following artistes were prevented from appearing by professional commitments, but send their best wishes to Derek and for the success of this evening:-

THE BACHELORS, THE BARRON KNIGHTS, TONY BRITTON, ROY CASTLE, RONNIE CORBETT, LES DAWSON, MICHAEL DENISON, REG DIXON, KEN DODD, VAL DOONICAN, CYRIL FLETCHER, DULCIE GRAY, THE GRUMBLEWEEDS, JOHN HANSON, BERNARD HEPTON, TREVOR HOWARD, TEDDY JOHNSON & PEARL CARR, ARTHUR LOWE, ALFRED MARKS, JOHN LE MESURIER, KENNETH MORE, PEGGY MOUNT, ANNA NEAGLE, DES O'CONNOR, LYNETTE RAE, BERYL REID. TED ROGERS, LEONARD ROSSITER, LESLIE SANDS, JIMMY TARBUCK, NORMAN VAUGHAN, MIKE & BERNIE WINTERS, NORMAN WISDOM, GLYN WORSNIP.

Brochure researched and compiled by **Jackie Swancutt** and **Alan Davies**.
Edited by **Michael Bullock**

No Cameras or Tape Recorders allowed in the auditorium

229

INDEX

For complete list of repertory actors, pantomime titles and casts see Appendices B (pages 199-219) and C (pages 220-227). The index does not include play titles, authors' names or theatres and theatrical companies.

Ada, 135
Addleman, Cecil, 53
Adey, Frank, 175, 189
Adey, Betty, 175
Agar Bates, 26
Alder, Karen Stanley, 13
Alderton, John, 112
Allen, Dave, 165
Allen, Mrs, author's note
Andrew, Doreen 177
Angers, Avril, 38
Anderson, Georgina, 100
Arlen, Stephen, 76, 95
Arculus, Peter, 194
Arnaud, Yvonne, 80
Arts Council, 8, 19, 91, 92, 93, 121, 135, 140, 147, 178, 187
Ashby, Peggy, 191
Ashcroft, Dame Peggy, 80, 91, 109
Askey, Arthur, 44, 45, 156, 162
Astley, Roy, 74, 171
Attenborough, Sir Richard, 106
Aubrey, Anne, 104
Audley, Maxine, 71, 109
Avenell, Bill, 112, 172, 173
Aylmer, Sir Felix, 109

Babbage, Wilfred, 39
Bachelors, 164
Badel, Alan, 127
Baddeley, Hermione, 70
Bailey, Robin, 71, 107
Baker and Douglas, 161
Bancroft, Jack, 93
Bancroft, Pat, 93
Bancroft, Judith, 94
Banks, Leslie, 70
Barbara, 87
Barlow, H.J., 70
Barnes, Fred, 6
Barrie, Sir James, 52
Barrington, Jean, 165
Barrington, Michael, 98
Barron, John, 41, 117
Barron Knights, 164, 168
Bartlett and Ross, 161, 175
Bastiman, Roy, 171
Bates, Shirley Ann, 104
Bayless, Jean, 166
Bayntun, Amelia, 116
Beaumont, 'Binkie', 94, 109
Beaumont, John
Beck, Maureen, 100
Belfrage, Bruce, 14
Bell, Mr & Mrs, 82
Bell, Sam, 175
Bennett, Billy, 44
Benson, Sir Frank, 51
Bentine, Michael, 165, 166
Benyon, Joan, 160
Beresford, Leslie, 175
Berner, Max, 194
Berryman, Gwen, 41
Bewes, Rodney, 146
Bird, Yolande, 76
Birmingham (Alexandra) Theatre Club, 82, 121, 132, 134, 192
Birmingham Arts Shop, 187
Birmingham Civic Society, 192
Birmingham Press Club, 10
Brimingham Weekly Post, 48
Black, Judy, 102
Blake, Joan, 98
Blakemore, Winnie & David, 96
Bleyer, Hon. Ald. Stanley, App. A
Bloom, Claire, 76
Bolam, James, 146
Borg, Neville, 122
Bosworth, Hon. Ald. Neville, 120, 134, 135, 136
Bowen, Ald. Teg, 121

Bowden, Betty, 28, 58
Bowers, Raymond, 115, 117
Bramham, Mrs, 86
Brent, Nicholas, 168
Brewer, Reg, 64
Bridge, Peter, 102, 104, 105
Bridge, Ros, 105
Briers, Richard, 77
Bright, Harry, 166
Britton, Tony, 127
Bronhill, June, 127
Brook, Clive, 76
Brown, Janet, 171, 174, 175
Brown, Rt. Rev. Laurence, 6
Brown, Pamela, 176
Brownrigg, Sheila, 58, 116
Bryan, Dora, 109
Bryan, Hal, 28
Bryant, Michael, 111
Bullock, Michael, 129, 144, 146, 171, 172, 191
Bullock, Laurie, 144
Burden, Billy, 164, 166
Burke, Pat, 73
Burley, Colin, 191
Burman, Nancy, 142, App. A
Bushill Matthews, Phyllis, 125
Byrne, Myles, 58
Byrne, Peter, 150

Cabney-Smith, Jack, App. A
Cadbury, Richard, 2
Calvert, Phyllis, 128, 156
Cameron, Earl, 77
Canning, Heather, 103
Capper, Sir Derrick, 6
Carey, Jan, 112
Cargill, Patrick, 169, 190
Carmichael, Ian, 150
Carroll, 164
Casson, Sir Lewis, 110, 111
Chandos, Viscount, 94, 95, 96
Chaplin, Charlie, 6
Chater, Geoffrey, 53
Cherry, Helen, 23, 79
Chester, Alan, 171
Chetwyn, Robert, 99
Chigwell House School, 21
Chissick, Jack, 21
Christie, Allen, 163, 167, 174, 175
Christine, 87
Church, Joe, 162
Clark, Lord Kenneth, 94
Clarke, Sir Ashley, 94
Claxton, Hedley, 175
Clements, Sir John, 76, 80, 91, 106, 109
Clifton, 20, 22, 34, 52, 60
Cliftonian, Old, 113, 114, 124
Cochran, David, 31, 56, 155
Coleman, Hughie & Ida, 42
Coleman, Richard, 149
Collingwood, Lester, 1, 4, 5, 6, 7
152, 154
Compton, Fay, 76
Condon, Richard, 187
Connor & Drake, 161
Connor, Jim, 62, 64
Cooke, Roy, 155, 171
Cooney, Ray, 180
Cooper, Yvonne, 171
Corbett, Mrs Freda, 94
Corbett, Ronnie, 147, 166, 171
Cotterill, Michael, 116
Coulthard, Arthur, 54
Counsell, John, 187
Courtneidge, Dame Cicely, 111, 126
Courtney, Virginia, 169, 171
Coutts, William, 2, 3, 69
Coward, Sir Noel, 81, 91, 110
Cox & Miles Twins, 164, 167, 169, 175

Coyne, Tom, 192
Craig, Wendy, 127
Cranmer, Peter, 52
Craven, Lady Anna, 21
Crickmay, Dennis, 115
Crocker, John, 71
Crosthwaite, Iris, 35
Crowther, Leslie, 168, 189, 193, 194
Cruickshank, Andrew, 126, 128
Cuff, Gerald, 41, 52
Cummings, Constance, 91
Curtis, Alan, 169, 193
Cusack, Cyril, 39

Da Costa, Ted, 62
Daker, David, 113
Dallas Boys, 162, 165
Danvers, Billy, 27
Dark, Hon. Ald. Beaumont, 132, App. A
Davidson, Jim, 169
Davidson, Tony, 88, 170
Davies, Alan, 192
Davis, Allan, 75, 101, 112
Davis, Eli, 49
Dawson, Les, 167
Day, Peter, 170, 193
Deakins, Leslie, 10
Dean, Basil, 68, 76, 104
Dee, Jasmine, 166
Delfont, Lord, 179
Dell, Martin, 162
De Manio, Jack, 192
Denison, Michael, 109, 125
Denyer, Maggie, 102
Devon, Keith, 157, 158
De Witt, 161
Dews, Peter, 71
Dietrich, Marlene, 129
Dixon, Adele, 161
Dixon, Reg, 167
Dobson, Bill. 60, 72, 107
Dodd, Ken, 126, 129, 145, 175
Dodimead, David, 79
Donald, James, 107
Donaldson, Rt. Hon. Lord, 93
Doogan, Terry, 169
Doolan, Ed, 192
Doonican, Val, 161
Doreen, 87
Dorritty, Elizabeth, 171
Dors, Diana, 100
Dorward, Helen, 103, 116
Dotrice, Roy, 145
Douglas, Jack, 167
Doyle, Bunny, 50
Draper, Ruth, 80
Draycott, Eileen, 28, 74, 75, 78, 98
Duckworth, Leslie, 136, 137
Duffy, Bernard, 25
Dumarte & Denzar, 158
Dunham, Christopher, 103, 117
Dunkerley, Herbert, 79
Dunlop, Frank, 103
Dunn, Leslie, 53, 98
Duxbury, Elspeth, 75, 79

Edison, Robert, 80
Edmonds, Christine, 117
Edwards, Geoffrey, 113
Edwards, Jimmy, 75, 148
Elsa, 190
Emerson & Jayne, 162
English, John, 96
E.N.S.A., 63, 66, 67, 68
Eric, 121
Erving, Lynette, 117
Espinosa, Eddie Kelland, 158
Essie, 87
Evans, Carol, 58
Evans, Dame Edith, 80, 107, 109
Everitt, Anthony, 1, 129, 192

Faith, Adam, 116
Fahy, Tom, 64
Farquhar, Malcolm, 58, 103, 113, 116
Fearis, Terry, 161, 162, 167, 173
Fellows, Fred, 62, 63
Fields, Gracie, 12, 68
Finch Fred, 15
Finch, Noelle, 115, 167
Finlay, Frank, 124
Finlayson, Michael, 105
Finney, Albert, 89, 125, 181
Fisher, Simon, 36
Flanagan, Bud, 12
Fletcher, Cyril, 59
Florence, Norman, 191
Forbes, Freddie, 159
Forde, Florrie, 12
Forder, David, 43
Formby, Beryl, 110
Formby, George, 45, 68, 74, 110
Forsyth, Brigit, 117, 146
Fortescue, Vernon, 80
Fox, Lee, 41
Francis, Dai, 169
Francis, Raymond, 74, 76, 127
Franklin, Coun. E.J., App. A
Fraser, M.F.K.E., author's note, 10, 47, 49, 155
French, Leslie, 99
Frost, Richard, 117
Fulton, Rikki, 165
Furness, Mark, 175
Fyffe, Will, 68

Gabriel, John, 73, 75
Gala Performance, Preface, 86, 184, 192, App. D
Gale, John, 179
Garner, Rex, 99
Geordie, 2
Gielgud, Sir John, 76, 81, 84, 91
Gilpin, John, 111
Ginns, Robert, 58
Gitana, Gertie, 11
Glenville, Shaun, 156
Godsell, Vanda, 41, 71, 104
Goodman, Lord, 19, 135, 140
Goodwright, Peter, 169
Gopsill, Coun. G.A., App. A
Gordon, Barbara, 45, 52
Gordon, Noelle, 157
Gordon, Oliver, 35, 53, 75, 76, 113, 159, 160
Goring, Marius, 114, 115, 139
Grade, Leslie, 66, 74, 110, 135, 140
Grade, Lord Lew, 66, 135
Graham, Bill, 171
Graham, Jill, 118
Grant, Cy, 165
Graves, Peter, 107, 110
Gray, Dulcie, 101, 109, 125
Grayson, Jill, 188
Green, Michael, 54, 55
Greene, Richard, 114
Greenwood, John, 181
Grey, Dame Beryl, 111
Griffin, Hon. Ald., 131, 134
Grumbleweeds, 168
Guest, Billy, 38, 48, 56, 71
Guinness, Sir Alec, 91, 106, 109
Gurney, Norman, author's note
Gwynne, Michael, 114

Hale, Sonnie, 51, 104
Hall, Terry, 161, 169
Hallatt, Henry, 13, 14, 15
Hammond, Kay, 76, 80, 101, 107, 109
Hammond, Rae, 58
Hand, Lizzie, 2
Handl, Irene, 111
Hanson, John, 127, 128, 146
Hare, Robertson, 111
Hargreaves, Janet, 114
Harper, Betty, 135
Harrison, Kathleen, 80
Harrod, Jane, 166
Harvey, Brian, 54
Harvey, Rupert, 14
Hayle, Brian, 111
Haynes, Arthur, 161
Heape, Dick, App. A
Henry, Paul, 116
Hepton, Bernard, 100, 115
Heslop, Charles, 108
Hewlett, Arthur, 102

Hill, Kenneth, 105
Hiley, Edgar & Ingrid, 97
Hiller, Wendy, 80
Hinsley, Carol, 50, 171
Hitchcock, Ray, 97
Hockridge, Edmund & Jackie, 162, 168
Hodgkinson, Jo, 91, 92, 135
Horstead, Hilda, 32
Horton, Hon. Ald. Ernie, App. A
Howard, Anthony, 112
Howard, Barry, 169, 175
Howard, Trevor, 23, 52, 53, 73, 79, 124, 135
Howerd, Frankie, 109, 125, 126
Howes, Peter, 171
H.R.H. Prince Charles, 96
Hudson, Harry, 170
Hudson, Len, 171
Hulbert, Jack, 111, 126
Huntley, Raymond, 15, 107
Hutchinson, Jeannette, 98, 99
Hyde-White, Wilfred, 150

Ifield, Frank, 163, 164, 169, 190
Illsley, Stanley, 58
Inman, John, 169, 175

Jackie, author's note, 191
Jackson, Alex, 66
Jackson, Sir Barry, 4, 39
Jackson, Nancie, 100
James, Sidney, 102, 145
Jay, Gordon & Bunny, 164
Jaynes, Rosemary, 101
Jeans, Ursula, 125
Jim, 109
John, Rosamund, 41
John, 109
Johnson, Noel, 59
Johnson, Teddy & Pearl Carr, 161, 174
Johnstone, Beryl, 58, 112
Jokel, Walter, 179
Jones, Emrys, 156
Jones, Griffith, 111
Jones, Philip Garston, 69, 75
Jones, Sidney, 14, 126, 155, 171
Junkin, John, 146

Keeling, Charles, 70
Keeling, Kenneth, 42, 177
Kelly, Hugh, 71
Kemp, Shelagh & Mrs 79
Kemp, T.C., 1, 79
Kennington, Lyn, 167
Kent, Brian, 102, 112, 114
Kenwright, Bill, 146, 148, 179
Kerry, Patricia, 117
Keswick, Sir William, 94
Key, Anne, 63
Key, Bob, 54, 62
Kidd, Delena, 100
King, Edmund, 25, 26, 70, 141, 144, App. A
King, G.C., 70
King, Hetty, 5
Kirk, David, 179
Knight, Albert, 163
Knight, Malcolm, 179
Kraus, Charles, 87, 191

Lacy, George, 161, 162, 164, 168
Laight, Eric, 171
Lambert, J.W., 93
Lancaster, Pat, 165
Landstone, Charles, 91, 92
Lane, Laurie Lupino, 158
Lang, Julia, 99
Latham, Tom, Snr. 42
Latham, Tom, Jnr. 42, 53, 54
Laurence, Colin, 77, 98
Lawson, Ennis, 11, 15
Lawton, Frank, 78
Laye, Evelyn, 50, 76, 78, 132
Leach, Rosemary, 105, 114, 139
Lee, Jennie, 93
Lee, Vanessa, 107, 110, 138
Leech, Richard, 76, 194
Leggatt, Phyllis, 96
Lehmiski, Madam, 4, 155, 171
Leigh, Vivien, 68
Le Mesurier, John, 77, 158
Leno, Dan, Jnr., 16
Lenore, Fay, 161, 165
Leslie, Eddie, 157
Levi, Joan, 60
Levy, Benn, 91

Levy, E. Laurence, 1
Lillie, Beatrice, 68
Lily, 87
Lineham, Barry, 115
Lister, Moira, 80
Little Titch, 182
Littler, Sir Emile, 57, 59, 73
Livesey, Roger, 125
Lloyd, Freddie, 138, 178
Lockwood, Margaret, 110, 127, 150
Lodge, Terence, 115
Logan, Sir Douglas, 94
Lohr, Marie, 110
Lorna & Gordon, 190, 191
Lotis, Dennis, 161
Lowe, Arthur, 77
Lupino, Barry, 154, 162
Lupino Wallace 158
Lutman, Glady, 10, 56
Lynn, Vera, 68
Lyttleton, Humphry, 146

McCallum, 52
McCowen, Alec, 71
McKellan, Ian, 127
McNae, Jennie, 114, 116
Mackintosh, Cameron, 179
Macklin, Larry, 170
Madge, 121
Madin, 121, 122, 123
Magill, Ronald, 102
Manderson, David, 40, 43
Manley, George, 17
Mann, Hastings, 72
Marjorie, Horstead-Stanford, 31, 32, 34, 56, 60, 85
Marklen, Paul, 112
Marlowe, Robert, 165, 166, 171
Marshall, Henry, 160
Martin, George, 161
Martin, Millicent, 167
Marwoode, Peter, 42
Marx Bros, 44
Master Betty, 182
Matthews, A.E., 107, 109
Matthews, Francis, 130
Matthews, Granny, 32
Matthews, Jessie, 51, 58, 106, 109
May, 121
Meadows, Hon. Al. Jim, App. A
Merchant, Vivien, 100
Michaels, Louis, 169
Michell, Keith, 127
Miki & Griff, 162
Miller, Joan, 71
Milligan, Spike, 145
Mills, Hayley, 127
Mills, Sir John, 106
Mills,, Lynn, 151
Mitchell, Barbara, 41
Mitchell, Mitch, 171
Monarchs, 158, 161, 165
Moody, John, 91
Moody, Ron, 145
Moore, Sir Henry, 94
More, Kenneth, 41, 59
Morecambe, Eric, 63
Morecambe & Wise, 65, 129, 162, 193
Morley, John, 28
Morley, Robert, 110, 145
Mort, Ray, 112
Mortimer, Penny, 151
Morton, Bill, 171
Morton, Clive, 130
Moseiwitch, 59
Mount, Peggy, 41, 113, 114
Mulhare, Edward, 53, 98
Mumford, Cecil, 55
Myatt, Dr. Connie, Frank, Mrs Taylor, 42

Naughton & Gold, 72
Neagle, Dame Anna, 193
Neale, Jimmie, 171
Nelson, Wal & Annie, 42
Newman, Greatrex, 63
Newman, John, 179
New Vaudeville Band, 165
New World & 'Fuzzy' Lee, 167
Nicholls, Sue, 117
Noble, Larry, 71, 74*
Norman, Liz, 118
Norris, Fred, 134, 146, 186, 190
Novellow, Ivor, 85
*Incorrect as he joined the company in 1947

O'Connor, Des, 165
O'Leary, Ursula, 99, 116
O'Neill, Terry, 161
O'Rorke, Brefni, 39
O'Sullivan, Richard, 146
Oliver, Joan & Vic, 82
Olivier, Lord, Foreword, 95, 109, 124, 129, 193
Orr, Aletha, 41
Osborn, Andrew, 71
Ost, Geoffrey, 112
Otto, Eric, 171
Oulsnam, Pat, 121
Oulsnam, Robert, 120, 121, App. A
Oulton, Brian, 108, 184
Overton, Gwen & Clive Stock, 164
Owen, George, 30, 57
Owen, John, App. A

Page, Paul & Peta, 165
Page, Tilsa, 198
Palmer, Margaret & Mrs, 82
Parfitt, Judy, 104
Patching, Morris, 148
Patrick, Nigel, 109, 128, 150
Pattons, Brian & Jimmy, 162, 168
Pavlova, 16, 182
Pearson, Adrian, 116
Pease, Sydney, 29
Peers, Donald, 166
Pegg, Joyce, 101, 193
Perry, Clive, 180
Peters, Gordon, 165
Pettingell, Frank, 14
Pichon, Anne, 58
Pinter, Harold, 100, 146
Plowright, Joan, 124
Polacks House, 22, 24
Poushinoff, 59
Powell, Peter, 52, 74, 77, 78, 79, 101, 102, 103, 113, 127, 176, 177
Powell, Sandy, 9, 27
Power, Tyrone, 109
Price, Miss, 42
Price, Gordon, 131, 132, 151
Price, Shirley, 132
Pringle, Bryan, 100
Purdey, P.J., 40, 41
Pursall, Alf, 64

Radd, Ronald, 98
Rae, Kenneth, 93, 94
Rae, Lynnett, 161
Rambert, Madam, 60
Randle, Mollie, 96
Ravel, Alfred, 166
Ray, Phil, 28
Redman, Joyce, 80
Redgrave, Sir Michael, 124
Rees, Harris, 178
Rees, Llewellyn, 91
Reeves, Fred, 171
Reid, Beryl, 110, 162, 163, 164
Reptiles, 51 to 54
Richards, Olga, 43
Richards, Sue, 151
Richardson, Sir Ralph, 106, 110
Rix, Brian, 110, 126, 127, 146
Roberts, Arthur, 88
Roberts, Ken, 167
Roberts, Nancy, 110
Robey, Sir George, 16, 57, 155, 156
Robinson, Cardew, 176
Robson, Dame Flora, 87, 111
Rocket Club, 6, 48, 49, 64, 156
Rodway, Philip, 4, 73, 85, 125
Rogers, Ted, 162, 165
Rosay, Francoise, 78
Rose, Clarkson, 30, 37, 38, 39, 49, 160
Rose, Tommy, 161, 162
Rosser, Peter, 58
Rossiter, Leonard, 41, 117
Rowland, Allen, 6
Royle, Derek, 102, 105
Russell, Sir Lionel, 113
Russell, Ronald, 113
Rutherford, Margaret, 109
Ryder, R.V., 10

St. Dennis, 171
St. John, 58, 60
Sagar, Anthony, 52, 98

Sal, 190
Salberg, Evelyn, 19, 39
Salberg, Jane (Chissick), 21
Salberg, Janie, 9
Salberg, Joan, 31, 32, 33, 34, 35, 39, 56, 60, 76, 77, 78, 84, 93, 95, 101, 142, 143, 172
Salberg, Joanna, 35, 36, 39, 44, 46, 76
Salberg, Judith, 22, 34, 35, 36, 39, 76
Salberg, Kate, 21
Salberg, Keith, 19
Salberg, Leon (father), 1, 8, 10, 12, 15, 16, 18, 28, 30, 31, 32, 37, 40, 41, 47, 48, 49, 137, 139, 154, 174
Salberg, Loretta (Guard & family, 19
Salberg, Louis, 32
Salberg, Noreen (Craven), 20
Salberg, Reginald, 17, 18, 19, 20, 32, 54, 58, 75, 76, 115, 143, 182, 183, 184
Salberg, Stanley, 18, 20
Sanderson, Michael, 118
Sandford, Stephen, 190
Sands, Leslie, 74, 77, 99, 100, 110
Saunders, Peter, 117, 180
Savage, Raymond, 169
Saville, Victor, 106
Scofield, Paul, 108, 110
Scott, Peter Robert, 117
Scott, Terry, 162, 166
Scully, Terry, 102, 111
Sears, Heather, 110
Seaton, Derek, 116
Selby, Nicholas, 41
Selema, 190, 192
Sever, Coun. John, MP, App. A
Sharman, Sam, 148
Sharp, Anthony, 105
Shaune, Denise, 171
Shaw, Penelope, 41
Shearer, Moira, 108
Shellam, Mary, 125
Shepley, Ida, 77
Sherwood, Henry, 114
Shiner, Ronald, 109
Siddons, Mrs, 86
Sim, Sheila, 106
Simpson, Hon. Ald., Charles, 83 App. A
Simeon, David, 114
Simmonds, Harry & Audrey, 82
Sinclair, Brook, 191
Sinden, Donald, 126
Slaughter, Giles, 194
Smith, Alan, 10
Smith, Dolly, 29, 38, 56
Smith, Maggie, 111
Smith, Norman, 101, 126, 171
Smith, Sidney & Florence, 62
Southall, Anthony, 41, 43, 174
Spencer, Dennis, 114, 115
Spencer, Rex, 158, 163, 171
Stainton, Philip, 66
Stanbury, Humphrey, 41, 88, 174
Standing, John, 101
Stanford, Jack, 161
Steedman, Tony, 53, 77, 98, 104
Steele, Tommy, 186
Stenson, Tony, 170
Stepham, Renee, 130
Stern, Liz, 64
Stone, John, 150
Sutton Coldfield Photographic Society, 192
Sutton, Randolph, 11
Sykes, Eric, 75, 148
Sykes, John, 52

Tarbuck, Jimmy, 168, 170
Taylor, Derief, 143
Taylor, John, 57
Terry, Jane, 169
Tewson, Josephine, 114
Thaw, John, 149
Thesiger, Ernest, 108
Thomas family,
Audrey, Betty & Myra, 18
Basil, 17, 24, 33, 34, 43, 44, 45, 46, 51, 54, 55, 60, 69, 70, 72, 106, 109, 184
Hedi, 45, 46
Joshua, 8
Jules, 8
Julius, 8, 58, 69, 72
Mim, 18
Myer, 20. 54
Sarah, 70
Susan, 45
Tim, 18
Thomas, Hon. Ald. Dennis, 122
Thomas, Stephen, 134
Thorndike, Dame Sybil, 80, 110, 111, 124
Thorpe-Bates, Peggy, 184
Three Squires, 168
Tilley, Vesta, 182
Tod, Peter, 115, 187
Todd, Richard, 125
Tolcher, Arthur, 170, 175
Tolcher, Beatrice, 170
Tomlinson, David, 109, 110
Tompsett, Jeannette, 116
Toye, Jacqueline, 167
Toye, Wendy, 72
Travers, Linden, 39
Trewin, J.C., 1, 124, 152
Trinder, Tommy, 45, 50
Tripp, Jack, 162, 163, 164, 165, 167, 168, 174, 175, 189
Truzzi, George, 167
Turner, Big Dick, 42, 135, 171
Turner, Joan, 116
Turner, Ken, 172
Tyler, Hon. Ald. Harold, App. A

Udloff, Maurice, 88
Ustinov, Peter, 80, 91

Valerie, 94
Vanbrugh, Prudence, 13
Vance, Charles, 179
Van Praagh, Peggy, 60
Vaughan, Norman, 161
Vaughan, Peter, 41, 53, 77, 98
Vaughton, Ira, 190
Vaughton, Joan, 86, 190
Vaughton, Mr & Mrs, 190
Viccars, Anthony, 30, 58
Vyvyan, Johnny, 168

Walker, Zena, 78
Walsh, Dermot, 114, 127
Ward, Dorothy, 5, 156
Warner, Jack, 109
Warwick, Billy, 171
Warwickshire Cricket, 44, 51, 52, 63, 96, 143
Waterhouse, John 75
Waters, Elsie & Doris, 50
Watling, Jack, 78, 114, 138
Watton, Hon. Ald., 122, 131, 138
Weedon, Bert, 174
Weldon, Duncan, 169
Westall, Claude, 99, 108
Wheeler, Jimmy, 159
Whitelaw, Billie, 96
Whiteside, Janet, 105, 112, 114
Willatt, Sir Hugh, 92
Williams, Emlyn, 66, 106, 109
Williams, Kenneth, 111
Williams, Linda, 168
Williams, Martin, 191
Williams, Pauline, 74, 98, 99
Williams, Simon, 150
Willis, Denny, 164
Willis's, The, 82
Wilmot, Lord, 94
Wilson, Keppell & Betty, 159
Winters, Mike & Bernie, 161
Wisdom, Norman, 157, 158
Wiseman, Alan, 142. App. A
Wiseman, David, 142
Wolfit, Sir Donald, 80
Wood, George, 27, 38, 41, 49, 156
Wood, Norman, 39, 86, 147, 191
Wood, Pam, 191
Wood, Peggy Ann, 113
Woodfield, Frank, 104, 112, 117
Wooldridge, Clifford, 52, 70, 121, 135, 140, 143, 144
Worsley, Arthur, 164
Worsnip, Glyn, 118
Worth, Kathleen 116
Wright, Angela, 82
Wyngarde, Peter, 146, 147
Wynyard, Diana, 108
Wynn Owen, Meg, 102

Yates, Pauline, 41